Interreligious Dialogue
Voices From a New Frontier

INTERRELIGIOUS DIALOGUE

Voices From a New Frontier

Edited by M. Darrol Bryant and Frank Flinn

A New ERA Book

PARAGON HOUSE
New York

First edition, 1989

Published in the United States by

International Religious Foundation
481 Eighth Avenue
New York, NY 10001

Copyright ©1989 by the International Religious Foundation
Chapter 22, "The What and the How of Dialogue," copyright © 1983
Augsburg Publishing House

Distributed by
Paragon House Publishers
90 Fifth Avenue
New York, NY 10011

A New Ecumenical Research Association Book

Library of Congress Cataloging-in-Publication Data

Interreligious Dialogue: voices from a new frontier / edited by M. Darrol
Bryant and Frank K. Flinn.
    p. cm.
Essays based on presentations made at the Assembly of the World's Religions
held at McAfee, N.J. in November 1985.
"A New ERA Book."
Includes bibliographies and index.
ISBN 0-89226-067-X
1. Religions—Relations—Congresses. I. Bryant, M. Darrol.
II. Flinn, Frank K. III. Assembly of the World's Religions (1985: McAfee, N.J.)
BL410.I574
291.1'72—dc20   89-7469
                                                         CIP

Contents

Part III — Resources at the Frontier

Part IV — Issues at the Frontier

Introduction

Scouting the Frontier

M. Darrol Bryant and Frank K. Flinn

Something new is happening in the religious traditions of humankind. After centuries of isolation from one another—and often hostility when they came into contact with one another—something different is occurring when people of different faiths meet. Scholars differ in their explanations of its origins and causes, but all agree that it is new. Indeed it is so new that we are still unsure how to name it. Here we will call it, simply, dialogue between persons of differing faiths, or interreligious dialogue. Even the phrase interreligious dialogue is not wholly happy since dialogue is always an event between persons, a meeting and sharing from the heart. Regardless of the difficulties of definition, what is important is that it is happening. This meeting of faiths signifies a new day in the history of humankind's religious life.

Attending these meetings is particularly important since hardly a day passes without our newspapers, radios, and televisions reporting stories of conflict and hostility between persons of different religious communities. We know of the tragic conflicts in the Middle East, in Northern Ireland, in Sri Lanka, and in India. These conflicts involve people of different faiths: in the Middle East the conflict is between Jews and Muslims; in Northern Ireland it is between Christians of different denominations; in Sri Lanka it involves Buddhists and Hindus; and in India, Sikhs and Hindus and Muslims find themselves in conflict. And yet it is in the midst of these conflicts—often arising as a response to these tragic relations between persons of differing faiths—that the desire for dialogue emerges. In all these traditions, there are, as the readings in this volume demonstrate, persons who do not believe that their faith leads them to conflict with others, but, quite the contrary, that it leads to dialogue as the way to mutual understanding and acceptance among persons of differing faiths. Indeed, in the midst of the conflicts and suffering of our century, some remarkable exponents of another way for people of differing faiths to meet and relate to one another have emerged. We can name people like Mahatma Gandhi, Rev. Dr. Martin Luther King, Mother Teresa, and His Holiness the Dalai Lama. With these well-known figures —and because of hundreds of lesser known persons from all faith communities—a movement towards a new era in the relations between the religious traditions has begun. While we do not deny that tragic conflicts between persons of different traditions persist, in this volume we want to turn our attention to another aspect or current in the present situation. We want to explore that emerging frontier where men and women of different faiths are meeting in ways that contribute to understanding, appreciation, and mutual respect.

All but two of the essays in this volume emerged from a meeting of persons from different religious traditions held at McAfee, New Jersey, in November, 1985, called the Assembly of the World's Religions. This meeting brought together over six hundred persons for a week of prayer and meditation, small group dialogues, plenary sessions, and cultural events. Several sections of the Assembly were devoted to the theme of interreligious dialogue. Participating in these sessions were religious leaders, scholars, monks, and lay people from the many traditions of faith around the world. It is our conviction that their contributions to that gathering deserve to be shared with a wider audience. One of the participants spoke for many when she remarked that "our Assembly was a beacon of hope in the midst of our religiously troubled world." Through these readings we can participate in the emerging dialogue of men and women of faith. We can hear the words of Buddhists, Christians, Hindus, Jews, Muslims, Sikhs, Shintoists, and many others as they present the resources in their respective traditions that can sustain dialogue, explore the difficulties and problems that arise when we meet across traditions, and struggle to articulate the implications of such meeting for their traditions. Thus we can hear these words from a new frontier, not as last words, but as the reports of those, albeit still a minority, exploring a new terrain where few have ventured. While the reports of these explorers are the primary substance of this volume, it might be helpful to anticipate some of the features of the landscapes that lie ahead.

Backgrounds to the Contemporary Movement

The contributors to this volume do not write in a vacuum. They are contemporary explorers in a journey that began, according to scholars, with the World's Parliament of Religions, held in 1893 in conjunction with the Columbia Exposition or World's Fair in Chicago. This event gave public visibility to efforts to build better relations between members of different faith communities. Several of the essays in this volume invoke that Parliament and especially Swami Vivekananda, who was its most noteworthy participant. As Swami Vivekananda remarked at the end of the Parliament:

> If the World's Parliament of Religions has shown anything to the world, it is this: It has proved to the world that holiness, purity, and charity are not exclusive possessions of any church in the world, and that every system has produced men and women of the most exalted character.[1]

This recognition has, unfortunately, still claimed few. Nevertheless, it was a beginning.

It was a beginning of a movement that has grown over the past century, yet is not widely known through the media of mass communications or within our respective traditions. In a recent publication, Francis Clark, former Head of the Religious Studies Program of the Open University in England, gathered the names of nearly 700 organizations and institutions around the world that are devoted to promoting understanding between members of different faith communities. His *Interfaith Directory* is impressive evidence that there is a growing commitment to interreligious dialogue. In his view, the *Interfaith Directory* is not exhaustive but rather indicative:

> In hundreds of different places around the world men and women have felt impelled in recent years to begin or to join associations which are inspired by the interfaith ideal. Usually their initiatives have arisen spontaneously and independently. Unknown to one another, they have been moved by the same motives, have felt the same urge to transcend religious rivalries and differences, and have formed societies with the same interreligious character and aims.[2]

The purpose of this volume is to make this growing movement known to a wider audience. The evidence Francis Clark has gathered shows that there is a widespread yearning among believers in all traditions to find a new way that overcomes the antagonisms that have too often characterized relations between religions in the past.

The essays here make clear that the way ahead does not involve either a lessening of commitment to one's own faith or a wholesale rejection of one's tradition. Sometimes people assume that dialogue with men and women of other faiths will undermine one's own faith. If this assumption were true, it would constitute a serious criticism of interreligious dialogue. But the clear evidence of these authors is that this is not true. While dialogue may lead to the revision of certain attitudes, or practices, that have arisen in a given tradition, the authors included here more often note how it leads to a deepening of faith in one's own tradition, and, simultaneously, a greater respect for the faith of others. Thus these essays make clear that mutuality is not opposed to loyalty to one's own tradition. Rather, the opposite seems to be the case: as appreciation for one's own tradition grows and deepens, so does a willingness to respect the depths in the faith of others.

Thus we arrive at the starting point for the journey into interfaith dialogue: a vital faith rooted in one's own tradition, the tradition from which the journey begins. The importance of one's own faith is emphasized time and time again in the readings in this volume—and in the distinctive style of each author. This point is crucial. It makes clear that interreligious dialogue does not flourish in a setting where the participants seek a lowest common denominator—a process that weakens the participants. Rather it grows where faith is grounded in the ultimate. Genuine meeting takes place, first and foremost, out of the depths of the respective traditions embodied in the participants. The faith of each participant is the foundation for the journey to interreligious dialogue that emerges in these readings. It is important to keep this point in mind as you read the papers in this volume: what is sought is a deepening of religious faith and its consequent virtues as the fruit of interreligious dialogue.

We have arranged these explorations of this new frontier along the following lines: Part I, Marking the Frontier; Part II, Journeys to the Frontier; Part III, Resources at the Frontier; and Part IV, Issues at the Frontier. Each section deserves introductory remarks.

Marking the Frontier

Every exploration involves an attempt to map the frontier that is being explored. Such first attempts are always tentative and open to revision by the work of subsequent explorers. But when we are charting a new terrain, the provisional sketches of what lies ahead, however limited, are always valuable. Provisional maps tell us what we can expect as we make our way into this new terrain. The writings in this first section serve this function: they scout the way and report provisional findings. This has been done in an impressive way by these explorers. Professor Ewert Cousins, a Christian from Fordham University, movingly shares his vision of the current situation. He believes that in the movement towards interreligious dialogue, we see the emergence of the distinctive spiritual journey of our age. According to Professor Cousins, we are on the edge of a new axial period, a new turning point in the religious life of humankind, one comparable in significance to that first axial period that the German philosopher Karl Jaspers located in the fifth to seventh centuries B.C. In Professor Cousins' view, we in this century are called to explore new ways of moving across tradition, not in order to abandon the faith of our fathers and mothers, but to renew it and recover it in relation to the other communities of faith.

In a complementary way, Professor Anantanand Rambachan, a Hindu teaching at St. Olaf's College in Minnesota, reaches back to the vision of Swami Vivekananda at the 1893 Parliament of the World's Religions. He recalls for us the vision that Swami Vivekanada articulated in the Parliament and in his too-short life. Vivekananda saw the different religious traditions as various paths towards a common goal: the absolute. Professor Rambachan shows us that Vivekananda's response to the faith of others grew out of his own Hindu and Vedantic commitments. The author urges his fellow Hindus and others interested in exploring the interreligious frontier to look critically at Vivekananda's vision to discover how it applies now and where it needs revision.

Another significant mapping of the interreligious frontier is found in the contribution of Father Thomas Keating, a monk from the Benedictine Monastery at Snowmass, Colorado. One of the founders of the North American Board for East-West Dialogue, Father Keating has long been in dialogue with monks and teachers of other religious traditions. Out of his experience, he has sought to articulate an understanding of the ultimate mystery that recognizes the integrity of faith as being open to and responding to the ultimate mystery wherever it is found. In his vision, such faith is found across traditions. For Father Keating, the source of unity lies in the ultimate mystery itself and not in the frames of reference that characterize particular traditions.

A similar mapping of the interreligious frontier is provided by Rabbi Rami Shapiro, who serves a Jewish congregation in Miami, Florida. Writing in part out of his experience of the Assembly of the World's Religions, Rabbi Shapiro argues that genuine meeting and dialogue lie at the heart of the interreligious frontier. And when we meet here, he continues, we must "place ourselves on the line in a mutual quest for truth." That quest, however, expresses itself not primarily in propositions but in a sense of wonder and an awakening to the whole that exceeds all our particular traditions. Writing with enthusiasm and vitality, Rabbi Shapiro seeks to plant the seeds of dialogue that can bring forth "a rich harvest of human dignity and peace."

An important survey of the current interreligious situation is found in Professor Durwood Foster's contribution. A systematic theologian at the Pacific School of Religion in Berkeley, Professor Foster has long been involved in interreligious dialogue. He is well situated to survey the current situation. Taking as his point of departure the 1893 Parliament, Foster assesses its goals and points to the developments since that have created "the new mood among world religions." A chief aspect of the new mood is "openness to mutual dialogue." These opening explorations provide us with five provisional maps of the new frontier of interreligious dialogue. These maps are not mutually exclusive, nor do they cover the whole terrain. Yet they are immensely helpful in providing some orientation towards that frontier that we are invited to explore along with believers from other traditions.

Journeys to the Frontier

The first section of this volume explores the frontier of interreligious dialogue in general terms. The contributors to the second section share in more personal ways their own journeys to this new frontier. Everyone involved in interreligious dialogue undergoes a personal journey in coming to this frontier. The frontier is not ready-made for habitation. Since we are among the first to explore this new terrain, we must find our way, in large measure, through our own experience. Two of the contributors to this section are Indian Christians: Father Ignatius Hirudayam and Father Albert Nambiaparambil. Father Hirudayam, from Tamil Nadu in Southern India, movingly recounts his own personal pilgrimage to interfaith dialogue in his own Indian setting. We in the West, especially those of us in the Christian tradition, have much to learn from Indian Christians who have always been a minority in relation to much larger Hindu and Moslem populations. But the issue here is not majority/minority relations as much as the recognition of the good of dialogue with persons of other faiths. Using the image of the "moving train," Father Nambiaparambil reflects upon his own experience in his journey to interreligious dialogue, reminding us that on that journey we will all be transformed in countless ways we cannot anticipate.

A similar point is made by Odette Baumer-Despigne, a Swiss Catholic who shares with us something of her journey. For her, the journey does not lead to an abandoning of tradition, but to a new plumbing of the depths of tradition. Thus, ironically, what seems to the outsider as a radical departure when the value of other faiths is acknowledged, turns out to be a radical recovery of the depths of one's own tradition. For the Protestant theologian from Drew University, Pieter De Jong, the journey to interfaith involves his own transformation as he incorporates what he learned from other traditions into his own personal life and discipline. While many theological questions remain open for De Jong, the personal transforming aspects of interreligious dialogue are highlighted in his contribution.

The last two contributors to this section do not frame their journeys in exclusively personal terms. One shares an outline of his own Shinto tradition, and the other, drawing upon his own Sikh faith, urges us to take care not to build fences around God. For Professor Yoshimine Komari, the first stage of the journey to interreligious dialogue is a sharing of one's own tradition. Komari does this by explaining a religious tradition that is little known in the West yet so central to the people of Japan. This contribution does not share the same journey motif as the others, but presents an essential aspect of the journey, namely, the encounter with traditions that are deeply and profoundly different from our own. This presentation of the Shinto tradition in the context of interreligious dialogue is one of the first of its kind. Komari kindly invites us to dialogue with him and the Shinto tradition. Similarly, Professor Avtar Singh from the Punjab shares his own Sikh tradition and some of its relevance for interreligious dialogue. Recounting his own experience of the partition of India, Avtar Singh reminds us that God always exceeds our limited perceptions. Thus in ways that recall the noble Sikh tradition to honor God above all else—even the religious traditions themselves—Singh urges us to discover in dialogue the reality of God beyond our fences, those human barriers to the divine that we often create. Thus both of these contributions, each in their own unique way, underscore the importance of sharing one's own faith on the journey to interreligious dialogue.

Resources at the Frontier

In this section, we turn to some resources for interreligious dialogue. In addition to mapping the terrain and making our own journeys, we discover at the frontier a wide array of perspectives concerning the importance and meaning of interreligious encounter and dialogue. These perspectives can provide further resources for interreligious dialogue. Professor Badru Dungu Kateregga, an African Muslim from Kenya, offers an important Islamic perspective. He outlines the resources for dialogue to be found within Islam, claiming that Islamic faith is in principle open to dialogue. This view will come as a welcome surprise to many in North America who perceive Islam in another way. Kateregga turns to the *Qur'an* itself to ground his openness to dialogue. Dr. Ki-Young Rhi, a Korean Buddhist, turns, on the other hand, to an earlier Buddhist sage, Won-Hyo, for an important statement about the frontier of interreligious dialogue. According to Rhi, the metaphysical views as well as the mental disciplines of Won-Hyo are important resources for the current dialogue.

Similarly, Professor K.L. Seshagiri Rao, a Hindu teaching at the University of Virginia, turns to Gandhi's experiments in interreligious dialogue to explore their meaning for today. According to Rao, Gandhi wanted "harmony and friendship to be established not merely between the Hindus and Muslims of India, but among the adherents of all the great religions of the world." Especially noteworthy is Rao's documenting of the practical dialogue that Gandhi lived in the ashrams he founded in South Africa and India. Here, in the luminous example of Gandhi, we can see the way dialogue can contribute to the creation of genuine community.

For Swami Devananda, a Christian who freely acknowledges his many debts to the Hindu tradition, the practice of dialogue leads to a recovery of the "experience of God." In dialogue, Devananda argues, we are driven to that which is the deepest ground of our religious life: a meeting at the level of heart and experience that is central to interreligious encounter. Likewise,

James Kodera, a Japanese Christian teaching in the United States, argues that dialogue moves us beyond a mere agreeing to disagree. For Kodera, mere tolerance is not enough. We must, Kodera believes, move toward "contemplation, not upon ourselves but upon One to whom many of our traditions attribute the beginning of our being." In these perspectives, then, dialogue is not a simply polite or tolerant meeting, but an invitation to plumb the deeper levels of religious life and contemplation.

Gokul Chandra Jain, from the Sampurnanand Sanskrit University in Varanasi, speaks to us from the Jain religious tradition. Though little known in the West, the Jain tradition has been an important stream of religious life and philosophical reflection in India, as Gokul Chandra's essay exemplifies. Here the emphasis falls on the resources of the Jain tradition for interreligious dialogue. Those resources include the Jain doctrine of "love for all beings." Added to this doctrine are views concerning the nature of reality and the relativity of knowledge that, according to our author, are Jain resources relevant to the dialogue between people of living faiths. The final paper in this section is written by an Indonesian Muslim, Djohan C. Effendi, who offers a Southeast Asian Islamic perspective on what can emerge from dialogue. For Effendi, what we might achieve is harmony.

The note of harmony is sounded often in these essays. It is an important metaphor drawn from music where several notes, standing in proper relation to one another, create harmony. This is a fruitful image for the goal of interreligious dialogue, even though such harmony is not easily achieved. Still, it is a fitting metaphor beckoning us toward that for which we strive. It stands as a counterpoint to the dissonance that characterizes our current situation. These several perspectives are written from the frontiers of actual dialogue among believers, but in the rhythms and scales of the Islamic, Buddhist, Hindu, Jain, and Christian traditions from which the authors come. They cast further light on the interreligious terrain. They point to resources within their respective traditions that contribute to the quest for mutual understanding and to the meeting at the deeper places that our respective traditions open up to us. As perspectives from the frontier, none of them claim a final word, but each points to a distinctive note that must be sounded if we would move from dissonance to harmony.

Issues at the Frontier

In the earlier sections of the volume, the contributors have sought to map the terrain of interreligious dialogue, to share their journeys to dialogue, and to offer the contributions of their particular perspectives, in order to illuminate what confronts us at the frontier of dialogue. But at this frontier we often encounter difficult and troubling issues, issues that remain despite the good will of those involved in dialogue itself. It is good for these issues to be explored, especially by people who see interreligious dialogue as both necessary and desirable. In this final section, then, the authors take up a range of issues that arise on the frontier of interreligious dialogue. Dr. Wande Abimbola, a Yoruba priest and Vice Chancellor of the University of Ife in Nigeria, calls upon the leaders of the religious traditions to enter into urgent and continuing dialogue with one another. Citing the often bitter experience of the traditional religions of Africa at the hands of Christian and Muslim missionaries, Abimbola movingly pleads for mutual regard and respect among adherents of religious traditions. Rejecting the notion of the adequacy of any single tradition to address the spiritual needs of the whole human family, Abimbola calls religious leaders to constant dialogue to reverse the devastating trends that have too often characterized relations between historic and primal religions in Africa.

Dr. Owen Cole, a Christian educator in the United Kingdom and a specialist in Christian-Sikh relations, raises the crucial issue of interreligious education in the schools. Citing the important example of the United Kingdom where considerable strides on this front have been made, Cole argues the case for bringing dialogue into the experience of students in the school setting. Can we educate the young in ways that respect the variety of traditions found in all societies? Cole argues that we need to attempt such education. The essay by the Tibetan Buddhist monk, Thubten Losel, raises a very different issue in relation to interreligious dialogue as a whole, but one with implications for the issue of interfaith education. For Losel, we encounter in dialogue real differences between traditions. The case he has in mind is non-theistic Buddhism and theistic Christianity. In such cases we should frankly acknowledge fundamental differences and explore the practical implications of differences. The fact of differences is a crucial issue to be faced both in the classroom setting and in the wider dialogue. As others have noted, we need not pretend that the differences do not exist. They do. But how can we experience these differences in ways that contribute to mutual enrichment rather than to antipathy? This is perhaps the greatest challenge facing the interreligious movement.

This issue is partially addressed in the contribution by Dr. Paul Mojzes, a Christian originally from Yugoslavia but now an American citizen and one of the editors of the *Journal of Ecumenical Studies*. Mojzes offers some "guidelines for dialogue" that have arisen from the explorations of this new frontier in recent decades. The cornerstone of these guidelines is the recognition that since dialogue is between persons, we must allow all participants in dialogue to define themselves and their own tradition. Only in this way can we undercut the stereotypes of persons of other faiths. Stereotypes are too often the basis on which we relate to people of other traditions. This issue is certainly central to interreligious encounter and dialogue. On a practical level, the breaking of stereotypes has been—and is being—achieved in the intermonastic dialogues that Sister Pascaline Coff speaks of in her contribution. Here the issue is the meeting of monks of different traditions. This experience has been wonderfully positive as monastics have lived at each others' monasteries and shared each others' monastic life. Again we see that depth of religious commitment is not an obstacle to interreligious dialogue but rather contributes to the richness and significance of the meeting of men and women of different faiths.

As a final contribution to this section, we have included the statement of Tsering Dhondup, a young Tibetan Buddhist, who addresses the issue of world peace. For Dhondup, interreligious dialogue is a way of creating peace, initially among believers from different traditions, but ultimately in relation to the whole family of humankind. This moving statement points to the way interreligious dialogue can contribute to the wider quest for peace on our common planet.

These are but some of the issues that arise as believers from different traditions come into dialogue with one another. It is important to recognize that when interreligious dialogue is authentic, it can lead to the exploration of crucial issues that confront and trouble us all. Again we should realize that the frontier of interreligious dialogue is being explored, in part, to find ways to go forward together to address crucial issues in our time. Dialogue is not flight from the world but a way to enter more deeply into life based on the mutual recognition of the integrity of one another's faith. From this spiritual foundation, perhaps the search for creative responses to troubling issues can be initiated and carried forward. Here at the frontier, then, we are invited not simply to observe, but to join these other explorers in a movement that can heal the tragic antagonisms that have characterized the religious life of humankind in the past and present. Fully aware of our differences, we can begin the long process of finding our way together, towards our common planetary future.

From our initial scouting of the terrain ahead of us in this volume, three points stand out:

First, faith is not the obstacle to interreligious dialogue, but its ground. Such faith must be rooted in the depths of our own tradition to be authentic because it is here that we are related to the ultimate that sustains us in our religious journey.

Second, the encounter with men and women of other faiths will be full of surprises as we move beneath and beyond the stereotypes that we too often have of one another. As we have seen in our anticipatory scouting, we can learn a great deal from how believers understand both their own traditions and the traditions of others. And these understandings are not always what we expect. As you listen to these voices from the frontier of interreligious dialogue, keep yourself open to surprise—and to delight as well.

Third, the terrain in front of you is only now being explored. Its contours, its valleys and heights, its obstacles and gently rolling plains, are not yet mapped out. Listen to these words of explorers, knowing that there will be revisions as new discoveries are made, but knowing also that you are invited to join this voyage of discovery. The journey is not only theirs but ours as well.

Notes

1. *The World's Parliament of Religions* (Chicago: Parliament Publishing Company, 1893), vol. 2, 1582.
2. *Interfaith Directory*, ed. H. Francis Clark (New York: International Religious Foundation, 1987), iv.

Part I
Marking the Frontier

1

Interreligious Dialogue: The Spiritual Journey of Our Time

Ewert H. Cousins

On the eve of the twenty-first century, we observe that many have embarked on a spiritual journey. In the West large numbers have rediscovered spirituality, awakened and instructed by teachers from the East. Some have turned to the East, following the paths opened up to them by the ancient wisdom of the orient. Others have searched for their spiritual roots in their own western tradition from which they had been alienated by the pressures of secular society. Still others have pursued a secular path which has drawn them into the spiritual journey. They have found their way through psychoanalysis, social concern, involvement in the movements for peace and justice. Or they have pursued careers in science or the arts, discovering there the spiritual dimension of the human.

Many of these, and others as well, have become drawn into another spiritual journey, which is not merely their own, nor that of their tradition. Rather it is the common, collective spiritual journey of the human community as we approach the twenty-first century. It is the journey that opens up through interreligious dialogue. In an unprecedented way, the religions of the world are meeting one another in an atmosphere of trust and understanding. The members of different traditions not only wish to understand the others, but to be enriched by them. As the traditions meet, each individual can inherit the spiritual heritage of the human community as a whole. With this enrichment, consciousness can expand its horizons to encompass the whole human community, with its global consciousness. Interreligious dialogue is the vehicle and the model for developing this new consciousness. In this sense, then, interreligious dialogue is the distinctive spiritual journey of our time.

In the present paper I would like to explore this notion, by examining: (1) the dynamics of the collective journey through interreligious dialogue; (2) the common roots of our heritage in what Karl Jaspers calls the Axial Period; (3) our common spiritual journey into the Second Axial Period.

Interreligious Dynamics

Interreligious dialogue, if it is to lead to a common spiritual journey, must take place on a deep spiritual level. This means that it cannot be merely a polite meeting of participants from different traditions who engage in swapping superficial information. Rather it must be a sharing from the heart—from the depths of each tradition, solidly rooted in its spiritual experiences and supported by centuries of accumulated wisdom. It means, then, that the tradition as a whole, and each member, must recover its classical heritage. They must return to the wellsprings of spiritual vitality—to the scriptures, to the teachings of the masters, to the practice of prayer and meditation—and bring this richness to the dialogue.

The recovery of one's heritage need not be an isolated task. Fortunately, on the eve of the twenty-first century, it can be a shared endeavor. Already Hinduism and Buddhism have awakened Westerners to the spiritual dimension of life and have spurred them to discover their own forms of meditation and spiritual practice.

As the traditions mutually support each other in the recovery of our classical heritage, they can open their horizons to each other in a creative phase of interreligious dialogue. In this phase, which involves a "passing over and coming back," participants from one tradition empathize with those of another. For example, a Christian will attempt to perceive and appreciate the spiritual values of Hinduism, not merely from his own perspective, but from within the Hindu experience itself. I believe that this is not only possible, but the necessary step into truly creative dialogue. We all have a capacity for this kind of empathy. We must activate and cultivate it. We need to develop what I call a "shamanistic epistemology." The shaman can leave his body and travel in spirit to distant places to gather and bring back information; so we have a capacity to leave the confines of our own historical horizon and travel into the value-world of another tradition returning with new spiritual insight and wisdom. When we return to our own tradition, we may find the same values there, which we had forgotten or overlooked. Or we may find these values were not present as such, but are compatible. For example, a Christian may find that the *atman* in Hinduism has remarkable affinity with his own doctrine of the soul as the image of God; or that the no-self doctrine of Buddhism has resonances with his teaching on dying to the false self. On the other hand, we may discover genuine differences which seem incompatible. This can be the most challenging moment in the dialogue. It is here that creativity must be awakened to proceed beyond what some might perceive to be impasses. Yet such differences can awaken new energies and open up new horizons for common spiritual journey.

If we follow this path courageously, we will find that we will not merely return enriched to our own tradition, but we will have established a network of relationships with the other traditions. We will have recovered our own classical heritage, it is true, but we will also have discovered and assimilated the classical heritage of the other traditions, and, most importantly, drawn these heritages into the emerging global consciousness of our time.

Axial Period

In order to understand this global consciousness, I would like to situate interreligious dialogue in a larger context. In our converging world, we need a vantage point from which to view our planet as a whole. Like the astronauts, who first traveled into outer space, we can now look at the earth as a single unit—a beautiful globe, blue and white, floating against the black background of space. For the first time in history human beings can have a sense image of the earth as a whole, not merely of our limited earth-bound horizons, but of the earth as a single organic unit. I believe that this new image of the earth is the symbol of the emerging global consciousness of our time.

But to understand this global consciousness, we must look back in history to another great transitional period: the first millennium B.C. In his book, *The Origin and Goal of History*, Karl Jaspers claims that around 500 B.C. a striking transformation of consciousness occurred in Greece, Israel, Persia, India, and China, without detectable influence of one area on another.[1] He calls this the Axial Period which, "gave birth to everything which, since then, man has been able to be." He continues:

> It would seem that this axis of history is to be found in the period around 500 B.C, in the spiritual process that occurred between 800 and 200 B.C. It is there that we meet with the most deep cut dividing line in history. Man, as we know him today, came into being. For short we may style this the 'Axial Period.'[2]

In the Axial Period there emerged great spiritual leaders, prophets and philosophers, whose teachings represent a change from mythic to self-reflective thinking, from union with the cosmos and the tribe to individual identity which stands apart from nature and collectivity. During the Axial Period, in China, Confucius and Lao-tze appeared; in India, the *Upanishads* and the Buddha; in Persia, Zoroaster; in Israel, the prophets—Elijah, Isaiah, and Jeremiah; in Greece, Socrates, Plato, and Aristotle. The great world religions, which endure to the present, were born in this period; for Christianity and later Islam emerged out of the transformation of Jewish consciousness by the prophets. Jaspers observes: "In this age were born the fundamental categories within which we still think today, and the beginnings of the world religions, by which human beings still live, were created."[3]

Second Axial Period

I believe that we are now going through a Second Axial Period, which will be as momentous as the First.[4] While the First Axial Period produced individual consciousness, the Second Axial Period is producing global consciousness. The First separated consciousness from the cosmos and the tribe; the Second is extending consciousness back into the material universe and encompassing the entire human community. I believe that a major dynamic of the Second Axial Period is the recapitulation of the cosmic modes of consciousness from the Pre-Axial Period, but with the preservation of the subjective, reflective consciousness of the First Axial Period. The archaic modes of consciousness—mythic, ritualistic, cosmic, and collective—must be reconstituted along with the individual, reflective, and critical consciousness in a new more complex form of consciousness.

The complex consciousness of the Second Axial Period is global in two senses: (1) in a horizontal sense it is encompassing the entire human community on the planet in all of its historical experience; (2) in a vertical sense it is recovering its rootedness in the earth. The encounter of world religions reflects the first sense of the global, with its corresponding form of of complex consciousness. In the second sense, the religions of the world must cultivate an awareness of our rootedness in the earth. They must recognize the value of the secular—the political, economic, social and biological dimensions of life; but this secular energy must be grounded in spiritual energy so that it will not become chaotic and destroy life on our planet.

In such a global context interreligious dialogue is not a mere luxury—it is a necessity! For the traditions must not only recover their classical heritage, they must do so together in harmony; and at the same time they must transform that heritage to meet effectively the problems threatening the survival of the human community. In this context, the image of the earth—moving peacefully through space—can become the symbol of interreligious dialogue and our common spiritual journey as we move into the global consciousness of the twenty-first century.

Notes

1. Karl Jaspers, *The Origin and Goal of History*, trans. Michael Bullock (New Haven: Yale University Press, 1953), 1-77.
2. Ibid., 1.
3. Ibid., 2.
4. For a further development of my concept of the Second Axial Period, see my article: "Les religions a l'aube du XXI siecle," *Cahiers des Religions Africaines*, vol. 18 (1984): 67-80.

2

Swami Vivekananda: A Hindu Model for Interreligious Dialogue

Anantanand Rambachan

> Sectarianism, bigotry, and its horrible descendant fanaticism, have long possessed this beautiful earth. They have filled the earth with violence, drenched it often with human blood, destroyed civilizations, and sent whole nations to despair. Had it not been for these horrible demons, human society would be far more advanced than it is now. But their time is come: I fervently hope that the bell that tolled this morning in honor of this convention may be the death-knell of all fanaticism, of all persecutions with the sword or with the pen, and of all uncharitable feelings between persons wending their way to the same goal.[1]

These were the words with which the Hindu monk, Swami Vivekananda (1863-1902), concluded his opening address at the World's Parliament of Religions in Chicago on September 11, 1893. Vivekananda's impact on the World's Parliament of Religions was impressive and resounding. It is documented that in order to retain a satisfactory audience for a particular session, the chairman's secret was to announce Vivekananda as the final speaker. The strategy always worked. The World's

Parliament of Religions marked the beginning of a career as remarkable for its influence as its brevity. The character and nature of contemporary Hinduism can hardly be grasped without reference to the interpretations of Swami Vivekananda. There is little in modern Hindu apologetic writing which does not bear the indelible stamp of his character and thought. It was Vivekananda who initiated and inspired the attempt to universalize the message of Hinduism and establish its relevance and meaning beyond the confines of India. This process, of course, continues today.

Vivekananda's thinking was shaped in an environment of religious diversity and difference. In addition to the pluralism within Hinduism, there were also the traditions of Jainism, Buddhism, Christianity, Islam, and Sikhism. Christianity, in particular, as part of a wider Western colonial presence, saw itself as a challenge and alternative to Hinduism. Christian missionaries questioned the validity of Hinduism and denounced it as a mass of superstitions. It was condemned as idolatrous and polytheistic. Vivekananda's response to this diversity, and especially to the exclusive and triumphalistic attitudes of the Christian missionaries, is important for several reasons. It is one of the earliest and most detailed attempts to formulate a Hindu response to religious plurality, and his interpretations have continued to exert a considerable influence on attitudes within Hinduism towards other religions. Many of the popular Hindu responses to religious pluralism can be easily traced to Vivekananda's formulations. Vivekananda's response is also important because it enables us to grasp some of the presuppositions of the Hindu approach.

In a time when we are being called more urgently to dialogue, it is necessary to critically assess and evaluate our respective standpoints. Hinduism is often, and with good reason, commended for its receptivity and openness towards other traditions, and its willingness to recognize and respond to the presence of truth in these. The Hindu approach, however, has not been subject to the detailed and rigorous criticism which is necessary for evaluating its advantages and drawbacks. It is still formulated in terms of well-rehearsed generalizations, with little attempt to explore the underlying suppositions and implications. If Hinduism is to contribute the many important lessons it has learned from centuries of growth in an environment of dialogue and pluralism, it must adopt a more critical attitude. It is hoped that this brief study of Vivekananda's interpretation of religious diversity will contribute greater clarification and evaluation of the Hindu approach. I will begin by outlining the principal arguments of Vivekananda, and conclude with a preliminary assessment of the relevance of these to contemporary interreligious dialogue.

Vivekananda's approach to the diversity of religious belief and practice outside the tradition of Hinduism was basically the same as his approach to the tremendous pluralism within it. Diversity and difference were not accepted as absolute and the same principles of interpretation were applied in the search for reconciliation and understanding. In trying to form a composite picture of his views on this subject, one initially recognizes that all the strands of viewpoint are held together by the premise that the goal of all religious quests is the same. Movement in religion, according to Vivekananda, is not a growth from error to truth, but from a lower to a higher truth. He sees all religions, from the lowest fetishism to the highest absolutism, as reflecting various attempts to grasp the infinite. The world of religions is, as he puts it, "only a travelling, a coming up of different men and women, through various conditions and circumstances, to the same goal."[2] For Vivekananda, the climax and goal of every religious quest is the appreciation of the non-dual reality underlying and uniting the entire universe and all life.[3] This knowledge, in his view, is attainable through different religious paths. Vivekananda, however, distinguishes between the paths and the goal. Each one is entitled to choose his path, but the path is not the goal.[4] This is the clue to his often voiced concept of unity in diversity, first expressed at the World's Parliament of Religions. The unifying factor is the common goal, and diversity is expressed in the variety of means adopted for its attainment. Religions, therefore can be positioned at points along the approach to the final non-dual truth.

> All religions are so many stages. Each one of them represents the stage through which the human soul passes to realize God. Therefore, not one of them should be neglected. None of these stages are dangerous or bad. They are good. Just as a child becomes a young man, and a young man becomes an old man, so these are travelling from truth to truth, they become dangerous only when they become rigid, and will not move further, when they cease to grow.[5]

This broad outlook, Vivekananda feels, offers the possibility of accepting all religious doctrines, not as an act of patronizing, but with the full conviction that "they are true manifestations of the same truth, and that they all lead to the same conclusions as the *advaita* has reached."[6] However crude an idea may appear from our present standpoint, its value as a necessary evolutionary step in our growth and the growth of others should be appreciated.

Vivekananda traces three evolutionary stages in the growth of any religion. In the first stage, God is omnipotent and omniscient, but extra-cosmic. He lives in the heavens and is invested with all the characteristics and qualities of his worshippers. God is distant, remote, and unapproachable. The second stage is a development of the idea of omnipresence. God is not only in the heavens, but also pervades the earth. Most importantly, however, is the appreciation of God's existence within the human person. In the final stage of religious evolution, according to Vivekananda, the human person discovers his unity and identity with the all-pervasive, non-dual reality of the universe:

> All that is real in me is He; all that is real in Him is I. The gulf between God and man is thus bridged. Thus we find, by knowing God, the kingdom of heaven within us.[7]

Any religion in the present, says Vivekananda, may reflect all three phases of its growth, for the discovery of a higher phase, in his terms does not mean the discarding of the steps along which it has travelled.[8]

Given this unity of goal and common inspiration of all religious traditions, how does Vivekananda account for the diversity of doctrines and practices? The answers to this question constitute the second dimension of his interpretation of religious plurality. He speaks of plurality sometimes as being the result of differences in expression, or of differing conditions of birth and association.[9] In the main, however, his thesis is the application of the traditional Hindu idea of differing natures and capacities in spiritual aspirants. He sees the many contradictions as arising from the same truth adapting itself to the circumstances of different human natures. In this sense, according to Vivekananda, the religions of the world are not essentially contradictory or antagonistic. In support of this claim, Vivekananda tenders the possibility that there may be almost contradictory points of view about a particular object, but that these could be all indicative of the same object. He uses the analogy of photographs of the sun taken at different points along an approach to it.

> Suppose a man is journeying towards the sun, and as he advances he takes a photograph of the sun at every stage. When he comes back, he has many photographs of the sun which he places before us. We see that no two are

alike, and yet, who will deny that these are photographs of the same sun from different standpoints?... In the same way, we are all looking at the truth from different standpoints, which vary according to our birth, education, surroundings and so on. We are viewing truth, getting as much of it as these circumstances will permit, coloring the truth with our own heart, understanding it with our own intellect, and grasping it with our own mind. We can only know as much of truth as is related to us, as much of it as we are able to receive.[10]

A number of examples are repeated in Vivekananda's lectures and writings to illustrate this concept. The examples of rivers struggling through different terrain to reach the sea is his most common and popular one. He also uses the example of taking vessels of different kinds to fetch water, the water in each case assuming the form of the particular vessel.[11] God here is comparable to the water being fetched and the vessels of different shapes and sizes indicate varying levels of individual understanding and receptivity. A less frequently used example is the idea of a bubble of air struggling through liquids of differing densities to join the mass of air without. The free air symbolizes infinity.

It is important to recognize in this context that Vivekananda did not see religious diversity, either within or outside Hinduism, as negative. On the other hand, it was something he positively valued. He saw differences of opinion as signs of the life of thought. A world with uniformity of thought is a dead one. His most important argument, however, for religious diversity is that it widens the choice for the religious person. Because of the rich variation in human nature and temperament, diversity holds out the possibility of the individual discovering a form of religious life suitable to his or her mentality.[12] While Vivekananda was thus ready to welcome diversity, he stood firmly against exclusivism. Religious discord was the result of the adoption by each religion of a narrow self-righteous position, refusing to take into account any other existing view.[13] His first utterance before the Parliament of Religions was on the theme of sectarianism and bigotry, which he strongly denounced. Because of what he believed to be the common source of all traditions, he saw religious antagonism as a form of self-undermining.

Vivekananda's own solution to the problem of religious conflict and dissension is his proposal of the idea of universal religion. This is one of the central concepts of his religious thought. As universal religion, however, he does not mean religious uniformity of the triumphing of one tradition over all others. Any attempt to achieve universal religious conformity has failed and will fail:

> Every man who starts a theory, even at the present day, finds that if he goes twenty miles away from his followers, they will make twenty sects. You see that happening all the time. You cannot make all conform to the same ideas: that is a fact, and I thank God that it is so.[14]

Vivekananda analyzed each developed religion as having three parts. First of all, there is its philosophy, presenting the entire scope of the tradition, delineating its basic principles, goal, and the means of attaining it. Second, there is its mythology. This consists of legends relating to human or supernatural beings and is concerned with making philosophy concrete. Still more concrete than mythology is ritual, consisting of various forms and ceremonies.[15] A universal religion in the sense of uniformity at any one of these three levels is an impossible dream, for there is no general consensus about doctrines, myths, or rituals.

What then does Vivekananda mean by universal religion? Universal religion, for him, seems synonymous with the absence of exclusiveness and fanaticism. In this connection, he distinguishes between religion and sect. The former is indicative of an all-embracing attitude, whereas the latter is exclusive.[16] The same distinction he makes between religion and creed and refuses to use the former appellation to designate Christianity because of its exclusiveness:

> Religion is the acceptance of all existing creeds, seeing in them the same striving toward the same destination. Creed is something antagonistic and combative.[17]

By universal religion, Vivekananda means, more than anything else, a particular outlook on religious diversity. A number of key attitudes constitute this outlook. The natural necessity of variation must be recognized and accepted:

> Just as we have recognized unity by our very nature, so we must also recognize variation. We must learn that truth may be expressed in a hundred thousand ways and that each of these ways is true as far as it goes. We must learn that the same thing can be viewed from a hundred different standpoints and yet be the same thing.[18]

In spite of this diversity, according to Vivekananda, religions are to be seen as expressions of a common struggle towards God.

> Through high philosophy or low, through the most exalted mythology, or the grossest, through the most refined ritualism or arrant fetishism, every sect, every soul, every nation, every religion, consciously or unconsciously, is struggling upward, towards God; every vision of truth that man has, is a vision of Him and of none else.[19]

In his view, it is wrong to denounce another man's religion as being false. He saw no tradition as having a monopoly of holiness, purity, and charity, since every tradition has produced men and women of the most exalted character. In this framework, Vivekananda saw the necessity of each tradition striving to assimilate the spirit of the others while reserving its own uniqueness and individuality. Uniqueness will be enriched by openness.

> The Christian is not to become a Hindu or a Buddhist, nor a Hindu or a Buddhist to become a Christian. But each must assimilate the spirit of the others and yet preserve his individuality and grow according to his law of growth.[20]

He often pointed out that contemplation of another tradition enhanced the understanding of one's own. In this concept of universal religion, he represented each of the major religions as having a unique mission wherein its individuality is expressed. These missions, however, reflect and emphasize different aspects of truth and are supplementary rather then contradictory. Each one utilizes its energy in typifying and embodying the dimension of truth which is its special concern. He portrayed the religions of the world as different forces in the economy of God, working for the good of mankind. Religions have survived because their missions have been kept intact.[21]

In his formulation of the concept of universal religion, two Hindu ideas have an extended role in the interpretation of diversity and the development of the spirit of acceptance. The first of these is the idea of the *avatar*, the incarnation of God from time to time in the human world. The application of the idea in this context, according to Vivekananda, would result in the recognition of the falsity of the assertion that any single prophet is alone true. Each prophet, like the religion he founded, represents and emphasizes an important ideal. The second idea is the principle of *ishta*, the freedom of the individual to choose a concept of God, a spiritual path or a means of worship consistent wih his own personality, needs and preferences. There is no urge to impose one's preferences on another.

In trying to assess the relevance of Vivekananda's interpretations to contemporary interreligious dialogue, one must bear in mind that these were formulated during the last decades of the nineteenth century. In the context of his own times and in the light of subsequent developments in interreligious dialogue, Vivekananda appears to be an inspired visionary. It is important to note also that his career was tragically short and afforded little opportunity for detailed development of thought and response to criticism. In view of his wide and continuing influence, the insights and inadequacies of his interpretations must be more thoroughly explored.

It seems to me that Vivekananda offers a positive orientation and proposes some of the indispensable conditions for meaningful and fruitful dialogue. His readiness and willingness to admit a common source and inspiration for the world's religions is indispensable. So also is his contention that truth is not confined to any single tradition. If we are to listen to each other authentically, the latter proposition, even as a hypothesis, must be accepted. Vivekananda was deeply convinced that the great religious traditions had important lessons to learn from each other and much to share:

> I do not understand how people declare themselves to be believers in God, and at the same time think that God has handed over to a little body of men all truth, and that they are the guardians of the rest of humanity.[22]

He saw the need to preserve uniqueness and individuality and to balance this with assimilation. The individuality of each tradition is not an accidental feature of its character, but the very condition of its existence and survival.

We need to ponder more closely Vivekananda's rejoicing attitude towards plurality and his justification of it by reference to the diversity of human nature and temperament. Too often religious unity is equated and identified with uniformity, and the tragic consequences of seeking to enforce religious conformity litter the history of humanity. "The unity of sameness," Vivekananda affirms, "can only come when this universe is destroyed." The unity he proposed lay in a common orientation to diversity and not in its abolition. Vivekananda's sketchy attempts to identify a unique message for each of the great traditions need to be pursued and his vision that these ultimately complement the insights of each other has to be clarified. Vivekananda offers us a number of rich and provoking images and analogies to explain the diversity of doctrine, myth, and ritual in the world's religions and to demonstrate their more fundamental unity. His perception that "there may be almost contradictory points of view of the same thing, but they will all indicate the same thing," may yet prove to be one of the most remarkable insights about our religious diversity and of inestimable value to contemporary interreligious dialogue.

In trying to trace an evolutionary pattern within the great religions, I think that Vivekananda is also pointing to an important quality of genuine dialogue. This is the openness to the possibility of change and growth. This, of course, is not possible if partners are unwilling to grant the possibility of discovering truth outside their respective traditions. While we are willing to admit the necessity and possibility of growth in relation to almost every field of human inquiry, our religious views and orientations are almost immediately fossilized and we resist change and challenge. "Religions," as Vivekananda so rightly testifies, "become dangerous only when they become rigid and will not move further." If we are sufficiently open and receptive, interreligious dialogue will undoubtedly prove itself to be a great stimulus to individual and collective spiritual growth.

A basic problem in Vivekananda's interpretations, however, is the extent to which we can apply the concept that the existence of every doctrine, ritual, and practice is justified because it is suitable to some individual. Taken to its limits, it would seem to eliminate critical evaluation of religious doctrine and practice. It could become a sanction for that which is manifestly cruel, irrational, and absurd. Interreligious dialogue must allow us to question and disagree with sincerity and respect. In fact, one does not have to go beyond Vivekananda himself to see the difficulty of consistently maintaining this position. He often questioned Christian doctrine and practice and applied *advaita* insights in his evaluation of Christianity.

Vivekananda rejects the patronizing attitude to religious diversity obvious in the idea that one religion is the fulfillment of all others.[23] He sees his position as being different from this in the sense that he is proposing a concept, not merely of tolerance, but of universal acceptance. He is arguing that all religions are true, and that religious growth is not from error to truth, but from lower to higher truth. It is very important, however, to note that Vivekananda takes his stand on a definite view of absolute truth and one to which he is committed. *Advaita* (non-dualism) is the ultimate goal towards which all religions are moving, representing, as it were, different points along the way. His interpretations of religious pluralism are founded on the assumption of a common goal. I emphasize this fact because the Hindu attitude towards religious pluralism too often mistakenly emerges as one which lacks firm claims about truth. The Hindu outlook, however, is difficult to understand without recognition of its affirmation of a common goal. In fact, interreligious dialogue does not seem possible without the participants possessing commitment to a particular understanding of the universe and feeling that this understanding is relevant for all people. Dialogue must be founded on religious conviction. While Vivekananda, in common with other religious traditions, adopts a firm position with regard to ultimate truth, there are certain significant distinguishing elements. These are also broadly characteristic of the Hindu approach. Vivekananda does not see the truth of *advaita* as available only within the Hindu tradition. It is not a truth "possessed" by Hinduism and over which it exercises proprietary rights. As we have noted, he felt that all traditions and individuals, by a process of natural spiritual evolution, would grow to *advaita*. It is neither necessary nor possible to impose one's viewpoint. Each individual, in Vivekananda's view, is growing and developing according to his own nature and each one in time will come to the highest truth.

> If it be true that God is the center of all religions, and that each of us is moving towards Him along one of these radii, then it is certain that all of us *must* reach that center. And at the center where all radii meet, all our differences will cease; but until we reach there, differences there must be.[24]

Vivekananda's patient stand has to be seen in the context of the impersonal nature of truth in *advaita* and the wider Hindu view of life as a long pilgrimage to truth stretching over many births and life experiences. Life's central tasks do not become less urgent, but one learns to wait and to share.

Notes

1. *The Complete Works of Swami Vivekananda* (hereafter abbreviated *CW*), 8 vols., Mayavati Memorial Edition (Calcutta: Advaita Ashrama, 1964-71). See *CW* 1, 4.
2. See *CW* 1, 18.

3. *Advaita Vedanta* is one of the leading systems of Hindu thought. Based on the teachings of the *Upanishads*, it was systematized and expounded by Shankara (788-820.) God, according to Shankara, is the only reality, not simply in the sense that there is nothing except God, but also in the sense that there is no multiplicity within God.
4. See *CW* 2, 321.
5. Ibid., 500.
6. Ibid., 347.
7. *CW* 1, 323.
8. In fact, Vivekananda seems to hold the view that in the present all religions have reached the one conclusion of an absolute and infinite existence. In this connection, he distinguishes between the essential truth and the non-essential casket of every religion, concluding that the essentials are the same in all religions.
9. See *CW* 2, 299; *CW* 1, 17.
10. *CW* 2, 366.
11. Ibid., 383-84.
12. Ibid., 368.
13. See *CW* 1, 5
14. *CW* 2, 363.
15. For full discussion see *CW* 2, 377-79.
16. See *CW* 3, 483
17. *CW* 7, 286
18. *CW* 2, 382-83.
19. Ibid., 383
20. *CW* 1, 24.
21. In Vivekananda's view, Islam emphasizes the ideal of human brotherhood. In Hinduism, the ideas of renunciation, religion as realization, and the definition of God and soul predominate. With Christianity, it is purity and the awaiting of the second coming of Christ.
22. *CW* 4, 182.
23. Ibid.
24. *CW* 2, 384-85.

3

The Search for the Ultimate Mystery

Thomas Keating

Many paths lead to the source. We call this source the ultimate reality, the absolute, the infinite God, Brahman, the Great Spirit, Allah, and other names depending upon our cultural or religious frame of reference. The term *ultimate mystery* has been chosen to designate what all these words are trying to signify.

All who seek to participate in the experience of the ultimate mystery, that is, the meaning of the reality underlying the cosmos, are united in the same search. An unprecedented awakening of transcultural human religious values has begun to take place throughout the world. The most fundamental contribution to this awakening is to cultivate the experience of one's own identification with the ultimate mystery, with all other human beings, and with the cosmos.

Those who seek the ultimate mystery relate to everything that is true and of genuine spiritual value in every religious and cultural tradition. They resonate to human values wherever they are found whether in religion, science, art, human friendship, or the service of others. This is not at all an attitude of eclecticism, a kind of homogenizing of human values; still less an abdication of one's personal convictions and experience. It is rather a centering of one's attention upon what unites rather than what divides; the developing of a hierarchy of values in which transcultural values come first, without denigrating the particular values of one's own race, culture, or religion. True unity is expressed in pluralism: unity in the experience of the ultimate values of human life; pluralism in one's unique response to these values in the concrete circumstances of one's life.

Those who seek the ultimate mystery are people of faith, even if they do not belong to a particular religion. Faith is deeper than one's belief system. Belief systems belong to the level of pluralism; faith to the level of unity. Faith is constitutive of human nature itself.[1] It is openness to the ultimate mystery as such, before the ultimate mystery is broken down into various belief systems. It is the acceptance of authentic living with all its creativity, and the acceptance of dying with all its potential for a greater fullness of life. The experience of the transcendent dimension in oneself is an expression of this fundamental faith at work.

One aspect of the search for the ultimate mystery requires special emphasis today. That is its identification with human beings and with their needs, rights, and heartbreaks. One must search for the ultimate mystery not only in itself, but also in its presence in individual human beings, especially in those who are suffering. In the Judeo-Christian tradition, these people are the apple of God's eye, and everyone will be judged on the basis of response to their needs.

Seekers of the ultimate mystery perceive themselves as citizens of the earth. Their first loyalty is to the human family as a whole. The particularities of race, nationalism, religion and culture can be transcended without reacting against them or trying to destroy them. Each culture enshrines human values eminently worth preserving and enhancing but not at the cost of dividing the fundamental unity of the human family. It is possible to belong to the emerging global community as well as to the nation in which one lives; to embrace transcultural religious values as well as to practice one's own religious tradition. Each religious tradition has developed teachings and practices designed to foster the full spiritual development of the human person. These common elements must be recognized as the gift of the ultimate mystery to the whole human family and made more available to the world community as a powerful means of promoting understanding and peace among the nations. Spiritual unity is the catalyst that facilitates harmony and cooperation on all the other levels of social interaction.

Seekers of the ultimate mystery need to be realistic in furthering the cause of unity. The modern world is extremely complex. The problems of peace, hunger, poverty, and justice are so interrelated today that they cannot be solved in isolation. What is required is the massive cooperation of the nations of the world, the world religions, and the worldwide scientific, medical and academic communities.

The question must be posed whether nationalism as a supreme value is healthy or even viable in the technological, cybernetic age. Nationalistic self-interest is becoming an anachronism in a world of increasing interactions in ever-expanding areas of global concern. The original idea of the United Nations as a world federation of autonomous nations designed to respect, foster and protect legitimate cultural differences is a model that deserves to be recognized.

World peace has become the greatest cause in human history. In the nuclear age if this cause fails, everything fails. At the same time a global program for establishing peace based on justice and the equitable distribution of the necessities and goods of the earth is essential for its success. One who is seeking the ultimate mystery can hardly be indifferent to the ultimate concerns of the human family.

The world religions have a special obligation to contribute to the cause of world peace. In the past their confessional differences have led to violence, injustice, and persecution. If they would pool their spiritual resources and give witness to the world community of mutual respect and understanding, political and nationalistic divisions might more easily be overcome.

What is the relationship of seekers to religion? To begin with, the world religions have an ability to respond to the seekers of our time. Are there truths on which the religions of the world are in substantial agreement? Having listened to the masters of other traditions, I am convinced that underlying the particular conceptual frames of reference is a unity that has never been sufficiently grasped. Such a realization could make an extraordinary difference for the future of the world. Here are significant points on which the world religions seem to be in agreement and which point to common understanding and experience of the ultimate mystery.

1. The potential for human wholeness—or, in other frames of reference, liberation, nirvana, self-transcendence, transforming union, enlightenment, salvation—is present in every human person.

2. The human mind cannot form any adequate *idea* of the ultimate mystery, but the ultimate mystery makes itself "known."

3. The ultimate mystery, however understood or experienced, is the source of all existence.

4. Faith is opening, accepting, and responding to the ultimate mystery.

5. Confidence in one's self as rooted in the ultimate mystery is the necessary corollary to faith in the ultimate mystery.

6. As long as the human condition is experienced as separate from the ultimate mystery, it is subject to ignorance and illusion, weakness and suffering.

7. Disciplined practice is essential to the spiritual life; yet spiritual attainment is not the result of one's own efforts, but the result of the experience of oneness with the ultimate mystery.[2]

Besides the immense spiritual resources which these basic insights constitute, the most precious value that the world religions have in common is their accumulated experience of the spiritual journey. Centuries of seekers have discovered and lived its conditions and temptations, trials, developments, and final integration. This wealth of personal experience of the transcendent bears witness to the historical grounding of our contemporary searching. It is not just a passing fad. It invites the spiritual masters of the various disciplines which have evolved in the various world religions to pool their common experience, resources, and insights for the benefit of seekers in every religious tradition.

This vast reservoir of practical wisdom inherited from the past raises an important question. Can one transcend the false self without plugging into the spiritual tradition of one of the world religions? Unfortunately, cultural differences and institutional structures create special difficulties in our time. It is not easy for a westerner to absorb the religion and culture which gave birth to a particular spiritual discipline in the East. Nor is it easy for seekers to accept the religious roots of western culture because that culture seems to be dying. On the other hand, without the experience and encouragement of a community rooted in a long tradition of spiritual discipline, how can one avoid needless mistakes and resist the back-sliding of human weakness? The spiritual renewal of the world religions and a restatement of their spiritual traditions in closer relation to modern conditions might enable seekers who come from a religious background, but who are presently turned off by the lack of spiritual instruction from their churches, to return to the religion of their youth. Then, together with their parent churches, they could work to revitalize the spiritual practices of their respective religions.

Demands of the Spiritual Journey

Certain requirements or characteristics of the spiritual journey seem to be present in every religious tradition. To focus on examples from the Christian tradition, the story of the Magi. described in the Gospel of Matthew can be taken as a parable of the spiritual journey. The Magi are symbols of seekers of the truth. They found what they were seeking, probably to their great astonishment, in the crib, but then Christianity is an astonishing religion. It teaches that the ultimate mystery became the tiniest and most helpless of human beings, a baby.

According to the infancy narratives, many paths lead to the crib. The Magi understood that the advent of a brilliant new star was a gracious reaching out of the ultimate mystery inviting them to search for its meaning and source. An outward revelation by spiritual beings directed the shepherds to the manger. An inward revelation of the Holy Spirit enabled Anna and Simeon to recognize the child when Mary and Joseph carried him into the Temple. Mary and Joseph evidently were led to the babe through their marriage. The babe himself was later to teach that serving the genuine needs of one's neighbor is the surest path to the truth. All true paths tend to converge at the source like the spokes of a wheel. To come closer to the source along one path, therefore, is to come closer to every other path. The main thing is to choose one's path in the light of the inner and outer signals coming from the ultimate mystery, and then to persevere in it regardless of the difficulties that may arise from the length of the journey, the politics of the time, or the opposition of other people.

The Magi returned to their homeland by a route different from the one by which they came. The parable may be hinting that once the babe has been found, the route itself no longer matters. In any case, in order to reach the goal of the Christian journey, the route at a certain point has to be transcended, not necessarily by leaving it, but by the inner freedom that attaches to the goal rather than to the path.

Joseph played a significant role in the preparation of the Gospel. His marriage with Mary seems to modify God's original commandment to Adam and Eve to "increase and multiply and fill the earth," giving that commandment a new dimension and a broader meaning. In Mary and Joseph, the ultimate mystery seems to be extending a new invitation to the human family, this time "to increase and multiply and fill the earth" with the experience of divine union and the expansion of the human power to love which that union brings about. The new commandment, later formulated by Jesus himself, is to fill the earth, that is, the human environment, in a qualitative manner, not just quantitatively. The marriage of Joseph and Mary signifies this new vision of the primary purpose of human life. Thus, according to the firm tradition of earliest Christianity, it was their spiritual union with God and with each other and not their physical union that brought the Son of God into the world and created the environment in which he grew to maturity.

Joseph had his heart set on taking Mary as his wife. Her mysterious pregnancy completely interrupted his marriage plans. He believed that God was asking him to give up the precious vision he had formed for his life. This incident might be described as the loss and finding of Mary. Later, both Joseph and Mary experienced the loss and finding of Jesus when he disappeared for three days in the Temple. For Joseph, each of these events represented a death and a resurrection.

Every seeker of the ultimate mystery has to pass through the experience of death and resurrection, perhaps many times over. Joseph's love of Mary and his vision of life with her—and later his love of Jesus and his vision of life with him—were his two great visions, both given to him directly by God, and both taken away from him through circumstances over which he had no control. These two visions were the two eyes that he had to give up in order to see with God's eyes; he had to surrender his personal vision and become totally blind to it in order to become one with vision itself.

Our contemporary world desperately needs persons of boundless generosity who dedicate themselves to great ideals; who wish to transform themselves and contribute to the transformation of the world. Commitment to a great vision is what gives ordinary daily life its direction and purpose. As one journeys across the desert or prairie or sea—all images in sacred literature of the tedium of ordinary life—one may come upon a place of rest: an oasis, a garden of spiritual delights or a harbor. This can be an occasion of terrible temptation for a person with a great vision. It seems as if one has arrived at the end of the laborious journey and that one's immense efforts are at last coming to fruition. Actually, unless one hastens to push on, the place of rest becomes a place of poison. Spiritual consolation is a trap when sought for one's own satisfaction.

But how does one push on? Is it by giving up the vision? Not exactly. It is rather by being willing to do so. Renunciation is the only way to move beyond what one thinks is the vision and to experience what it actually is. The struggle to attain the land of vision leads inevitably to disappointment, even to what is close to despair. This is because in order to get to the place of vision, it is necessary to give up one's own ideas about how to reach it. It is like dying. The world as we know it must be broken, and ourselves with it. Our idea of the spiritual journey, of service to humanity, of the church, of Jesus Christ, even our idea of God must be shattered. The crux of the human predicament is not the personal wrong-doing for which we are responsible. It is rather our sinful condition, all that causes us merely to reflect about the vision rather than to experience it.

There is another story that speaks to the hearts of those engaged in the spiritual journey, the raising of Lazarus from the dead described in the Gospel of John. Lazarus' illness is a parable of the human condition. According to John's testimony, Lazarus was a special friend of Jesus. But when he fell ill, Jesus did not come to heal him. What is the nature of this mysterious illness that comes upon friends of Jesus? It is the recognition of one's false self and the sense of spiritual poverty which results from this awareness. The false self might be described as the constellation of all the self-serving habits that have been woven into our personality from the time we were conceived. It includes the emotional damage that has come from our upbringing and environment, all the harm that other people have done to us, knowingly or unknowingly, at an age when we could not defend ourselves; and all the methods we acquired, many of them now unconscious, to ward off the pain of unbearable situations. The story of Lazarus is a kind of psychodrama; it is the acting out of Jesus' teaching that one has to lose one's life, one's false self, in order to save it; that is, to find one's true self. The healing of the division in one's self can only come about if one identifies with the illness of Lazarus.

At a certain point in the spiritual journey, one's unconscious motivation begins to surface and the truth about oneself, whatever that may be, has to be faced. In the past one may have been a pillar of strength for one's neighbors, friends, and family, or may have worked for some great cause. But there is a new sensation, a strange gnawing question inside: "Why did you do all those things? Where was it all coming from?" All the good that one struggled so hard to accomplish in the past seems trifling compared to the evil that one recognizes in oneself. It may be impossible to believe in one's own goodness because there is no longer any experience of it. A terrible feeling of dread may arise as one questions what to do with this pervasive sense of the absence of meaning in one's life. And there is the temptation to think that no outside power can help.

In this situation there is only one support: hope in the compassion of the ultimate mystery. But that support is not felt. This is the time to hope, continuing to hope against hope; the time to wait. According to the story Lazarus died and was laid in the tomb, a striking image of the psychological state of one who feels alienated from the ultimate mystery. It is at this point in the spiritual journey that one encounters head-on the existential anguish of contemporary society.

Abandoned to what seem to be uncontrollable forces of political and social change, our contemporary world groans under pervasive despair, of being abandoned by the ultimate mystery, or at least of experiencing it as absent. This absence of the ultimate mystery is accompanied by the loss of the sense of value in life itself. One has only to read a book like *The Autobiography of Malcolm X* to realize what this means concretely for countless numbers of people. At the very least, it involves loneliness, confusion, powerlessness, frustration, fear. If these people are to find the ultimate mystery they have to search for it in a society in which, to all appearances, it has been almost totally forgotten. Those in search of the ultimate mystery must be willing to share in the agony of our time. The sense of alienation from the ultimate mystery, from human values, and from oneself is very deep in our time. Hence, participation in that experience is also bound to be very deep. It may involve an inner poverty so intense and so complete that no word can describe it except death. Although Lazarus was not aware of it, Jesus had come to the place where he was laid and was about to call him from the tomb to life. The symbol of Lazarus challenges those on the spiritual journey to go the whole way in letting go of the false self with its illusions and hang-ups. The inner resurrection of one's true self moves the whole human family in the direction of transformation. In this perspective, the spiritual journey is the very reverse of selfishness. It is rather the journey to selflessness.

Aim of the Search

What needs to be emphasized by those in search of the ultimate mystery is the contemplative dimension of human life, whether they identify the aim of their search as self-transcendence, transformation in Christ, enlightenment, union with the ultimate mystery, or whatever. By the contemplative dimension of human life I mean the growth of faith to the point that one's actions are motivated by an abiding sensitivity to the presence of the ultimate mystery with insight into its secret workings in all that happens both inwardly and outwardly. The growth of the contemplative dimension leads to the stable perception of the presence of the ultimate mystery underlying and accompanying all reality like a fourth dimension of ordinary sense perception. To dispose oneself for this awareness, one needs a discipline that engages all the faculties and a structure appropriate to one's life circumstances that can sustain it.

To begin, one needs to cultivate a practical conviction of the primacy of being over doing. Our society commonly values what one can do and this becomes the gauge of who one is. The contemplative dimension, however, is an insight into the gift of being human that enables one to believe unhesitatingly in one's own basic goodness. It also perceives the basic goodness of everyone else. It enables one to accept physical death as a step in one's evolution to the fullness of life. And finally, it perceives the presence of the ultimate mystery at the heart of all reality because it no longer gets stuck on the meaning of symbols but goes through the symbols to the reality.

Our world is at a crisis point because so many structures that supported human and religious values have been trampled upon. To discover the ultimate mystery at the center of so-called "secular" occupations and situations is essential because for most people today it is the only milieu that they know. Humanity as a whole needs a breakthrough into the contemplative dimension of life. This is the heart of the world. There the human family is already one. If one goes to one's own heart, one will find oneself in the heart of everyone else.

Notes

1. Raimundo Panikkar, *Faith, Myth, and Hermeneutics* (Ramsey, N.J.: Paulist Press, 1980.)
2. These points of agreement were drawn up by a group of twelve spiritual teachers from Buddhist, Hindu, Jewish, Native American, and Christian traditions meeting at St. Benedict's Monastery, Snowmass, Colorado from October 21 to 24, 1984.

4

Moving the Fence: One Rabbi's View of Interreligious Dialogue

Rami Mark Shapiro

Not in Heaven: A Prerequisite for Dialogue

During the past ten years I have been involved, to one degree or another, in interreligious dialogue. Through books, study, formal meetings, and informal encounters, I have made my life and learning an arena for cross-cultural meeting and exchange. I have done this out of the firm belief that through authentic interreligious dialogue we can help each other overcome the sense of separateness and alienation that keeps us from awakening to the unity and wonder that is at the heart of ordinary living. It is my belief that genuine dialogue can be a means for centering, awakening, and enlightenment.

Genuine interreligious dialogue is not a safe ecumenical gathering. Genuine dialogue demands that we place ourselves on the line in a mutual quest for truth. Certainly we can sit down together and share information. We can learn from each other about each other—in this there is much merit, but it is not yet authentic dialogue. Authentic dialogue demands a special kind of freedom that only people truly at home in their given faith traditions can achieve. Genuine dialogue demands that we look into the blind spots of our traditions through the eyes of another; it demands that we are secure enough in where we come from to risk venturing where we have never been. Genuine dialogue requires a commitment to our personal "ism" that is strong enough to allow us to suspend belief and step beyond the "ism" to meet what "is." All of this is a prerequisite for genuine dialogue, and all of this falls under the heading: "Not in Heaven."

In the Book of Deuteronomy, Moses addresses the people of Israel saying:

> Surely, this Teaching which I enjoin upon you this day is not too baffling for you, nor is it beyond reach. It is not in the heavens, that you should say, "Who can go up to the heavens and get it for us, that we may observe it?" Neither is it beyond the sea, that you should say, "Who among us can cross to the other side of the sea and get it for us and impart it to us, that we may observe it?" No, It is very close to you, in your mouth and in your heart, to observe It. (Deuteronomy 30:11-14)

"It is not in heaven" means that truth is not far away, that it is "very close"; "in our mouths" if we would but speak honestly; "in our hearts" if we would but open to one another in fellowship and with compassion. Moses is saying: "There is no excuse for not living justly and with truth. Reality is not alien to you or hidden from you. It is you just as your mouth is you, your heart is you. It is not in a book or a teacher, it is not restricted to one path or way. It is very close to you if only you would but meet the world with the fullness of your heart, mind, body, and soul. In meeting the world you will encounter truth."

"Not in Heaven" as a prerequisite for authentic interreligious dialogue also means that we recognize the limitations of our images and the ineffable quality of reality. "Not in Heaven" removes the hubris from institutionalized faith and restores our humility in the face of the humor, wonder, sadness, and grace that is ordinary living. "Not in Heaven" assumes a common humanity, a common quest, a common strength and limitation. "Not in Heaven" allows us to dialogue.

Authentic Dialogue

The Jewish philosopher Martin Buber (1878-1965) set forth the following six criteria for authentic dialogue.

1. When people interact authentically, when they move beyond themselves to encounter the other person as an equal, they discover a basic reality, a "sphere of between" that links humanity in some greater wholeness.

2. This sphere of between is a primal category of human reality available to us through human dialogue.

3. Genuine dialogue happens when one contributes one's spirit without abbreviation or distortion: everything depends upon the legitimacy of what one has to say.

4. Genuine dialogue requires the overcoming of appearance. If the thought of one's effect as a speaker outweighs the thought of what one has to say, then one inevitably and irreparably deforms what one has to say: it enters deformed into the conversation, and the conversation itself is deformed.

5. Genuine dialogue does not require that everyone present has to speak, but that no one can be there as a mere observer. Each must be ready to share with the others, and no one can know in advance that he or she will have something to say.

6. Genuine dialogue can be either spoken or silent. Its essence lies in the fact that each participant turns to the others with the intention of establishing a living mutual relationship.

Buber's position is that through authentic dialogue we enter into the sphere of between linking each of us to the other in a greater unity without erasing our personal uniqueness. Authentic dialogue should not blur distinctions, but honor both similarities and differences. Just as a magnet needs both positive and negative poles, so reality needs both unity and diversity. The One does not preclude the Many; it embraces it. But for this honoring to happen, participants in authentic dialogue must be willing to risk all. This is what Buber means by "one contributes one's spirit without abbreviation and distortion." Participants must put themselves and their traditions on the line. If we hold back, if we are afraid to let others examine us and our beliefs then we will distort the truth and "deform" the dialogue. This does not mean that we come to these dialogues with a vehement desire to "bear all," indeed we must come to them with a humility that frees us from having to speak at all. We need not be heard. We need not defend. We need not make our case or win our point. We need only be present, fully and passionately there, offering through silence or words our bit of wisdom to the unfolding whole. Authentic dialogue cannot be preplanned, it cannot have established taboos, it cannot have limits other than the limits of human kindness and respect for one another. Genuine dialogue must be an open-ended meeting of daring individuals who trust themselves, their traditions, and their partners-in-dialogue enough to risk all that they might discover something more, something new.

The goal of genuine dialogue is not simply to share competing platforms and dogmas, but to partake of a much more powerful opportunity for awakening. This awakening is not simply an appreciation of another's point of view, but the stepping beyond fixed points of view in hopes that reality might be encountered in a manner that is fresh, evocative and rich with new possibilities for human growth, unity, and enlightenment. This is both the beauty and the danger of authentic dialogue.

The beauty of authentic dialogue is its capacity to open participants (and through them their constituents) to new ways of seeing the world and the wonder implicit in it. The danger is that new ways of seeing are often received with fear, and the seer is suddenly suspect of having been tainted by the encounter with other faith traditions. To bolster the former and lessen the latter, it is essential that all concerned foster the attitude of "Not in Heaven." But can we?

Who participates in authentic interreligious dialogue? Do we ever see the Pope sitting down with the Ayatollah, or either sharing with the Chief Rabbis of Israel? No, we do not. Why? Because these men cannot accept "Not in Heaven" as a prerequisite for genuine dialogue. As defenders of particular and mutually exclusive faith traditions, the best these men could hope for is a cordial exchange of doctrine. Indeed, this is precisely what the Second Vatican Council calls for in its statement on ecumenical dialogue.

> Dialogue [takes place] between competent experts from different Churches and Communities. In their meetings, which are organized in a religious spirit, each explains the teaching of his Communion in greater depth and brings out clearly its distinctive features. Through such dialogue everyone gains a truer knowledge and more just appreciation of the teachings and religious life of both Communions.[1]

While there is nothing "wrong" with this approach to ecumenical encounter, it should not be mistaken for genuine dialogue. In the beginning it may be necessary for participants in authentic dialogue to make sure all concerned understand the various faith traditions represented, but the goal is to go beyond comparative religion and see if through the mutual exchange of insight one can get outside one's particular "ism" and glimpse the "is."

The conventional Vatican II model of ecumenical encounter is analogous to an international delegation of gourmets meeting over a sumptuous meal who simply exchange menus from their respective countries without ever tasting the food set before them. Certainly much would be learned, but the wonder of the meal and the communion that could be established by sharing it is lost.

Given the risky and daring nature of genuine dialogue, those who participate fully in such encounters are rarely, if ever, the establishment spokespersons of their respective faith traditions. Rather, genuine dialoguers, while deeply rooted in their faith, are the risk takers, the radicals, the prophets who are not afraid to affirm wonder wherever it is revealed. While participants may be and often are abbots, roshis, gurus, priests, imams, established scholars, rabbis, and others whose positions in their respective communities may well be exalted, they are nonetheless not the official spokespersons of their faith. They represent not so much the tradition to which they belong, but themselves and the spiritual quest they personally undertake. They choose of their own accord to participate, to risk, to put themselves on the line spiritually and existentially in hopes of experiencing the wonder that meeting entails. Genuine dialoguers are rare and wonderful people, and while I cannot claim to fit the mold, I am honored nonetheless to have been invited to share with such gifted and loving teachers.

Personal Reflections

While participating in a variety of interreligious encounters over the course of my rabbinate, two stand out as examples of the potential for awakening that genuine dialogue offers. One occurred at the Assembly of the World's Religions held in McAfee, New Jersey, in 1985, another at St. Benedict's Monastery in Snowmass, Colorado, in 1983. While these two encounters differed in both size and scope, a common thread of the "sphere of between" ran through each.

In both cases the participants were secure in their respective traditions. While recognizing that "It is Not in Heaven" and that there is no path, let alone one true path to the truth, each of us felt comfortable with the symbols, histories, rituals, and traditions of our respective faiths. We were not threatened by others equally committed to their own way. We were not afraid to discover similarities, nor embarrassed to stumble over differences. Even when there were sharp and unbridgeable gaps between traditions and teachings, still the sphere of between bound us together.

I remember one particular discussion during the Assembly of the World's Religions. A Jain monk was explaining that in his tradition the soul is fundamentally independent and on its own; there is no union with God or connection with other beings. Those of us in attendance did our best to rework what the monk was saying so that it more closely matched our own teachings about unity and unification. But try as we might the integrity of our dialogue refused to permit us to pretend to some agreement that was not in fact there.

As this point dawned on me I began to laugh. Not loudly. Perhaps, as I think back on it now, not even outwardly. Yet deeply and powerfully. I laughed as an expression of "something awakening." I laughed as the idol of a false unity was toppled and the wonder of diversity was affirmed. I laughed with joy at our different paths and the fundamental pathlessness of Truth.

At that moment, I realized in a deep and powerful way— though not one given to reason or words on a page—that regardless of Jainism and Judaism, regardless of sutras and scriptures, regardless of all the words spent on explaining our differences—there was in fact common ground: the here and now dialogue and sharing that we were involved in made a greater statement of Truth than any doctrine we might take up and examine. There was something in the act of listening, of speaking, of taking the other to heart that opened my heart to ineffable wonder.

The key term here is ineffable. The whole cannot be reduced to a neat and marketable package of information. It can only be met and encountered and embraced. It must actively engage the self, subsume the self into the other as an act of both submission and affirmation. Even as I submit myself to the whole I am affirmed and made aware of my uniqueness. It is the paradox of reality that unity necessitates diversity. Thus even as I embrace the infinite I am confirmed in my finitude. This is why reality is ultimately ineffable—it includes its own opposite and cannot be abstracted from the goings-on of any given moment.

A similar insight was given me during my stay at St. Benedict's Monastery in Snowmass. Because of the small and intimate nature of our gathering, we moved very quickly beyond a study of comparative traditions and into the much more fruitful sharing of personal experiences. Each of us told the story of our spiritual quest. Some chose to tell the tale through the tales of their teachers. Others chose to weave their story on the loom of traditional teaching tales, but each of us told our story. For me that is the heart of religion: the telling of stories, powerful tales that open the listener up to holiness.

So often in interreligious dialogue we engage in apologetics. We speak at each other and not to each other. At Snowmass we strove for intimacy. We spoke softly, intensely, personally of the pain and burden of spiritual journeying and leadership. We spoke candidly of the turmoil we and our traditions and our communities are undergoing. And we spoke of the awesome respect we had for the paths each of us had chosen. Our respect grew not from the historicity of a given tradition, not from its politics or piety, but from our growing awareness that all religions are partial articulations of truth.

Each tradition has its blind spot. Yet by genuinely dialoguing with people deeply rooted in other faith traditions we might look for a moment through their eyes and see what our own blind spot prevents us from seeing. And in this is sheer joy.

One morning the conversation turned to Jesus, the suffering servant nailed to a cross. While the Jewish prophet Isaiah introduced the concept of the suffering servant, referring to the people Israel rather than one Jew in particular, I admit to having trouble with Jesus. The history of abuse against my people and other "non-believers" that finds excuse and rationale in his name makes the very figure of Jesus suspect to me. And yet here was a man I admired and respected telling me of his love for this martyred messiah.

At first I couldn't hear it. The words were there, but I wasn't truly listening. Then as the passion of my friend's convictions broke through the barriers of my own fear, disbelief, and anger, I began to listen and to hear and to know Jesus through the heart of another.

Not Jesus the God; not Jesus the Messiah; but Jesus the man, the crucified servant who died for his belief and his right to speak it freely. I sensed the faith of my friend even though I could not share it. I saw through his eyes what I could not see with my own. I cannot pretend to understand the mystery of faith in Christ crucified and resurrected, but I did open my heart to that of another and found there new insight into the human grappling with suffering and meaning, and a renewed sense of purpose and peace. Without words to map it out, I stepped on foreign shores and beheld some of its beauty and grace. And from that brief meeting came a deeper appreciation

for Christian faith and a renewed bonding with humanity arising from my having entered the sphere of between.

We took a break shortly thereafter, and I remember walking
outside to take in the glory of the Rocky Mountains in winter.
Not too far from me was a photographer eyeing the mountains
through his viewfinder. The cliffs were draped in new snow,
thick clouds hugged the mountains' peaks. It was an incredible
sight. But the photographer couldn't capture it. He would put
his camera to his face, focus, refocus, scowl and put the camera
aside for a moment to look again with his own eyes. Time after
time he sought the right angle, the perfect point of view that
would reveal the grandeur of the mountains. But he couldn't
find it. He grew frustrated and eventually walked away without
taking a single picture.

The photographer's frustration was inevitable. There is no
perfect angle or point of view that can reveal the Whole.
Whether we are talking about a range of mountains, a range of
teachings, or the ineffable wonder of reality itself, no lens can
capture the big picture. The camera could not capture the essence of what the photographer saw because that essence arose
not from the mountains themselves but from his personal meeting with them. Meaning, wonder, awe, and grace arise not from
within or without but from the sphere of between that is established when we meet. The camera can record an object, but not
the meeting that makes for wonder. It can record the mountain
and the man, but not the inbetweenness that so powerfully
linked the two. Great photography never captures an image,
but rather frees it to dialogue with others. The same is true of
great stories and great religions.

The potential and power of authentic dialogue and interreligious meeting arises not from the sharing of traditions or
the explaining of doctrine; the power for healing, for unity and
fellowship comes when the participants genuinely meet and
dialogue with each other as equals and together enter the
sphere of between.

To What End

Several times a year I participate in formal interreligious
events. The worst of these is simply a smorgasbord of religious
traditions. A topic or theme is offered as a focus and representatives of various faith traditions articulate their official positions on the matter at hand. There is no real communication.
Nothing is learned that could not be learned from a book or en-
cyclopaedia.

The best of these events are those that go beyond the expected. These begin with the premise that genuine dialogue is unprecedented, unpredictable, open, honest, and daring. Here the emphasis is not to state positions, but to understand the person. Here the emphasis is not on doctrine or dogma but on the human quest for meaning, purpose and wonder. It is at these meetings that true meeting happens, that participants enter into the sphere of between and discover a greater unity that makes us all one humanity. There is no need for apologetics or defensive posturing; no need to rationalize or compromise one's beliefs or faith tradition—rather with all our differences intact we step beyond tolerance and the implications of superiority that tolerance maintains, and enter into a deep understanding of plurality and diversity as a necessary aspect of unity.

And yet even with the best of these events I am often asked a very simple and provocative question: Why bother? Is the world really a better place for our having had our dialogue?

No it is not. And yet...and yet....

It is true that the meeting of religious teachers and way-pointers does not in and of itself make the world a safer or more benign place to live. It is true that the problems I leave at home when I travel are waiting for me when I return. It is true that anti-Semitism seems to persist no matter how often rabbis speak out and share the heart of Judaism. And yet....

And yet there is a bit more knowledge now than there was before, a little more understanding. There is a sense among some that religions can be gateways to healing rather than obstacles to peace. By sharing the Way of meeting there is hope that religions and people can recapture the art of peace and free themselves from the pretense that God's blessing rests upon unjust and inhumane behavior. There is a feeling that participants will go home and teach the common heritage of humankind's quest for truth, putting an end to slanderous accusations against religions and those who uphold them whenever and wherever they are encountered.

It is true that no gathering in and of itself makes for a new world. But it is also true that only through meeting, genuine meeting that leads to the sphere of between, is there any hope at all for a new world. Interreligious dialogue plants the seeds of new thinking, new understanding, new ways of being in the world. These seeds need the nurturing of time and study, spirit and grace. They need the continued care of those who plant them and those who take responsibility for their nurture and growth. But there is every hope that the seed will outlive the planter and bring forth a rich harvest of human dignity and grace.

Conclusion: Moving the Fence

Douglas Steere, the patriarch of modern Quakerism, and one of the participants at the Snowmass conference, told a powerful and elegant story about an American Quaker woman who went to Poland in the 1920s to help care for the poor and the hungry. The woman labored for years among the peasants, ministering to their needs: medical, emotional, and spiritual. She cared for them when no one else seemed to care. Her service and devotion won her the love of the people. After so many years of working with the ill and ill cared for, she fell sick with typhus and died within a day's time.

The rule of the Roman Catholic Church forbade the burial of any non-Catholic in a Catholic cemetery. But there was no other cemetery anywhere nearby. The best that could be done for her was to bury her outside the cemetery gates near the fence that encircled the cemetery and marked it as hallowed ground. She was buried there with a simple ceremony early the next morning.

When evening fell, villagers from the surrounding hamlets made their way to her grave under the cover of darkness. Quietly they removed the fence that marked this part of the cemetery and, working throughout the night, moved the fence to include the grave of their friend within the boundaries of the cemetery. This is what genuine interreligious dialogue is all about. Without confrontation and ecumenical harangue, we build bridges and recover unity. Quietly and with love, we move the fence to include us all within the hallowed ground of this fragile planet we call home.

Notes

1. *Documents of Vatican II*, ed. W.M. Abbott, S.J. (New York: America Press, 1966), 347.

5

Current Interreligious Dialogue

A. Durwood Foster

What are the aims of interreligious conversation, and how well are these being accomplished by the actual dialogues that have been and are underway? The epoch-making World Parliament of Religions in 1893 announced ten proposed objects, as it addressed invitations throughout the earth. Since many will be preparing to commemorate the centennial of that notable congress, it is interesting to review what the ten objects were, and how they have fared over the intervening century.[1]

The first was "to bring together in conference for the first time in history the leading representatives of the historic religions of the world." Let me comment here that while the Chicago Parliament drew some 7,000 persons, many hundreds of them from around the world, and while it was monumentally successful in including spokespersons from the major historic traditions, it still fell far short, inevitably, of covering the vast diversity of existing religion. For one thing, deliberately, it did not include the new religious movements like the Baha'i World Faith or Christian Science or Mormonism. Nor did it adequately reflect the internal divisions of historic faiths subsumed under common labels like Hinduism or Buddhism. Because the meeting took place in America, the varieties of Christianity were by far the best represented. Nevertheless Eastern Orthodoxy, for example, and Roman Catholicism were greatly underrepresented; and no one was there at all from such historic and distinctive Christian bodies as the Egyptian Coptic and the Malabar Syrian Church. With respect to Hinduism and Buddhism the situation was much worse. Hindu Vedanta was superbly represented by Swami Vivekananda, who became in fact the outstanding star of the whole parliament, but Saivist and Vaisnava Hinduism, much more typical of that religion as a whole, were completely absent. Buddhism was best featured in its Mahayana expression, though far from thoroughly; while there were few Theravadins and, so far as I can discover, no Vajrayanins at all. In short, the proposal to bring together "leading representatives" of the world's religions was at best only partially fulfilled; and subsequent efforts toward "the wider ecumenism," as it has come to be called, have continued to try to make good what was lacking. This has been done, and is being done, both by involving the new religious movements—there was never any good excuse for omitting them—and by attempting more thorough coverage of the distinctive types within the great historic traditions.

The second stated goal of the 1893 World Parliament was "to show…in the most impressive way, what and how many important truths the various religions hold and teach in common." This intention stimulated a wave of books expounding what were taken to be significant agreements among the religions. Paramount among such agreements were precepts like the following: that ultimate reality is benevolent; that selfishness is the root of human misery; that relief and release from despair is possible through humility and compassion; and that the highest axiom of moral behavior is the so-called golden rule, or its counterpart, the silver rule of Confucius, which says "Do not do unto others what you would not have them do to you." However, already in 1893, and much more so in the following decades, the results of interreligious encounter did not appear to show nearly as much agreement as many had anticipated. On the contrary, profound differences among religions seemed to become more pronounced. One of the most conspicuous of these was and still is the prima facie antithesis between Buddhist atheism and Judaeo-Christian (as well as Muslim) theism. Another cleavage was and still is the understanding of the human self: whether the self is an illusion, as both Buddhists and Hindus have tended to believe, or whether the self is real and good. A third crucial difference concerns the value of human life in the world and the positive meaning of history. Biblical faith, with its controlling idea of the Kingdom of God, has strongly affirmed the goodness of creation and the meaningfulness of history, whereas both of these have seemed to be denied in the classical expressions of Hinduism and Buddhism. Therefore the intervening century since 1893 has considerably complexified the objective of exhibiting the agreements of the religions. We realize today that there are both unities and disunities among the faiths of humanity, and neither end of the stick is superficial or unimportant.

The third goal posited by the sponsors of the 1893 World Parliament was "to promote and deepen the spirit of human brotherhood among religious men of diverse faiths, through friendly conference and mutual good understanding, while not seeking to foster the temper of indifferentism, and not striving to achieve any formal and outward unity." It can be claimed, I think, that the aim of promoting brotherhood and sisterhood among persons of diverse faiths was fulfilled to an appreciable degree by the Chicago meeting, and has continued to be advanced since then by the process of interreligious dialogue. Consistently the wider ecumenical movement, like the intra-Christian World Council of Churches, has affirmed that it does not wish to foster indifference to specific confessional identity and allegiances; and the notion of an all-encompassing single religion, like that of a single super church, has been more or less universally repudiated.

Nevertheless, over the last decades there has become increasingly manifest through the interaction of religions a different kind of result than that foreseen or intended by the 1893 Parliament. This is well expressed in the title of a recent widely acclaimed book by Professor John Cobb of the Claremont School of Theology. His book is titled *Beyond Dialogue: Toward A Mutual Transformation of Christianity and Buddhism*. One version of what Cobb means is illustrated by the growing number of scholars who discover themselves as having today a double (or maybe a multiple) religious identity. Cobb argues that it is perfectly possible for a Buddhist to be a Christian and a Christian a Buddhist. However one may assess this in theory, I have been meeting lately quite a number of persons who do think this way about themselves. I think, for example, of three rather well known American professors who were at a conference I attended not long ago. Each of these professors is a recognized expert on Buddhism. Each of them is also a serious practicing Christian (Lutheran, high church Anglican, and Baptist, respectively). Yet each confided to me that he has appropriated Buddhist insights to a degree that significantly shapes his religious self-understanding. Each says he is a Buddhist as well as a Christian. Looking in the other direction, at the same conference, the person who a couple of times stood out as advocating Christian views was a distinguished Buddhist philosopher. Someone quipped that this man was the best Christian theologian at the conference; and the quip, I think everyone agreed, was in some respects not merely a quip! The upshot of this kind of thing is that we can no longer assume the 1893 objective of dialoguing between faith positions which remain fixed in their distinctive integrity. Faith is both powerful and subject to suasion and mutation under the impact of other faiths. While today's wider ecumenism decidedly repudiates any kind of imperialism, dynamic transformation and resynthesizing is occurring in many traditions; and no one can predict at this point what new varieties and unities within world religion will be emerging next.

The fourth proposed object in Chicago ninety-two years ago was "to set forth, by those most competent to speak, what are deemed the important distinctive truths held and taught by each religion and by the various chief branches of Christendom." The principle involved here has in the interim been more and more strongly confirmed: that is, that the only adequate or authentic way to gain insight into a religion is through the explanatory witness of one who is a participating believer in the religion. Again and again in the kind of dialogues in which I have taken part, one will discover that one's "book knowledge" of Hinduism, for example, is grotesquely misleading in the light of what a living and present Hindu can elucidate about his or her own faith. The bottom line is that there is no substitute, if one seeks valid understanding, for actual interpersonal dialogue with persons of other faiths. Of course, dialogue does not guarantee understanding. Nothing can do that. But most scholars agree today it is a *sine qua non* for it.

The fifth objective of the Parliament is the one that sounds the most dated. It reads as follows: "To indicate the impregnable foundations of theism and the reasons for man's faith in immortality, and thus to unite and strengthen the forces which are adverse to a materialistic philosophy of the universe." The phrase "impregnable foundations" connoted an invincible philosophical or rational basis for religious doctrines, but in the intervening century most theological thinkers have come to acknowledge that the axioms of faith cannot be proved or disproved by reason. Moreover, it has become quite clear that neither theism nor immortality of the soul is universally affirmed by the religions of humankind. Within Christianity itself, panentheism has tended to replace theism as a philosophical concept of God's relation to the world; and resurrection, rather than immortality, has been seen as the distinctive biblical way of symbolizing human participation in eternal life. Furthermore, the fifth objective of the Parliament sounds as though religions are being rallied to oppose materialism. There has been a good deal of this in the air over the last century. However, many contemporaries who pursue interreligious dialogue are interested in understanding materialism more deeply and doing more justice to the aspect of truth it represents. This attitude informs, for example, the Christian-Marxist dialogue, and also the Buddhist-Marxist dialogue that has lately been desiderated by the Dalai Lama. There is a strong feeling afoot, even in Hinduism, that religion in general has to overcome a kind of ghostly idealism, a one-sided tendency to be otherworldly. And this issue looms quite large in current interfaith discussions.

The sixth goal of the Chicago Parliament was "to secure from leading scholars (representing the Brahman, Confucian, Parsee, Mohammedan, Jewish and other faiths, and from representatives of the various churches of christendom) full and accurate statements of the spiritual and other effects of the religions which they hold, upon the literature, art, commerce, government, domestic and social life of the people among whom these faiths have prevailed." This project requires little comment. Essentially endless in scope, it has been intensively under way during the intervening decades and has made possible the already mentioned explosion of knowledge in the field of religion. At the same time, the secularization of modern culture has tended to make precarious the place of religious studies in our philosophy of public education, so that the possibility of society at large being engulfed by religious illiteracy, just when scholarship offers unprecedented knowledge, is a real possibility.

The seventh stated purpose of the 1893 meeting was "to enquire what light each religion has afforded, or may afford, to the other religions of the world." This shows that the Chicago Parliament also anticipated what was said above about mutual transformation, beyond mere dialogue. There were undoubtedly two parties involved at Chicago in formulating the goals of the Parliament. The more dominant party was responsible for the third goal, which reaffirmed the integrity of existing denominations and traditions. But what must have been a minority party, supported as well by unsatisfied sentiments in the larger party, succeeded in adding this seventh goal regarding the sharing of light. Shared light does not leave things the same but inevitably brings about transformation of religious existence and identity.

The eighth Chicago objective was "to set forth, for permanent record to be published to the world, an accurate and authoritative account of the present condition and outlook of religion among the leading nations of the earth." Two thick volumes of the proceedings were published in the aftermath of the Parliament. Their accounts were as accurate and authoritative as could be hoped for in 1893, though needless to say, besides being incomplete, they were quickly out of date. The effort to keep track of what is happening to religion in various regions of the planet has been fairly diligently pursued since then, but is not, I think, particularly successful at this time, because of turmoil and rapidly changing conditions. Lebanon, for example, is religiously, in any deeper sense, largely an enigma at this time. Cambodia (Kampuchea) is more so. The Soviet Union and China are religiously extremely difficult to comprehend; and so is Japan, for that matter, even though it lies completely open to empirical study. In sum, we probably know a good deal less about the actual condition (as distinct from the content) of religion around the world today than was known in 1893.

The ninth proposed object of the world parliament was "to discover from competent men what light religion has to throw on the great problems of the present age, especially on important questions connected with temperance, labor, education, wealth, and poverty." Methodologically this sounded an important note. It pledged interreligious dialogue to what Paul Tillich has named the method of correlation. That is: the real meaning and value of religious beliefs must be sought in intimate connection with the concrete problems experienced by human beings. The list of problems interestingly overlaps the pressing agenda of our own day, especially if we construe "temperance" as pointing to the massive, baffling threat of narcotics. Certainly we have not resolved any of the problems our 1893 forebears mentioned. "Wealth and poverty," and the systems of oppression entwined therewith, are the principal issues, for example, to which current liberation theology addresses itself. However, some whopping problems have been added to the list, such as the threat to the environment, the spreading malignancy of organized crime, the pathology of racism and sexism, and the impact of depersonalizing technology as well as demoralizing secularization and profanization throughout the earth. Current interreligious dialogue reflects all of these concerns and many, as already suggested, turn to it in the hope of dealing more effectively with them.

However, no concern today is paramount to that sounded in the tenth and last stated objective of 1893: "to bring the nations of the earth into a more friendly fellowship in the hope of securing permanent international peace." In view of the horrendous intervening events of the last ninety years, this aspiration of our grandparent or great-grandparent generation carries for us a heavy pathos. The least that can be said is that our need for peace today is far more urgent than could possibly have been foreseen in 1893; yet in the sober judgment of many of our brightest minds the prospects for peace, and for human survival, have never been as precarious as they now are.

Historically it seems that religion has often done a great deal to foment, not peace, but strife and warfare. Lamentably, this cannot be denied. Religion is the dimension of our ultimate concern and commitment; it is the locus of that meaning and power that enables us to "go for broke," to offer everything, including our lives, for a cause. And when we absolutize our own cause, religion gives us the freedom of conscience and the fanatic resolve to take life—to destroy others, not just randomly but rationally and systematically, as on the "killing fields" of Cambodia, as the current film depicts so horrifyingly.

It is for this reason, I want to point out, that many today take interreligious dialogue with new seriousness. Imperialistic religion, self-contained and unchecked by any counterpart, is indeed historically the spawning bed of crusades and jihads, of inquisitions and pogroms. It is because dialogical religion might be, could be, an antidote and counterforce to imperialistic religion that some see it as an integral component in our desperate search today for peace.

There is a special problem, though, in the fact that the antagonists who most threaten peace and human survival today do not readily open themselves to interreligious dialogue—that is, to an earnest give-and-take regarding ultimate values and commitments. I am referring to the communist and anti-communist polarization that runs so acrimoniously and dangerously through our world. It is in this context that the dialogue with Marxism, inchoately undertaken already by Christian groups, by some Buddhists, and incipiently by Hindus and Muslims, is so significant. It forms without question one of the most indispensable sectors of the religious dialogical enterprise.

These then are some of the goals, aspects, and problems of current interreligious dialogue, as compared with where the process was a century ago. Before concluding I also want to address the question, albeit very briefly, of what positive results may be emerging from the give-and-take within world religion.

I believe progress is being made in mutual understanding and appreciation, and I cite the following examples. First, there is a widening tendency for religions, not only to recognize, but to adopt into their own frames of meaning and value, the internal history of other religions. Jesus has an honored place in the *Qur'an*; this has always been a wholesome leaven in Muslim-Christian relations, and theologians of both these communities are lately appreciating it afresh. Gautama the Buddha has been accorded the status of an incarnation of the Hindu God Vishnu, and is more and more widely esteemed as such in India. For a good deal of emerging Christian theology, Krishna, as well as Gautama and Muhammad, are "Christ figures," that is, significant anticipations or replications of the "christic process," the liberation and healing which the word "Christ" means.

As the mutual recognition of founders already illustrates, progress in interfaith appreciation also occurs today through deeper insight into the symbolic nature of religious language. As Paul Tillich used to insist, literalism, in all traditions, is the greatest single obstacle to religious understanding. Flat literalism fails to comprehend that religious concepts and images point beyond themselves to mysteries and meanings that cannot be univocally expressed in ordinary language. It leads to the caricature of exotic symbols like the Hindu monkey god Hanuman or the elephant god Ganesha, worship of whom has frequently been abhorred by Christian and Muslim missionaries as disgusting idolatry. In contrast, deliteralizing such symbols uncovers that depth of meaning in which they express the power of natural vitality to mediate the divine, for which Hinduism has unique sensibility.

The final illustration I want briefly to give of current intercommunicative progress among religions has to do with reciprocal acknowledgment of conceptual diversity within traditions. It has frequently been asserted that Buddhism is atheistic and that Christianity stands or falls with its belief in the existence of God; therefore never the twain shall meet. What this simplistic antithesis ignores is that in Buddhism there are also theistic elements, and in Christianity there are atheistic elements. In and through its many schools and denominations, Buddhism affirms that the ultimate is "emptiness" (or sunyata), but it also holds that the threefold body of the Buddha savingly mediates this ultimate truth, and that savior gods, like Amida Buddha, validly symbolize this for humanity at large. Christianity on the other hand, in the teaching of many of its leading theologians through the centuries, has affirmed that God is beyond essence and existence, that the divine in itself is apophatic or inexpressible. This strand in the Christian tradition is intriguingly close to what Buddhist thinkers appear to mean by "ultimate emptiness," just as Buddhist theism corresponds functionally to the way many Christians understand the trinitarian symbols and God as personal Father/Mother.

I am, of course, just scratching the surface of a very complex discussion, requiring much time, careful study, empathy and patience. My only point at the moment is that dialogical explorations of this sort are now occurring among Buddhists and Christians; and that they have already shown how superficial and misleading, as a way of portraying Buddhism and Christianity, is the simple-minded opposition that says one tradition "believes in God" and the other does not.

John Wesley, whenever approaching a theological issue or project, strongly enjoined the use of four basic sources: scripture, tradition, reason and experience. He had in mind, of course, the Bible and the Christian tradition; he also meant specifically Christian experience; and reason, too, for him, while he assumed its logical universality, was eighteenth century European reason. Given his unconscious parochialism, Wesley was a remarkably ecumenical spirit who affirmed "the whole world as [his] parish" and said in principle to everyone: "if your heart is as my heart, give me your hand."

Relieved of their Christian fences, Wesley's proposed sources for theological work are quite apt and apply, I believe, also to our exploratory venture in wider ecumenical understanding. The scriptures we will need to study are of course the Bible of the World (not just Robert Ballou's edition but a far more adequate one including the philosophical classics). All of our traditions are in principle eligible to contribute, and their input is sought. Reason for us will be world reason, logically universal but with lots of illuminating surprises in its multiform instantiations. "Come, let us reason together" about our varied canons and heritages. And by all means let us likewise share our experiences, in their concrete particularities and their human universality. Out of this, I am confident, we will move appreciably closer to one another and to what our respective traditions are most basically about.

Notes

1. I follow the convenient listing of these in Marcus Braybrooke, *Interfaith Organizations, 1893-1979: An Historical Directory* (Lewiston, N.Y.: Ediwn Mellen, 1980), 179-80.

Part II
Journeys to the Frontier

6

My Spiritual Journey Through the Highways and Byways of Interreligious Dialogue

Ignatius Hirudayam

I was born in a village in Tamilnadu in South India. It was the central village of a parish comprising seven villages. The majority of the people of the village were Hindus. They had a large temple and held frequent festivals. There was also a community of Muslims traders with their mosque who held their usual festivals. The Roman Catholics were non-brahmin upper caste people from the northern districts of Thanjavur and Tiruchrappalli, who, on converting to Christianity, were transported and settled on the border of this village. They had to pass through the Hindu and Muslim quarters to go to the river Vaigai. Financially most of them were landless poor, dependent on their own middlemen who exploited them and who flouted all efforts to organize the community into a cooperative society for the betterment of all.

Religiously very devout, they practiced a veritable medieval monastic spirituality from dawn to dusk. A French missionary had found a benefactor and had worked himself to blindness in building a gem of a gothic cathedral, in brick and mortar in imitation of the stone cathedral of Rheims. It had two cylindrical towers connected by an attic. The multi-pillared and heavily decorated porches and portals with plastic reliefs were indeed Christian doctrine in Indian brick and mortar. The three naves were multi-pillared gothic structures, each pillar with an arabesque capital, crockets and corbels supporting statues of saints, not like Rheims and Chartes, but reflecting the concept of French beauty of the nineteenth century. The wall behind the main altar under the vault and arch sported iconographic representations of the trinity and angel choirs. The gothic altar and the lamps hanging or standing carried by figurines, the slender masonry and tracery supports of the sharp arched windows on the sidewalls fitted well with the exquisite nineteenth century French stained glass representations of the mysteries of the Christian faith and made this church the pride of the Tamil country. None of the larger later gothic churches could compare with it. The bigger bell, the biggest in the country, called the far flung seven villages to gather for worship. The music was Tamil and Gregorian chant, the prayers and readings were of the chant style that gave birth to the Gregorian. The annual enactment of the Tamil rendering of the Passion Play of Oberammergau, all these helped sensitive children to imbibe a deep vibrant faith of liturgical, devotional, musical, and artistic richness.

Colonial Attitude

This faith, however, had its drawbacks. It was overprotective in a ghetto atmosphere. The mass of the surrounding non-Christians were considered a *massa damnata*. All things of non-Christian origin, be it custom, culture, philosophy, art, architecture, music were believed to be from the devil and to contain nothing good. The Protestants proclaimed it. Marshman of Calcutta called the famous Raja Ram Mohan Roy an educated heathen. But it was not their monopoly. Such an attitude was and still is to be seen among Catholics of Tamilnadu, Bombay, Goa and other regions.

Already over a century ago, even before the Parliament of Religions in Chicago, General Lew Wallace had written in his famous epic novel *Ben Hur*: "A certain facility of accommodation in the matter of religion comes to us after much intercourse with people of a different faith; gradually we attain the truth that every creed is illustrated by good men who are entitled to our respect but whom we cannot respect without courtesy to their creed."[1] Down the decades thoughtful men have repeated similar sentiments. But we were taught that these "good pagans" were good and might be saved not through their religion, but in spite of their religion. Theirs was at best a "natural religion" whereas Christianity alone was a supernatural religion, the only true religion and unique way of salvation. Hence an Asian bishop has said recently that the "Asian soul has been deeply wounded by the last four hundred years of the Church's missionary effort to make it Christian." There are still today Christian and Catholic fundamentalists, not only ill-informed laymen but also churchmen, clergy and religious who are "saving their faith," adding insult to injury against non-Christians under the umbrella of the freedom of speech given by the secular republic of India. Communal conflicts and riots naturally thrive in the soil of such a mentality. And Hindu fanatical organizations find ample justification for any such conflicts in the misguided speech and acts of these Christians.

Double-Decker Theology

Mr. Narayan was a blameless Hindu brought up by a blameless devout Hindu mother. He fell in love with Christ and accepted Christianity. But he could not accept the pastor's doctrine of paganism vs. Christianity. He could not accept that his beloved mother whose training had brought him to accept Christ was a condemned pagan. He approached a Catholic priest who initiated him into the dichotomy of nature and supernature. Non-Christian religions were man's natural gropings for God whereas Christianity is God seeking out and raising man above himself to a life of divine grace. This satisfied Narayan and he became a Catholic. But the Catholic Church, thanks to theologians like Henri de Lubac, has outgrown this dichotomic theology.

Pluralistic Surroundings

In early childhood I moved to the capital town of the district and was thrown amidst a congested housing system and neighborhood where many religions and sects hobnobbed with one another. I moved also amidst vast convents, European and Indian and the Romanesque-Baroque cathedral fully covered inside with frescoes. Here, inhibition against Hindu social lifestyle was shed, and certain Hindu social customs were adopted for the sake of social acceptability and official contact with Hindus and Muslims, though this attracted mild censures from conservative priests and religious. But the Christian institutions helped cultivate deep faith and perhaps westernized forms of piety and devotion. A certain aversion to Hindu religious manners and style persisted. In early boyhood moving from village to village with elders who were government officials, I came into close contact with living Hinduism, its iconography, ceremonials, its myths and its epics, learned as bedtime stories from neighbors and bards. Some time spent in a village with a very famous Hindu temple—later on studied by the Lutheran Bishop Diehl, Paul Younger, and others—gave a great insight into Hindu praxis.

Fulfillment Theology

In October, 1922, Father Dandoy, S.J., and Father P. Johanns, S.J., sent out the first issue of *Light of the East*, from Calcutta.

It entered our household. It proclaimed "The East has lights already: religious, philosophical, moral. We have no intention to put out these lights. Rather we shall use them to guide both ourselves and our readers on the path that leads to the fullness of the light. We shall try to show the best thought of the East is a bud, that, fully expanded blossoms into Christian thought."

To me a boy of twelve, it gave the first twist away from the colonial missionary attitude that non-Christian religions were the products of the devil to be wiped out and their adherents were unbelievers to be redeemed by the Christian faith. It proclaimed the fulfillment theory which had been hesitatingly spoken by Protestants in 1910 in the World Missionary Conference of Edinburgh and clearly enunciated by them in 1920 and 1928 by the International Missionary Conference of Jerusalem, and elaborated by writers like J.N. Farquhar in *Christ is the Crown of Hinduism*, written already in 1913.

Too small to delve into the depths of "To Christ through the Vedanta" by Father P. Johanns, I went about captivated by the mere titles of his articles. The second issue in November, 1922, carried the first of the "Followers of the Light" series about Swami Upadhyay Brahmabandhav who had died twenty-five years before *Light of the East* appeared. The Bengali Brahmin Sannyasi Brahmabandhav was convinced that he could establish the Kingdom of Christ in an independent India without quitting the Hindu Samaj. And the article ended with the prayer "May the grace of God inspire the best youth of India to take up his work, renounce all, get the All, and rejuvenate India." The third number of December, 1922, started the series of articles on "Catholicism and National Customs," and later in

October, 1923, the series "Catholicism and Non-Christian Philosophies."

Fathers Dandoy and Johanns were not solitary Catholics holding this fulfillment theory. In *Light of the East*, May 1924, 8, they quoted Rene Grousset's *Histoire de le Philosophie Orientale* (Paris, 1923, 366): "Thus starting from the most opposed directions, and following the most unexpected round-about ways, Oriental thought invincibly moves towards one and the same goal—towards the God whom Aristotle, St. Augustine, and St. Thomas declared to be the supreme object of human intelligence and of philosophical wisdom. And this movement is, in our opinion, the more remarkable that the evolution which that thought has pursued is not only a historical evolution, but, as we trust we have shown, a logical evolution."

But the contrary missionary attitudes and their formulations were not silenced. The illustrious editor of the *Bombay Examiner* started a series of articles entitled, "The Great Antithesis," controverting the attitude of the *Light of the East*. It came under attack especially from the missionaries of the Madurai Mission and by their over-protected high caste converts. But my elders held to the policy of the Calcutta monthly, and I followed them.

This orientation, vaguely received and stoutly held since 1922, directed my enquiry backward to the non-baptized lovers of Christ of the Brahma Samaj: Keshub Chandra Sen, Raja Ram Mohan Roy, Mazumdar, and others.

Father Johanns in 1922 began his first article "To Christ Through the Vedanta" with, for me, the surprising words "Every Catholic student of Vedanta philosophy is soon struck by the fact that there is no important philosophical doctrine of Saint Thomas, the standard philosopher of Catholicism, which is not found in one or other of the Vedanta systems."

But twenty-five years of study of philosophy, theology, Indology, as well as the vast Tamil religious literature convinced me to go further than Father Johanns and write in the late 1940s that there was nothing deep, profound or soul stirring in the writings of the Christian church which could not find a parallel somewhere or other in the vast Tamil literature.

Forty years later and after nearly twenty years of indepth interreligious dialogue experience, I am absolutely convinced of this fact. Give the most striking verse from any of the vast Christian literature of the past twenty centuries and right away comes our dialogue partners' rejoinder and confirmation in a quotation which parallels it in content and often excels it in a poetic form and rhythm that penetrates our mind and heart. But I shall not repeat what I did in the late 1940s, i.e., start writing a series of articles "To Christ Through the Saiva Siddhan-ta." I have outgrown that fulfillment theology.

In the late 1920s there entered into my life a big-hearted noble scholar, my guru, Rev. Father Heras, S.J., of Bombay. He started a veritable crusade to convince Catholics that they cannot be truly Catholic if they are not yet truly and fully Indian. Father Heras read the Hindu scriptures with a profound reverence that made our hearts reverberate with the deepest resonance. A Protestant group uninhibitedly began speaking and writing on "Rethinking Christianity in India." A few respectable Indian theologians were emerging from among the Protestants. Then bang came the Missionary Conference of Tambaram (Madras) in 1938. Hendrick Kraemer with his theological axe of biblical realism pushed back Protestant thinking, which spoke of subversive fulfillment, reverse continuity, and eschatological convergence. Theological focus shifted to the relationship of Christian revelation to non-Christian religions. But the relation of religious experience and revelation in Jesus Christ was not properly probed. If even the concept of Christianity being the fulfillment and crown of Hinduism struck men like Radhakrishnan as "intolerably patronizing," what could be the non-Christian reaction to Kraemer's arrogance? They laughed in their sleeves at the Christian impudence and ignorance while keeping up diplomatic protocol on the surface.

Enter Dialogue

After the war, political decolonization had its impact on the church's thinking and praxis. The concept of missions yielded place to that of local churches. In 1948 the World Council of Churches was inaugurated. And since 1952 the question of Christian attitude toward those of other religious traditions was raised anew. Protestant theologians in India wrote on "Preparation for Dialogue." Even Kraemer revised his Tambaram position and wrote on "The Coming Dialogue." The search for a suitable basis for interreligious dialogue began. Kenneth Cragg's *Call of the Minaret* inspired the series of "Christian Presence." Theologians like Bishop Leslie Newbegin advised that dialogue could be tried with people of other religions not on the basis of their religion but on the basis of our common humanness, our anthropological solidarity against the background of the Western dualistic mentality.

The church's self-understanding was broadening, deepening, changing. Catholicity was no more conceived as geographical or statistical expansion but as the dynamism to assume every truth wherever and whenever found. But it required the good Pope John XXIII to awaken the church to a new self-understanding in maturity. He collected over 2,600 prelates, theologians, and non-Catholic observers and challenged them to update the church. Inaugurating the first session of Vatican Council II he eliminated heresy-hunting, anathema-mouthing, and recommended cooperative theological research and expressing its results in thought and language that could communicate to the modern world. He closed the first session on December 8, 1962 conscious that he would not live to see the second session. He was also conscious of the confusion that would follow the Council. His expertise in the history of the previous councils convinced the dying Pope that what had to be done had been done, i.e., to teach over 2,600 prelates to dialogue with one another so that the seven hundred million Catholics could begin dialogue with four billion human beings.

Most of humanity experiences its fundamental humanness and expresses it in diverse creeds and cults in the major world religions and innumerable regional folk religions. The main world religions are Judaism, Christianity and Islam which are called prophetic on the one side and Hinduism, Jainism, Indian Buddhism, Confucianism, Taoism, and Chinese Buddhism which are more experiential. The Second Vatican Council familiarized the word 'dialogue.' But it did not define it nor describe it. We became increasingly aware that this had to be the style of life for the church in the future. The Pope created the Vatican secretariate for the conduct of interreligious dialogue. But Rome is geographically and culturally outside the area of thought and aspirations of non-Christian religions. At best Rome could collate and coordinate the findings forwarded to it from other centers. Hence the need for establishment of such centers in regions where those religions are being reborn in their struggle against materialistic atheism and missionary expansion.[2]

Hence I was given the work of founding Aikiya Alayam in Madras. This institution has been cooperating with the Commission for Dialogue of the Catholic Bishops' Conference of India for the past fifteen years. Through direct contact in dialogue we have learned that Judaism, Christianity, and Islam are similar as regards their main problem of sin and their struggle for salvation from sin. They also concur in their belief in the transcendent and benevolent God who saves man from sin through his grace. Yet when delving deeper into these realities we discover great differences of understanding which make intellectual dialogue very difficult.

In the Indian religions of Hinduism, Jainism, and Buddhism the main preoccupation is not sin but the problem of the ego and ways and means of eliminating it. For Taoism and Chinese Buddhism the main problem is the alienation of man from cosmic or true nature and for Confucianism it is lack of humaneness. And their goal is harmony with cosmic nature or the realization of true nature. It is a formidable task to create a language and symbol system which could function effectively as a means of communication between these disparate creeds.

Sign and Sacrament

Pope John XXIII had given the Second Vatican Council the orientation that would lead the church to a self-understanding and a self-definition as the sign and sacrament of the unity of all humankind. This definition was destined to change the priorities of the church, bringing interreligious dialogue to the center of its preoccupations. As an instrument and sign of unity and peace of all humankind, the church could make the prayer of the seraphic Saint of Assisi its own.

Against the backdrop of Vatican II, the All India Seminar on the Church in India Today in 1969 recognized "the role of non-Christian religions in the divine redemptive plan. In Jesus Christ, who is God's word to man, we have the saving dialogue between God and all men, irrespective of their religious loyalties, for Christ is the head of all mankind and in him all men receive God's word and respond to it. This attitude allows members of the Church to be partners in the divine-human dialogue, with an openness and honesty of purpose which would be respected by all. Once it is realized that, by engaging in dialogue with other religions the Christian heritage itself can be fully appreciated and actualized through the reflections found in other religions of the same riches, whose common source is Christ, the door is open for a true dialogue, each side wishing to know and learn from the other whatever is worthy of emulation."[3]

The All India Seminar on the Church in India Today recommended the simultaneous meditation of our twin heritage of the Bible and the Indian Scriptures. And such a meditation did have a great impact on our spiritual journey.

Complementarity of Religions

The International Theological Congress at Nagpur in 1971 and the All India Consultation on Evangelization at Patna in 1973 developed the theology of interreligious dialogue further and further. The findings of all these meetings were summed up by the Catholic bishops of India in their meeting in 1973. This summary was communicated by their President, Cardinal Picachy to the Synod of Bishops in Rome in 1974. His statement is worth quoting at some length.

> India has cradled and nourished many ancient creeds which even now are a source of inspiration for the religious life of millions of their followers. We in India are daily witnesses to the religious experience of these men whose deep sincerity often puts us to shame. We can testify from experience to the presence of the Holy Spirit in the aspirations and undertakings of the adherents of these great religious traditions.

> Thus circumstanced, the church in India sees interfaith dialogue as a normal expression of a sharing between religious souls of their experiences. Through this dialogue God calls on each of them, drawing them onward to a higher spirituality and a profounder commitment to Him. We see interfaith dialogue, then, as something good in itself. Through mutual edification and communion men evangelize one another.

The International Interreligious Meeting in New Jersey (March, 1983) at which Archbishop Jadot, the President of the Vatican Secretariate for Non-Christians, delivered a remarkable speech reached a high watermark. And the International Interreligious Praying Live-together at Pariyaram, Cochin, and elsewhere, live-togethers, pilgrimages, and fast-togethers, etc., have taken us to ever soaring levels of interfaith experience.

In the practice of such interfaith dialogue, we have discovered ever deepening levels of spiritual living. Interfaith dialogue in depth flows from interfaith dialogue lived as one's personal existential spirituality. A genuine Indian ashram, living out its interfaith dialogue in word, thought, meditation and worship has been found the most suitable place to engage in periodic interreligious conversation in depth.

This requires that the dialoguers or ashramites sincerely practice one or other of the *sadhanas* or means of spiritual life given by acknowledged masters of spiritual life in these religions, that they first read meditatively the outpourings of the great mystics and spiritual masters of all the religions with which they wish to dialogue and try to imbibe the experience of others by spiritual symbiosis. This is helped if a native cult is created to suit the type of spirituality they live. This is a permanent spiritual style of life we have to maintain. If we do so, we find we are able to exchange pulse with people of the other faiths, and engage in enriching dialogue whenever an opportunity offers itself. In India a series of anthologies have been published to be added to the official prayer of the church. Raimundo Panikkar's *Vedic Experience or Mantra Manjari* is an eminent work of this kind. We, in our ashram, have published three anthologies from the mystic poetry of the Tamil religions and are producing more. Portions from these anthologies are read meditatively along with relevant portions of the Bible in our periodic ashram prayers as well as in our personal prayer. Thus we have in our Aikiya Alayam Ashram during the past fifteen years experimented and created a form of worship which is as authentically Catholic as it is fully Indian. This is enhanced by the liturgical use of our Tamil classical carnatic music which is best suited to lead people to the high reaches of contemplation. All participants and observers, Christians and non-Christians, witness to their being enriched by this. Such reading is ever changing and enriching. Our dialogue of life and conversation illicits a warm response from our non-Christian friends.

In reply to a questionnaire from Father Mason, Consultor to the Secretariate for Non-Christians, Rome, about Aikiya Alayam, the late Justice S. Maharajan of the Madras High Court wrote already twelve years ago: "This is the most important and useful thing your Church could do in the world at large and in India in particular today. Unfortunately not many exist as the one we have at Aikiya Alayam, Madras. Reverential approach and profound scholarship of the world scriptures as is found in Aikiya Alayam is rare to find. We have approached any and every topic fearlessly and with profit. The spiritual enrichment that every participant gains is remarkable."

Conclusion: Global Spirituality

Aikiya Alayam in Madras, therefore, is an ashram in an urban setting. It aims at integrating the ancient Indian tradition of ashram life and the life and needs of an urbanized society today and offering a haven of peace to the busy city dweller who seeks ardently the contemplative foundation for action and involvement in the present day struggle.

The heart of Aikiya Alayam is its chapel and sanctuary. It is in South Indian architectural style inviting the paschal mystery to incarnate itself. The paschal mystery is the abyss of divine compassion and the attitude of triumphant love. It is utterly incomprehensible to the human mind and inexhaustible by the human heart. This is witnessed to by the great number of the rites and liturgies of the Christian churches both in the East and the West. The ancient liturgies of the Eastern Churches were enthralled at the transcendent mystery of the divine presence. The ancient western churches tried to give expression to this by the magnificence of ceremonial. The Gothic traditions emphasized the sacrificial aspect of the eucharist. The present liturgical movements focus on the communal aspect of the Lord's Supper.

Aikiya Alayam's chapel and liturgy tries to combine all these and draw them into the profound silence of the Hindu (yogic) and Buddhist meditation and contemplation. Interfaith dialogue thus ripens into a global spirituality and worship of the universal Divine Presence in spirit and in truth.

Notes

1. Lew Wallace, *Ben Hur* (New York: Bonanza Books, 1978), 314.
2. Cf. A.M. Varaprasadam, S.J., *In Spirit and In Truth* (Madras: Aikiya Alayam, 1985), 12.
3. Cf. *All India Seminar on the Church in India Today* (New Delhi: B.C.I. Center, 1969), 523-524; cf. also 256-59.

7

A Pilgrimage to One's Own Roots—A Precondition to Religious Dialogue?

Odette Baumer-Despeigne

As a preamble I shall say a few words about the beginning of my own spiritual journey as regards interreligious dialogue, a journey which began half a century ago! I was brought up in a convent in Belgium. Among the subjects taught was of course "Religion." At the end of one year's dogmatic study on the mystery of the Holy Trinity given by a well known theologian of the day, our teacher said: "Mesdemoiselles, I have taught you all that can be known about God's mystery." My reaction was immediate: if at the age of seventeen I already knew all that one could know about God, what was I to do all my life? And I began to weep.

Fortunately the next year our teacher was a university Professor from Louvain, P. Charles S.J., who lectured on the then new science: "Missiology," concerned with the questions connected with the mission. P. Charles was a pioneer in the subject and is still quoted today.

For his lectures the whole convent was assembled, not only the pupils from the upper forms but also all the nuns. He began with these words, which pierced through the depths of my heart : "In missiology one has to begin with the learning of the great world religions, so I am going to introduce you to those religions existing outside Christianity." From that very second I knew what I was going to do all my life! The lectures went on for a few weeks giving us the rudiments of Hinduism and Buddhism. Alas! The nuns found this way of teaching missiology much too revolutionary and he stopped coming. The excuse: "He no longer had time."

But for me it was enough, a direction had been given; study, contact, and dialogue with non-Christian religions. So as soon as I left school I joined the l'Ecole des Sciences Philosophiques et Religieuses of Louvain University for I felt the need to deepen my own Christian roots. At the same time I began to read everything I could find on Hinduism and Buddhism, especially Hinduism.

For various reasons it was only much later that I had the opportunity to go to India. I have been there sixteen times and in Japan four times.

The Pilgrimage to One's Own Roots

I am not going to write an exegetic, dogmatic academic paper on this topic but I want to summarize those few points among many which in my opinion are most important, texts from the Scriptures which are too often overlooked by many Christians and which are the ones which could widen their horizon, show them the way to interiorize Jesus' message and thus prepare them for a fruitful interreligious dialogue.

First of all I think it is necessary that each one of us Christians tries on his own to retrace the main events of the founder Jesus, his central message, and above all to reflect on what he said of himself, the consciousness of his particular identity. Thus we would retrace the source from which our roots are nourished, and confront our personal attitude towards it. This, of course, requires a drastic purification of the conceptual fortress we have built upon him.

A Jewish scholar, A. Chouraqui, who was formerly Deputy Mayor of Jerusalem writes in the introduction to his translation of the New Testament into French: "When presented with the New Testament the interpreter is facing a musical partitur of which the original has been lost."[1] Therefore his endeavour was to retrace underneath the Greek texts the original words and thoughts in Hebrew and Aramaic. And this he did in an attempt to recover "the lost partitur," the one elaborated by the Semites in Semitic categories even if they wrote in Greek. For myself I found it most instructive to rediscover the evangelical message in these original garments.

The first of the evangelical texts I want to stress and propose for a deeper consideration is Jesus' baptism, because it reveals to him and to us his own identity. It makes us realize who the Son of Man is.

> As Jesus was in prayer after his own baptism—immersion in the Jordan—heaven opened and the Holy Spirit descended on him in bodily shape, like a dove. And a voice came from heaven: "You are my Son, the Beloved; my favor rests on you" (Luke 3:21-22).[2]

Is it not at that moment that Jesus discovered fully who he was, the most inward mystery of his relation with Yahweh ?

Of course the term 'Son' as well as the word 'Abba, Father,' with which he later answered are only symbolic, for Yahweh is ineffable, beyond the all names we are able to attribute him. The deepest discovery that Jesus made at that time is that, while discovering the Father, through the Spirit he did not discover 'Another,' for in John we read: "I and the Father are One" (John 10:30). Therefore we can affirm that the experience of his baptism was at once an experience of relation: Father-Son, and at the same time an experience of identification, of non-duality. He and his source were one.

Later, Jesus will speak of his identity in a very incisive manner when he declares: "I am He...I tell you most solemnly, before Abraham ever was, I Am" (John 8:58). This 'I am' that Jesus proclaims himself to be is identical with the 'I am' of Yahweh revealed to Moses: "I am who I am" and the command "Tell the sons of Israel: 'I am' has sent me to you" (Exodus 3:14). So we can conclude that Jesus' name is pure being, existence, and this introduces us to his eternal dimension beyond the historical personality who lived on earth two thousand years ago. This has a very important consequence in regards to our own human identity, we who are created "in the likeness of God."

As the Benedictine monk Henri Le Saux/Swami Abhishiktananda once wrote: "Too often Christians are frightened by certain statements of the Bible...they cannot believe that God really meant to do this or say that and thus bestow such dignity upon men. Theologians even reinterpret the texts and carefully tone them down."[3] For instance the words of Paul: "He Who unites himself to the Lord becomes one spirit with him" (I Corinthians 6:17,RSV), or "everyone moved by the Spirit is a son of God." (Romans 8:14) .

Another biblical text which can help us understand something of the eastern spiritual experience is Moses' saying: "Yahweh, your God, is a consuming fire" (Deuteronomy 4:24). The experience of this by Paul which makes him say "I live now not my own life but the life of Christ who lives in me" (Galatians 2:20) which means nothing less than the Spirit reduced Paul's 'small I,' his peripheral 'I' into nothingness. In a letter written to me Swami Abshihiktananda, our contemporary, said something similar: "To feel oneself in the presence of the True is too powerful an experience. It scorches one!"[4]

It seems to me important to stress that the Hebrew word *ruah* is feminine in Hebrew and that we never translate it as feminine when we say 'Holy Spirit.' In many languages Spirit is masculine. That means that we should read those texts of the Bible with new eyes, and first of all with the terms used to describe the creation of man in Genesis 2:7: "Then God breathed into his nostrils a breath (*ruah*, a feminine element) of life."

To meditate on the texts concerning the Holy Spirit as 'a feminine divine power,'[5] would help theology to grow out of its exclusive masculine conception of God and conclude that he is as Mother as well as Father. Through the words of Genesis 1:26-27 God revealed himself as such for it is said: "He created man in the likeness of himself...in the image of himself...male and female he created them."

Bede Griffith, in his book *The Marriage of East and West*, gives interesting information on this topic: "The feminine gender of *ruah* has been preserved in the Syrian Church to designate the spirit, so that they could speak of the Holy Spirit as Mother."[6] And the author adds:

> There is also in the Old Testament the beautiful figure of Wisdom—Hochmah which is also feminine. In this we can find a truly feminine aspect of God when it is said in the Book of Wisdom, Chap.7:25: "She is a breath of the Power of God and a pure emanation of the glory of the Almighty...She is a reflection of the eternal light, untarnished mirror of God's active Power...Although alone she can do all, herself unchanging she makes all things new."

Connected with this question of the feminine in God, one could also mention Jesus' own conduct towards women, especially the fact that after crucifixion he appeared first to a woman.[7] Luke 24:11-12 adds, "Having risen in the morning on the first day of the week, he appeared first to Mary of Magdala...She then went to those who had been his companions, and who were mourning and in tears, and told them. But they did not believe her when they heard her say that he was alive and that she had seen him. Peter, however, went running to the tomb."

Elisabeth Schüssler-Fiorenza says: "A total theology will be possible only when dualistic theology, the contradiction between the total liberating vision of the Gospel and the hierarchic structures of the Church, born out of the patriarchal culture, has been uprooted."[8]

At this point it seems necessary to find ways and means of arriving at such a state of 'evangelical liberation.' We find the answer in Paul: "Your mind must be renewed by a spiritual revolution" (Ephesians 4:24). Yes, each of us has to pass through such a 'revolution,' through such a *metanoia*, but in fact it is easier to say this than to do so! But let us not forget Jesus' promise: "I have still many things to say but these would be too much for you now. But when the spirit of truth comes he will lead you to the complete truth" (John 16:12-13).

It would be of immense value in trying to discover the "entire truth" to glance at the Orthodox Church which has certainly preserved and developed some aspects of the evangelical message that we have overlooked in the West. The vision of Christos-Pantocrator, the Omnipotent, described in Colossians 1:15-17 is:

> He is the image of the unseen God and the first-born of all creation, for in him were created all things in heaven and earth, everything visible and everything invisible...all things were created through him and for him. Before anything was created he existed and *he holds all things in unity.*[9]

To reflect on such texts broadens our conception of Jesus Christ and helps us to see the cosmic Christ, the "light that enlightens all men," of whom John speaks.

It also helps us to get a better understanding of the hebraic conception of the presence of God in the middle of his chosen nation, the *shekhinah* which "filled the tabernacle in the Tent of Meeting" (Exodus 40:34) and whose "glory fills the whole earth" (Isaiah 6:3).

This notion of the Presence of God at work in the creation has been remarkably preserved in Byzantine theology which differentiates between "divine energies penetrating all that exists" and the essence of God which is unreachable: "The divine and deifying grace-power is not the essence of God but his energy." This theological saying of Gregory Palamos is based on the second Epistle of Peter, in which we read: "Through the divine power...you will be able to share the divine nature" (2 Peter 1:3-4).

However we should never forget that our 'theandric' nature cannot be reduced to any category or absence of category. "Just as the butterfly discovers the secret of the fire in throwing itself in it," so we have to interiorize and live this sharing of the divine nature in our human condition.

Reciprocity and Encounter

If we are to hold a dialogue, either between Christian denominations or with members of other religions, it is necessary that both partners undergo the same process of searching for their own religious roots and reflecting on the implications of their faith and fundamental religious experience.

Above all both must be convinced that neither of them has monopoly on truth and both must have so much regard for one another's point of view that they stand ready to be challenged and to discover new aspects of the Divine—of the Reality—that they did not perceive before. Raimundo Panikkar has said: "Intellectually no religion can boast that it has deciphered fully the mystery of man and God."[10] "Thus one of the primary tasks facing theology," he continues elsewhere, "is the tremendous one of finding parallels and features in other religions that complement each other, as well as points of conflict."[11]

This is precisely what H. Le Saux/Abhishiktananda tried to do when he wrote "Here in India Christian theology of our time has to be a theology of the Spirit based on the fundamental intuition of being, on the pure self-consciousness...the theologians will have to face new problems: the confrontation of concepts with experience."[12] Here is one example of this necessary reformulation of Christian western theology in Indian terms—an example which is valid for the whole East: "Do we have to say that the theology of incarnation-redemption is totally dependant on the Jewish concept of bloody sacrifice? A Christian-Indian theology taking as its starting point the spiritual experience of *advaita* (non-duality), the simple awareness of being, instead of the bloody Jewish covenant would find other ways of expressing the human-divine (theandric) mystery. But the time has not yet come to outline such a theology...."[13]

As another example of reformulation one should not forget to mention the Second Vatican Council which developed for the first time a pluralistic view of religions. In response Abhishiktananda said: "Those who not knowing Christ endeavour under the influence of grace to accomplish the will of God in all their actions are saved *in* and *through* their religion."[14] "All the implications of such an affirmation," he added, "have not yet been examined, i.e., the working of the Spirit beyond all institutional boundaries."

A mutual exchange in the spirit between East and West could be most fruitful: "East could give to the West a more acute sense of the eternal, the primacy of being over becoming. The West could give to the East its sense of the human being as a person and a sense of brotherly love."[15] Even if wells of living waters are numerous in Christian revelation perhaps the East could give us more means to draw them out of our own Christian wells!

Humanity is an organic whole, all elements are interdependent. The have a common source 'in the cave of the heart' as the *Upanishads* say. It is there that we are able to meet one another. "Don't we all come from him who created the whole human race so that they could occupy the entire earth...It is in him that we live, and move, and exist...We are all His children" (Acts 17:26-28). "There is only one God who is Father of all, over all, through all, and within all" (Ephesians 4:6).

A Kind of Conclusion

The first step asks that both partners in an ecumenical encounter retrace their own religious source is certainly a precondition to dialogue and requires a drastic purification on the conceptual level.

The second step is to go beyond one's own roots to discover the constitutive religious dimension of man: "Man's religious root, which grows, flowers, and gives fruit in the most multiform way. Only the walls may fall, and private gardens open their gates. Such a philosophy results only from the mystical adventure of seeing truth from within more than one religious tradition."[16]

The third step is to meet present spiritual needs, each partner taking into account both the "riches and the burdening weight" of his or her past. Each religion has to build its future on this dual basis. In the words of Raimundo Panikkar: "The religious encounter must deal with the historical dimension, not stop with it. It is not an encounter of historians...but a living dialogue, a place for creative thinking and imaginative new ways that do not break with the past but continue and extend it."[17]

Maybe one day every religion will be able to join in St. Bernard of Clairvaux's intuition which prompted him to write:

"What is God? That without which nothing exists. Just as nothing can exist without him, so he cannot exist without himself: he exists for himself, he exists for all, and consequently in some way he alone exists who is his own existence and that of all else."[18]

Notes

1. *Un pacte neuf*, The New Testament translated by A. Chouraqui, (France: Brepols, 1984), 8.
2. All biblical quotations, when not otherwise stated, are from the Jerusalem Bible.
3. Abhishiktananda/H. Le Saux, *Saccidananda, A Christian Approach to Advaitic Experience* (Delhi: ISPCK, 1974), 118.
4. Letter dated May 22, 1972.
5. *Bible Lexicon*, ed. Herbert Haag, (Köln: Benziger, 1951), 527.
6. Bede Griffith, *The Marriage of East and West* (Springfield, Ill.: Templegate, 1982), 191.
7. Mark 16:9
8. Elizabeth Schüssler-Fiorenza, "Pour des femmes dans des univers masculins," in *Concilium* (French edition), no. 191, 1984, 69.
9. Col.1:17; italics added.
10. Raimundo Panikkar, quoted by G. Coward in *Cross Currents*, vol. 29, (1983), 184.
11. Raimundo Panikkar, *The Intra-Religious Dialogue* (New York: Paulist Press, 1978), 19.
12. Cf. *Saccidananda, Hindu-Christian Meeting Point; The Further Shore*.
13. Letter to O.B.D., June, 1969.
14. Italics added.
15. J. Monchanin in a letter to A.E.D., January, 1955 in *Mystique de l'-Inde Mystère Chrétien* (Paris: Fayard,), 211.
16. *The Intra-Religious Dialogue*, 52.
17. Ibid., 28.
18. *De Consideratione*, L.V. 6.13. Trans. John D. Anderson and Elisabeth T. Kennan in *Cistercian Fathers Series* vol. 37 (Kalamazoo, Mich.: Cistercian Publications, 1976), 155-56.

8

Interreligious Dialogue: My Pilgrimage of Hope

Albert Nambiaparambil

The Running Train

It was just one more day in my life-in-the-running-train. My official commitment to the cause of interreligious dialogue as secretary to the Catholic Bishop's conference of India took me to different townships, temples, and shrines of India, to areas often marked by communal conflicts. My job was simple, but delicate: to tune the different communities to sing the song of interreligious harmony. The train was running at full speed from Bangalore to Cochin. On that November evening, with the tropical sun spreading its golden rays in one unitive embrace, this cosmos of believers—Hindus, Moslems, Christians, Sikhs—and the running train became one symbolic expression of our unitive pilgrimage. Pensive, I started writing a few verses about my own life-in-the-train.

> I sit in the running train, leaning against the window.
> I run, in that running train with well set goal.

I had at that moment the heavy weight of memories: many years, almost fifteen, spent in the delicate task of bringing together the followers of different religious traditions into one pilgrimage of hope! This was very hard, with almost all of us well enshrined in our own language of having the last word, the seal of prophesies, the best religion. It was an effort at an exodus from the isolation of self sufficiency into the communion of the religiously felt need of another. I had been back in India after the third international session of the World Conference of Religions for Peace, held at Princeton, in the U.S.A. Sitting in the running train I recalled that beautiful sight of pilgrims, Hindus, Muslims, Jains, and Christians all standing in a prayful mood at the monument to Lincoln. Ah, these pilgrims are all one at the beginning, they will be one again at the end; but, now in the middle of their journey all of them are scattered!

Sitting in the "running train" (the title of the poem that was subsequently published in a journal of Kerala), I saw passengers with suspicious looks as they entered the train soon becoming members of the great family. But there were others who could never get out of their own built in prisons of hatred, distrust, and isolation in spite of the fact that they are all put together in this great running train. The bitter memories of Aligarh, of the communal riots, the sight of that bus in which over one hundred children and women, so I was told, were burned alive as victims of the communal hatred led me to write these lines:

> Blood of Abel is flowing in the streets of Aligarh,
> The cry of Abel is rising from the streets of Aligarh.

Soon the picture changed, the memories and the wings of imagination too. Looking out to the horizons through the windows, I saw birds flying up and down, with the green carpets spread out below, the rice fields all green, and the coconut trees hoisting the flags of the cosmic harmony, hillocks around, responding to the song of the birds:

> We are the guests, we are the guests, in the running train.
> We are Hindus, We are Christians, We are Muslims.
> We are guests, in this cosmos, in the running train.
> We are becoming one in the running train.

I wrote the poem in 1979. These lines are being typed out for the Assembly of World's Religions. Now one question remains unanswered. This question was raised again and again by many in sympathy with dialogue work. More often the same questions were raised by those with dubious attitudes, who did not want to be disturbed at all. This is the question: What have you achieved?

Yes, I have achieved nothing grandiose, but for a few steps made here and there towards the confluence of religious streams. Turning back on the twenty years of dialogic activities I have no achievements to count, but for that growing fellowship among followers of different religious traditions through the interreligious sessions, on "values in a fast-changing world," through the deep spiritual "satsungs" or meditation, shared reflection sessions, through the prayer sessions, through the joint celebrations of festivals. Have we converted anyone? Yes, we have converted ourselves. All the partners in the pilgrimage of hope went through mutual conversions.

Models Come, Models Go

As I started on this journey, I pictured myself as belonging to the center of the universe, as belonging to a privileged community and my effort at that time was to accommodate others, my fellow pilgrims into this picture, without disturbing my central position. Reflecting on what was happening in the dialogue scene I turned to writers who were "experts" on dialogue. There I found many models for the partners in interreligious dialogue. There was this preoccupation: to reconcile identity and openness, faithfulness to one's own religious faith and the dynamic of openness to other currents. These models helped me to place the partner in dialogue around me, along side of me. Organizing the World Conference of Religions on "Religion and Man," in 1981, in Cochin, Kerala, India, we looked for a symbol that would not disturb any of the partners. Those who took part in that fellowship were not so much experts "on" dialogue as persons actually involved in interreligious dialogue. Well, we came upon the atomic structure of mutually inclusive movements drawing a starlike picture. If each of these movements stand for the different religious traditions, who among us were at the center? All of us are at the center. Rather none of us is at the center in a possessive way, in a having way. We brought this out by placing a burning lamp at the center. Under this symbol we placed our prayer, the prayer of the Hindu sacred scripture: Lead me from darkness to light.

Is this picture expressive of all that we are involved in? Not at all. No picture, it seems, is all expressive of the pilgrimage of hope that is interreligious dialogue. At times one might pick up the rainbow model, of different colors of the one ray to outline the unity in diversity, or the unitive diversity. A few of my friends put the different symbols of religion in circular positions. My Hindu friends often pick up on the models of rivers flowing into the ocean, of different paths leading to the top of the mountains etc. The other day, at the end of a dialogue session in which a Christian and a Muslim shared their spiritual experiences tracing them to the sacred scriptures, I found a friend of mine, a good Christian, disturbed. For, he could not reconcile all that he heard with his faith in the "uniqueness" of his own religious tradition. No wonder that no one model alone is all expressive.

Life in Death

The prayer of St. Francis of Assisi, "Lord make me an instrument of peace" ends with this statement that it is in dying that we can be born to eternal life. What was perhaps the most rewarding experience in the pilgrimage of hope was this "life in death" experience. In January 1985 a conference was organized in Madras at the Lutheran Theological Seminary on the theme of the "Emerging Consciousness of Mankind." Reflecting on the ongoing dialogue, I narrated an experience at Allahabad. There the boat people take you to the confluence spot where the holy river Ganga and Jamuna meet. Your guide will point to the two different currents, one all muddy and the other all clear and say that the two currents flow side by side, as distinct currents. Are the different religious currents flowing side by side?

To answer, I show the face of a Muslim friend of mine, the most consistent partner in the dialogue that we organized. At times to express our fellowship symbolically we gave every partner a candle that we light from the central candle as part of a prayer service. A Hindu friend of mine recently remarked very personally in a sense of wonder and surprise: why is it that this Muslim friend alone has no lighted candle? All of us had our lighted candles in our hands to express symbolically the emerging consciousness. But this Muslim friend sitting in deep prayer, unable to light the candle along with us, is precisely pointing to the same reality. What is important is this faithfulness to the reality. Faithfulness in dialogic contexts often demands from the partners that one die to a word or expression to be faithful to the reality. At other times we have to look for expressions to celebrate our emerging fellowship spiritually. In any case any sincere partner in dialogue is opting for such life in death situations.

One result, a painful one indeed, for the one who takes to interreligious dialogue seriously is his exposure to misunderstanding by both those at home in his fellowship and by those outside. Those of his own fellowship observing him, the dialogue partner, externally, accuse him of unfaithfulness. They see him using different postures, praying in a different way, using other symbols, etc. Those who are of other religious traditions mistake this his openness as a hidden attempt at proselytization. Perhaps this would be the best result of this life in death option: the option for interreligious dialogue is an option to live in tension.

Transcendence Lost, Transcendence Regained

The poet G. Bankarakurup, who was awarded for the first time in the history of the "Gnanapeedhaam Award" the prize for the best poetry, narrated to me one incident that reveals his outlook. A rationalist writer of Kerala criticized him for the otherworldliness in his poems. In response the poet told him of two outlooks of the bird. The bird soaring high up in the heavens may look down and measure the heights achieved and declare aloud about the heights achieved. The same bird may focus the gaze on further heights, on the beyond. The poet then added that his poems are symbols of this second look.

Well, in dialogue situations what is at stake is not so much the uniqueness of this or that religion as the transcendence that is lost by many a believer in the language of comparisons that they too easily pick up in interreligious gatherings. They sit and count their possessions and also the possessions of other religions, of their fellow pilgrims and would be happy if they could convince themselves that they are better off than those of other faiths. But in dialogic exposure what is at stake is the pain of sacrificing this first self sufficiency look, of the look downward, for the look of the pilgrimage to the further shores and the further heights. Only when the partners dare to look to the further heights can they become real partners in intra-religious dialogue and interreligious dialogue is and should always be intra-religious dialogue as Raimundo Panikkar maintains.

Similarly, without in any way relativizing your own faith in this look to the further horizons, you learn that the only way to redeem your faith, the transcendence that is lost in the having language, in possessive language, is by relativizing all the languages about that very faith. In hope, in the *saranam gaccami* (I take refuge, I cry out, *saranam*—hope) the partners in dialogue meet. It is only in hope that crucial openness is maintained without becoming victims of religious indifferentism and of relativism in faith. So too parallelism in religion is avoided. All that is called for is an effort at regaining the transcendence in the very act of interreligious dialogue. In this process the not yet attained, the unknown, becomes more meaningful than the known and the known, the revelations received, become for the partners, signs to transcend. Here, again, the believers go through the process of exercising the very same faith as an effective transcending function and not the preservative function. To return to a Hindu way of saying the same, the partners reach for that language, "that word from which all words return without being able to reach it" (*yatho vaco nivartante aprapya manasa saha*).

9

Transformation Through Interreligious Dialogue

Pieter de Jong

By nature I am not the meditative type. As a young person, whenever I felt the need for inner peace I used to take a walk in the countryside near the city where I lived. That was as far as I had gone in that discipline.

My introduction to an oriental kind of meditation took place in Canada. It was on a late summer afternoon, I had been lecturing to a group of people on a university campus and at the end of the session I decided to have a run around the field. While I was jogging one of the participants in the conference came up to me and asked if I was enjoying it. I told him that after a day of talking and discussing in order to feel refreshed I had to do some form of exercise and this one was readily available to me. Then he asked me if I had ever done yoga. I did not know much about it but was interested in learning more and so he suggested that I should read and use a booklet he would bring to my room. Later on he brought me a paperback called *Yoga in Ten Lessons* by Father J.M. Dechanet who had become acquainted with yoga practice during his stay in India and had written a booklet about it in order to share his experiences and the benefits of practice. He also had written a book called *Christian Yoga* in which he adapted yoga practice to Christian meditation on Scripture passages like the Lord's Prayer and the Sermon on the Mount.

That evening before retiring I tried the "tree pose." I remember trying to balance myself on one leg and become aware of my breathing. I found that it was far from easy although it looked simple in the pictures of the book. The rest of the *asanas* were even more difficult. I slowly tried to master them over a period of time and have more or less continued practicing yoga since that day which is more than twenty years ago, although I have never succeeded in being able to sit in the full lotus position.

What were the effects of practicing yoga? Having been exposed so far only to Western calisthenics and sports I was puzzled as to how this form of exercise could make any difference. First of all I began to notice a greater flexibility and deeper breathing. Gradually, as the years went by I began to experience myself in a different manner, as a unity rather than a conglomeration of fragments like body, soul and spirit. I found that if the body lacks harmony or is ill the whole person suffers. I also felt that if the body is more relaxed the mind is more free and open to the spirit. But after several years of practice it was still a puzzle to me.

In my teaching and philosophy I could not explain it because I had been raised in the Cartesian paradigm, in which mind and body are opposites. Consequently, if I was ill or had a cold, I felt that I was (or was supposed to be) alright but that my body was in need of recuperation, my body which was not me but something out there. In Christian circles one was not supposed to pay much attention to the body because it was only the physical shell of the precious mind or spirit which really counted. And had not Paul said in one of his epistles (I Timothy 4:8) that physical exercise is of little use?

I remember how a professor at the University of Utrecht in his introduction to church history used to spend a lecture period giving us a picture of the ill health of most of the great leaders in the church. He would begin with the mysterious illness of the apostle Paul (the "thorn in the flesh"; II Corinthians 12:7) and proceed with the problems the church father Origen had with his body. He would elaborate on the nervous breakdowns of Augustine, on the obesity of Thomas Aquinas, on the effects of asceticism on medieval saints like St. Francis of Assisi. He would give illustrations of the digestive troubles of Martin Luther and describe the impact of John Calvin's temperament on his physical health, all with the implication that those who are called to work in the realm of the spirit are doomed to suffer ill health and have to pay a heavy price for it.

The same professor, however, discovered my potential interest in mysticism which at that time was dormant. During one of the oral examinations he asked me if I had read any of the medieval writings which were different from the ones quoted in the course. My answer was that during high school in a class on the history of Dutch literature I had come across the work of the flemish mystic Jan van Ruysbroeck called *The Spiritual Espousals* which fascinated me but to which I had paid no further attention. He encouraged me to pursue this interest saying that very few of the students had ever read anything along that line.

My background and theological training as a whole were far from positive toward this trend. It is true that my mother was mystically inclined. Whenever she would read the Scriptures she would turn to the Gospel of John but my father was quite rational, almost rationalistic, in his religious outlook. He regarded mysticism as too subjective and pathological and was suspicious of the elitist attitude of those who stressed the experiential aspect of religion. Both of them had been acquainted with "conventicles" or small groups of a pietistic nature in which people exchanged their spiritual experiences or lack of them in an emotional manner. The mystically inclined regarded these groups as the true church and had little regard for institutional religion.

The theological climate in the Netherlands after World War II was deeply influenced by Karl Barth who had played an important role in the resistance against the Nazis. I was familiar with the section of his dogmatics on human religion and divine revelation. In this part he criticizes both atheism and mysticism. Atheism, according to Barth is an adolescent reaction against the Christian faith but at least atheists take doctrine seriously and grapple with it even if they end up denying it. Mystics, however, he finds far more dangerous because they claim to go beyond doctrine and simply ignore it. They can be compared with anarchists. An anarchistic party ignores the government by the grace of which it is able to function. So the mystics live by the doctrines they relativize or reject.

When I came to Union Theological Seminary in New York City after the war, I was surprised that the theological climate was quite similar to that in Europe at the time. Many of the veterans had gone through crisis experiences and were attracted by existentialism which had a profound influence on European dialectical theology. Paul Tillich who was one of my teachers had a more positive appreciation for mysticism and integrated it into his theological system. In his doctrine of divine revelation he taught that the mind "stands out from itself" when receiving it. In his lectures I heard for the first time names like

Meister Eckehart and Jacob Boehme, mystics of great influence on the spiritual life in Europe.

During my career as a pastor in Canada my preaching was strongly influenced by the theology of Karl Barth with his emphasis on the objective character of the word of God. But in my work with the Student Christian Movement, after I had gone into teaching, I had my first encounter with the work of Pierre Teilhard de Chardin. Through his book *The Phenomenon of Man* I learned how theological truths can be expressed in terms of a dynamic worldview. In him I met a person who had been trained in a dualistic view of human nature and who was struggling to give expression to a unitary view. Here I found emphasis on change and he became my guide into the world of process thought to which I had not yet been exposed. In his *The Divine Milieu* I found a deep appreciation for the world of matter not as opposed to spirit but as its basis. He made a plea for a new asceticism in which the body is respected and provided an outline for a spirituality from a holistic viewpoint, taking seriously the doctrines of creation, incarnation, and the resurrection. His emphasis on the importance of the created world appealed to my appreciation for the world of nature and the sense of unity with it which I had always experienced. Teilhard meant a lot to me as a bridge to a more future-oriented worldview and a constructive approach in theology.

After having moved to the United States and having joined the faculty at Drew University, my wife and I spent our sabbatical leave in the orient. There were a number of experiences which deeply impressed me. While I was visiting a Buddhist temple in Rangoon, Burma, I noticed a man who was praying in front of a statue of Buddha and totally absorbed. While I watched him the question came to my mind: is this what the Buddha intended? Then the thought came to me: what would a Buddhist feel if he visited the Christian West and, let us say, the cathedral of Chartres in France? Would he catch the spirit of Christ or be lost in the trappings of the cult? What would Jesus think of the worship patterns which have developed?

I vividly remember the faces of two women. One was a nun in a Buddhist sanctuary in Korea who showed us around: her face quite radiant and her personality outgoing. The other was a gatewatcher in a sanctuary in Kyoto, Japan: her waxen face so detached from the world that it frightened me because of its other worldliness.

On one occasion while visiting a Buddhist temple I was struck by the enormously long ears the Buddha statue had. I asked my guide why Buddha is often represented that way and was told that it was an expression of enlightenment. I wondered why large ears rather than big eyes. In Geneva, Switzerland, I had seen the statue of the reformers who had all had been given big ears to express their openness to the word of God and for a long time I had thought that only Protestants had a right to big ears. Later I was told that some say that Buddha's long ears are a reminder of his luxurious upbringing in which he was accustomed to wear heavy earrings.

Upon our return to the United States my wife found out that she had a rare kind of cancer. After having it removed twice she decided to embark on a nutritional program which in addition to nutritional supplementation stresses the importance of detoxification, diet and fasting. I decided to join her in a fast and was surprised to discover the impact it had on my mind and spirit.

That fall I decided to teach a course on Christian mysticism. Involvement in oriental practices of meditation had led me to explore the mysticism in my own tradition. In preparation for the course I was introduced to the teaching of Eastern fathers on the Jesus prayer. I noticed that they paid attention to breathing and physical postures because of their importance for the practice of meditation. So far my praying had mainly consisted of conversation with God in which I did most of the talking. Now I was introduced to another type: the prayer of the heart. Through endless repetition of the words: "Lord Jesus Christ, son of God, have mercy upon me, a sinner," and by allowing it to become one with our breathing pattern, the prayer descends from the head to the heart and becomes one with the person who learns how to pray unceasingly, even if not repeating the words consciously. My main problem was that rather than repeating the prayer from within I tended to theologize about the content. In my Protestant background I had been conditioned against praying without understanding the words rationally.

Next I came across the work by an unknown author of the fourteenth century called *The Cloud of Unknowing*. The title intrigued me because knowledge was important if not all important to me. I had started my career as a minister and theologian with the hope that by refining my concepts I would come to know God better. Here was a book suggesting that the true way is one of unlearning or unknowing. I was even more surprised when I continued reading. So far my meditation had been the moving kind as in yoga *asanas* or sitting meditation, always with an object in mind, either a theological idea, image, or a passage of Scripture. Now I was introduced to objectless meditation or contemplation, in which the mind goes blank and leaves behind rational ideas and pictures of the imagination derived from the use of the senses. I found this extremely difficult. My mind kept racing and whenever it stopped I thought about the way it came to a halt or how I could get back to the stage of not thinking.

Again I read about paying attention to one's breathing and I tried the use of mantras like "God," and "Love," prayers of a single word, as the author calls them, and not to be used as objects of theologizing but rather as a way of opening up to ultimate reality. It was my first introduction to what Evelyn Underhill calls the purgation of the mind corresponding to the apophatic way of theologizing as introduced by Dionysius the Areopagite of the sixth century. I read his *The Divine Names* in which he speaks of God by using the *via eminentiae*, saying that God is to the degree of perfection what we are in a very small and imperfect manner. Then I read his *Mystical Theology* in which he concluded that all we say about God is really not adequate and he applies the *via negationis* or the way of negation. In the negative way we say what God is not or that he is nothing as contended by Meister Eckehart who lived at about the same time as the author of *The Cloud of Unknowing*. It was a profound shock to me as a systematic theologian to learn that the author of *The Cloud* praised his novice because he was dissatisfied with the dogmatic formulations and encouraged him to leave all that behind in the cloud of forgetting, experiencing nothing in order to leave room for the beam of light or the knowledge in love; the direct and immediate experience of God.

The question arose in my mind: how do we reconcile this with the faith of the church as it has been formulated in the creeds? Is it the same as faith or does it go beyond it? I read Thomas Merton's *Ascent to Truth*, one of his earlier works in which he answers the question by saying that doctrine can be compared with an airstrip from which the airplane takes off in order to reach its destination. I asked myself: does it ever land again?

Another problem posed itself to me. If part of the cloud of unknowing is the cloud of forgetting all that the senses have observed, how does this mysticism relate to God's creation and the way he is expressed in it? Also: if the pictures of Jesus we have formed on the basis of reading the New Testament are to be left behind, what does this do to the use of scripture?

Something else bothered me in this book: what about all the people who serve God and Christ in their fellow human beings. Are they on a lower step of development than contemplatives? The author tells the novice that he may be called to a higher degree than faith, namely perfection. Is he implying a dual morality, one for the common people and one for the mystics? He actually distinguishes four classes of people: common, special, singular, and perfect. He says that the common people lead an active life, removed from God. The special people have some desire for a spiritual life. In the singular people a love for the solitary, contemplative life has been kindled which may lead to the life of perfection which can only be completed in the hereafter. Many of the medieval mystics agreed with him and had some classification in which the contemplatives ranked at the top. They interpreted the well-known story of Jesus visiting Mary and Martha in such a way that Mary was the symbol of the contemplative, seated at Jesus' feet, listening to his words and absorbing his wisdom. Martha was busily engaged in the lower pursuits in the kitchen, preparing a meal for her family and their guest.

Meister Eckehart has a different interpretation. He claims that Martha and not Mary was the better Christian. Mary, he says, still needed the time apart while Martha had already gone through that stage and was now able to express it in a life of service, which is the goal of the contemplative life. If contemplation is a way of being or becoming more deeply engaged in life, the full time contemplative may have a prophetic function in witnessing to the need for meditation and contemplation as a necessary part of everday life.

For me Dionysius and the negative or apophatic way do not have the last word. Meditation or the way of silence is a way of detachment from theological formulations which we tend to consider as final and adequate. My appreciation of doctrine, however, was not just an intellectual exercise. During the war we had suffered severe oppression by the Nazis. On one occasion when I was interrogated by a member of the "Grüne Polizei" the conversation turned to the topic of religion. Many of them claimed to be religious people. Hitler used to refer in his speeches to the power of providence. We know that some of the people who committed atrocious and cruel acts were meditators. Single-mindedness can be used for all sorts of purposes. The ideology of "race, blood, and soil" had to be met head on by the church as in the Barmen Declaration which raises the issue of criteria of true revelation. Meditation does not abolish the need for criteria of the truth. The apostle Paul then faced by a confusion of spiritual gifts in the early church spoke of the need for the gift of "discernment," or of "testing the spirits." At the time of the reformation there were political mystics who claimed that their inward guidance had been directly inspired by God and who ended up as fanatics and dictators.

The issue of meditation and ethics is a very important one. By their fruits you will know them, and the fruits are those of love, compassion and justice.

When I began to teach a course on western mysticism I thought that I might talk myself out of a job, but gradually it became clear to me that meditation enabled me to teach doctrine with greater freedom and from a new perspective. All mystics agree that the experience of the ultimate is ineffable. Yet most of them proceed to talk or write about it, even if it is claimed to be a form of stammering. The stammering at times grows into several volumes. My Benedictine colleague and I like to discuss the question as to whether Thomas Aquinas wrote his *Summa* before or after he had his mystical experience. If it is after then it surely is some stammering.

Meditating together is a form of non-verbal communication. If our dialogue is preceded by meditation together we are reminded of the fact that the word is born of silence. We are being trained in the art of listening in the spirit of genuine openness. At the same time we will have the freedom and the courage to share with others those things which move us on the deepest level of our lives. We are deepened in our own faith by opening ourselves to the experience of others discovering similarities of structure where at first we thought there was no point of contact.

Real dialogue makes room for authentic witness on the part of the participants. How else can we learn from each other unless we are willing to make our contribution as people committed to a particular tradition? In finding out how adherents of other traditions are time and culture bound in the expressions of their faith we become aware of the degree to which we ourselves are influenced by our social, cultural, and political environment.

In my own case the introduction to mystical religions led to the recovery of a trend in the Christian tradition to which I had hardly been exposed before. Following that the interreligious dialogue led me to a renewed intra-religious conversation. Under the impact of becoming acquainted with perspectives of other faiths I began to ask questions within my own tradition in a new light. They are often the same questions and the differences run right through the various faith traditions rather than between them. Thomas Merton felt greater kinship with some adherents of the Buddhist tradition than with many of his own faith.

In interpreting our experiences the differences arise. These need to be discussed if we want to grow in our understanding of each other. Is God-realization the goal, as for many in the Hindu faith, or experiencing emptiness as in the Buddhist tradition? We also think of the variety within the Christian tradition: Is the goal divinization (*theosis*) as Eastern orthodox mystics describe it and union with the divine? Or do we hesitate to speak of union for fear that it may lead to absorption of the person into the all and rather call it communion with God and unity with nature and other human beings?

Not all Christians, however, are mystics. Many would claim that mysticism is only a fringe phenomenon within Christianity. So the question arises: what is the place of mysticism in the Christian faith? As a person who was raised in the reformed tradition and who has a deep appreciation for the prophetic element in the faith I began to grapple anew with the problem of revelation. What is the relationship between word and silence? What is the place of Jesus Christ in a world of religious pluralism? How do we relate discipline and grace? What is the meaning of the doctrines of creation and history? How are evil and sin to be taken seriously?

Dialogue with adherents of religions in which the divine is experienced in discontinuity with the human, like Judaism and Islam, reminds us that the divine-human encounter is a miracle of grace opening the perspectives of judgment and mercy. As in the dialogue with adherents of mystical religions, so in the dialogue with followers of prophetic faiths questions arise which are also asked within the Christian tradition: What is the authority of the holy scriptures and what does the doctrine of inspiration mean? How are the transcendence and immanence of God related? Are those who begin with the transcendence able to conceive of the immanence? Are those who begin with the immanence of God capable of getting to the transcendence? How does the awareness of an unbridgeable gulf between the human and the divine, between the creation and the creator relate to the mystical experience? Above all: how does a prophetic religion, Christianity included, solve the problem of exclusiveness and universality?

A question sometimes asked among Christians is whether a person committed to the Christian faith is able to participate in interreligious dialogue. Is a Christian able to be truly open to other faiths if he or she is committed to the Christ as God's decisive revelation? There are some who give a negative answer and others who believe that the only purpose is that of proselytizing. This, however, can hardly be called dialogue. Genuine dialogue means taking a risk. It implies embarking on a journey of which the end is not known. It requires on both sides the willingness to change and from a Christian point of view it implies trust in the Holy Spirit which is the spirit of truth and "blows where it wills." Commitment without openness leads to fanaticism. Openness without commitment ends in relativism. The answer lies in the balance between commitment and openness.

10

The Shinto Way to Dialogue

Yoshimine Komori

Japanese Culture and Shintoism

Located at the eastern end of the Eurasian continent and as a Far Eastern island nation surrounded by the Pacific Ocean and the Sea of Japan, today's Japan has her own traditional culture of diversity and uniqueness, such as *ikebana* (flower arrangement), *chanoyu* (tea ceremony), Zen Buddhism, *waka* (31-syllabled poems), *haiku* (17-syllabled poems), *noh* dramas, *kabuki* dramas, *judo, karate, aikido, mihonga* (Japanese painting), *ukiyo-e* prints or *kimono*, as well as her own unique style of architecture, gardening, cooking, and dancing. As the common features among these traditional cultural elements of Japan, one can say that they all contain: (1) the spirit of *wabi* (quiet taste) and *sabi* (elegant simplicity); (2) the spirit of respecting harmony with nature; (3) simplicity (or plainness); (4) the spirit of respecting the definite form or tradition; (5) broadness of capacity; (6) reality or possibility of creation and development, etc. Shintoism, as the root of Japanese traditional culture, maintains in itself these features in the purest form.

Shintoism is the spiritual and cultural root of Japan and has been so from very ancient times and, hence, is the source of her uniqueness. In the early sixth century Confucianism and Buddhism were introduced to Japan through the nation named Paekche (Kudara) which was located on the Korean peninsula. It was in 600 A.D. that the Japanese government dispatched the first envoy to the Sui (Zui) dynasty (589-618 A.D.) ruling the Chinese continent at that time. This was followed by an age of vigorous diplomatic relations between the two countries, which rapidly brought foreign (Chinese) culture into Japan. As a result, the so-called "Taika Reform" was carried out in 645 A.D., and subsequently, the new system of laws and ethics (Ritsuryo system) was put into practice in imitation of the Chinese laws and ethics of that time. As a religion and accompanying criterion of living, Shintoism has been popular within our nation since very ancient times even before the foreign cultures of Confucianism, Buddhism or Chinese laws and ethics were introduced to Japan. Therefore, Shintoism is the original spiritual culture of the Japanese nation with a history of more than 2,000 years.

The "Diversity of God" in Shintoism

Shintoism can be simply defined as a principle of living to improve the wealth of real life through conforming to God's will by worshiping him. "God" in Shintoism does not mean God as the absolute who created heaven and earth and dominates all things, but means god as the divine spirit or deity dwelling in everything in the universe, including human beings. Shintoists consider every human being is a god because he possesses divine spirit or deity. Moreover, that divine spirit universally dwells in every being in the cosmos: in mountains, rivers, fields, seas, stones, trees, forests, animals, insects, and even in germs. Therefore, they call the gods who exist in countless numbers "the Eight Hundred Myriads of Deities" (*Yaoyorozuno-kamigami*).

Shintoists grasp "god" essentially in the same manner as Buddhists who recognize a Buddha-nature (deity) not merely in every human being but in every creation such as dogs, cats, trees, stones, water, etc. The first words spoken by Gautama Buddha, the founder of Buddhism, at the moment he obtained spiritual enlightenment after six years in pursuit of the Way, were said to be "how surprising, how curious that every creature is endowed with a Buddha-nature without fail." The same view can be found in the opening of "The Song of Meditation" (*Zazenwasan*) by Hakuin-zenji (1685-1768), a celebrated Zen reverend of the Kinzai Sect, who noted that "all sentient beings are from their very beginning 'Buddhas': it is like ice and water; apart from water no ice can exist; outside of the sentient beings, where do we seek the Buddhas?"

It is one of the remarkable features of oriental thought in general to grasp absolute and relative things not as different, separated, and mutually opposing but in inseparable relation, both harmonious and unitable. Among them, the absolute is named "Buddha" by Buddhists, "Heaven (*Ti'en*)" by those who follow Chinese thought such as Confucianism or Taoism, and "God" (*Kami*) by Shintoists. These are, however, different merely in name, having no affect on their common conception about the relation between the absolute and ourselves, the oneness and inseparability which are like water and ice. God and man, man and nature, monarch and people, parent and child, husband and wife, I and you, society and individual, mind and body, subject and object—all these pairs are regarded as dual and thus mutually opposed in Western thought, while oriental thought grasps them not in opposition but in oneness and unity. Thus, to speak frankly, God and man are completely heterogeneous for western people, while the two are perfectly homogeneous for orientals.

Among the myriads of Shintoist gods, which include "nature gods" like the sea god *Watatsuminokami* or "idea gods" like *Omoikanenokami* who is said to administer human consideration and judgment, human ancestral gods who are centered upon the supreme god *Amaterasu-omikami*, the Sun Goddess, who is believed to be the ancestor of the emperor, are superior in number. Here, it must be noted that the first one who became god at the beginning of the world was *Ameno-minakanushino-kami*, not *Amaterasu-omikami*, according to Shintoism.

The place where gods usually stay is called the "shrine" (*jinja*), or more correctly "temple" (*shinden*). Shintoists in very ancient times, however, did not have a concept of gods usually staying at a fixed place. Rather, they made holy places, for example, *himorogi* (a sacred tree of life) or *iwasaka* (a sacred enclosure) whenever they celebrated festivals, to invite the gods' advent and to offer prayer.

The god dedicated in each shrine is called the "*matsurigami*" (dedicated god), which are of great variety because there are eight hundred myriads of gods in Shintoism. In Ise Shrine, for example, the inner shrine (*naiku*) is dedicated to *Amaterasu-omikami*, while the outer shrine (*geku*) is for *Toyoukeno-okami*, a god of food administration. In Tokyo, the Oeiji Shrine is dedicated to the Meiji Emperor, while Yasukuni Shrine is for the souls of the departed heroes of wars or other national crises after the Meiji Restoration (1868 A.D.). Togo Shrine is for the heroic Admiral Heihachjro Togo, and Sogi Shrine is for General Maresuke Sogi. Among many shrines in Kyoto, the Kamo Shrines (both of upper Kami-kamo and lower Shimokamo Shrine) are dedicated to the ancestors of the Kamo clan who were the first cultivators and governors of Kyoto; Kitano Shrine (or Kitano-Temmangu) is for Michizane Sugawara, a notable scholar in the ninth century who was set up as a god of study after death; and Yasaka Shrine is for a legendary ancient adventurer Susanono-mikoto, a younger brother of Amaterasu-omikami. The Grand Shrine of Izumo in Shimane prefecture is dedicated to Okuninushino-mikoto, the legendary ruler of Izumo area during the mythological age. Omiwa Shrine in Nara prefecture, which may look like an exception because of the absence of a temple, consists of only a front shrine (oratory), but the whole Miwayama hill behind it is regarded as the object of worship.

The Capacity of Shintoism

Shintoism is so rich in the sense of tolerance and harmony that it has experienced fusion with Buddhism or Confucianism in the past, and with Christianity and Islam in the present. When Dr. Arnold Toynbee, a notable British historian of civilization, visited the Grand Shrine of Ise on November 29, 1967, he was asked to make a registration remark with a writing brush, he wrote: "Here in this holy place, I feel the underlying unity of all religions." It was none other than the broad capacity of Shintoism that let him intuit "the underlying unity of all religions."

The broadness of its capacity is closely related to the fact that none of the Shintoist gods are the unique and absolute God of exclusivism, and its doctrine is not exclusive nor self-righteous but natural and reasonable. This point forms a remarkable contrast with Christianity or Islam. A typical example in Christianity can be found in the revelation from God to Moses on Mount Sinai, where you have the warning: "You shall have no other gods before me. You shall not make for yourself a graven image, or any likeness of anything that is in heaven above, or that is in the earth beneath, or that is in the water under the earth; you shall not bow down to them or serve them for I the Lord your God am a jealous God, visiting the iniquity of the fathers upon the children to the third and the fourth generation of those who hate me, but showing steadfast love to thousands of those who love me and keep my commandment" (Exodus 20:3-5). And the Islamic Koran strictly warns that "those who deny (their Lord), for them will be cut out a garment of fire: over their heads will be poured out boiling water. With it will be scalded what is within their bodies, as well as their skins. In addition there will be maces of iron to punish them" (*Qur'an* 22: 19-21).

This character of religious tolerance is not only contained in Shintoism but is also recognized to exist within oriental cultures in general, such as Confucianist or Buddhist culture. In this, the oriental cultures are quite unlike the western cultures of exclusiveness.

Reality and Super-Religionality of Shintoism

Shintoism as a principle of living to improve the wealth of real life and as a religion allows its followers to worship or pray to gods in order to improve their real lives more richly, not only to seek spiritual peace or enlightenment nor to obtain their welfare in the next world. Every human being, without exception, seeks happiness. It is from our natural emotion that people pray to gods for bumper crops and pray in thanks for the harvest, they pray for the happy life of a newly-wedded couple at a wedding, celebrate a gala day for children of three, five, and seven years of age in order to pray for them to grow up in good health, or in case of an examinee, to pray for his success in an entrance examination, or make various kinds of ceremonies such as ground breaking ceremonies, commencement ceremonies, or ship launching ceremonies. This shows us the direct relationship between gods' service (i.e. ceremonies) and human affairs.

The word *tabemono* (food) that Japanese people use in daily life originally meant "godsent," while a common salutation *uokagesamade* is an expression of thanksgiving that means "but for plenty of grace and favors from the gods and nature we cannot survive." Shintoists emphasize a concept of *musubi* which means the source of life, formation and development. Since ancient times this *musubi* has been believed to be administered by a couple of gods named *Takami-musubino-kami* and *Kami-musubino-kami*. They have been especially worshiped by the Japanese nation as the principle of generation and development and as the source of life to improve real life more richly.

This realistic attitude of Shintoism gives it a certain suprareligionality, that is, Shintoism is a religion without a tinge of religion. Whereas it is commonly recognized among religions such as Christianity, Islam, or Buddhism that it is appropriate to seek and long for the ideal world named the "heavenly kingdom," "paradise," or "elysium" outside of this real world, Shintoism places so much emphasis upon the real world that its concept of mythological *Takamagahara* (the abode of gods) written in the oldest national literatures *Kojiki* and *Nihonshoki,* is given less value than the real world. Moreover, *Yominokuni* (the land of death), a concept corresponding to the next world, is described in Shintoism as a dirty and abominable place. Thus Shintoism, with such a strong secularism may be more suitable to morality or principles of living rather than a religion.

Another example of Shintoist realism and supra-religionality is a word *naka-ima* found in the part of *Semmyo* (Declaration of Imperial Decrees) in *Shoku-nihonshoki,* another doctrinal text of history for Shintoism. The nuance of this word indicates that the Shintoist view of life and world is targeted to make the best efforts to find the greatest value neither in the past nor future but in the present life.

The Supreme Virtue of Shintoism

As mentioned above, Shintoism is a principle of living conformable to "god's will." Then, how can we know the will of the gods? Outwardly it can be known in the descriptions of *Kojiki* and *Nihonshoki,* in the teaching bequeathed by the imperial ancestors, or in other teachings of ancient sages, while inwardly one can keep contact with it by making his heart sincere. One of the *waka* poems the Meiji Emperor composed says that "it is by sincerity of the human heart that one can have contact with the invisible will of the gods." Another example is found in the ancient Chinese Confucianist scripture titled *Chuyo* (the Doctrine of the Mean), which says that "sincerity is the way of heaven, and to keep a sincere heart is the way of man." This "sincere heart" is none other than the will of the gods. Therefore, since ancient times Shintoists have respected sincerity, honesty, and purity as the supreme virtues of the human heart.

The same point has been made by others too. In *Tamakushige* written by Moto'ori Norinaga (1730-1801), a Japanese classical scholar, it is noted:

> Though there is only one way of truth throughout all the nations, in heavens and earth, it has been correctly bequeathed only in our Empire, whereas in all other nations it was lost already in very ancient times. In each of these nations some other way has been accepted as if it were the original way of truth. However, none of them is the same with the true one; they are all its offshoots or byways, though they have some similar points. Offshoots can never be a match for the original trunk.

Takamasa Okuni (1792-1871), a Shintoist thinker in the latter days of the Tokugawa Shogunate, wrote in his *Amatsunoritono-futonoritokou* (On Shintoist Congratulatory Addresses) that:

> Shintoism is to settle the cause, help the world and to save people. It has no other purposes than these three, which can be put together into one idea of making oneself humble. To settle the cause with a humble mind, to help the world with a humble mind and to save the people with a humble mind, this is what the original human heart of sincerity means.

Both of the literary pieces quoted above teach "sincerity" as the highest virtue for Shintoists. *Misogi* (bathing) or *harai* (litany) are Shintoist ways to wipe off or clean away the sins and impurities of the mind. But they are also a means to bind one's heart with gods by making it sincere, so that one can live in conformity with god's will. This way of living is called *kamunagarano-michi,* or originally *kamisanaganano-michi* (to live just as gods do), which is, the proper way of nature everyone should follow and tread upon. It is the way of "sincere heart." To summarize, let me quote the words of Dr. Tsuji Sato, former president of Kogakukan University.

> It is the self-evident truth for every human being living in reality that parents love children and children adore parents. This is called *makoto* (truth) throughout heaven and earth. Shintoism is establisheded to unify, or bring harmony into, the world and human life by this truth as a principle.

Shintoism and the Tenno (Emperor) System

Shintoism has been preserved in its purest form continuously from ancient times by successive emperors, from the first Emperor Jimmu to the 124th Emperor Hirohito of today. The first Emperor Jimmu was said to be a great-grandson of Niniginimikoto who was a grandson of the goddess Amaterasuomikami. All the successive emperors were, in this religious and spiritual sense, endowed with deity and divine spirit as descendants, letting people call the emperors *akitsu-mikami* or (personal god) since olden times. The fundamental difference of the Japanese emperor system from those of other foreign empires is its single family lineage not only of blood, but also in the spiritual aspect through the execution of various ceremonies such as *kenjitogyonogi* (a ceremony of the enthronement for new emperor to succeed to the sacred treasures of throne symbols), *daijosai* (the great thanksgiving service after the enthronement), etc.

Theocracy in Shintoism has been an original attitude of the Japanese since the beginning. This is reflected in the fact that a letter meaning "policy" is often read *matsurigoto* (literally meaning "worshipping affairs"). A *waka* poem the Meiji Emperor composed says, "it is only after worshiping at the Ise shrine in the morning that I can effectively manage the affairs of my Empire." Surely many emperors were converted to Buddhism as private persons after it was brought into Japan, but in the public eye even these emperors of Buddhist faith put priority on divine services by executing various Shintoist ceremonies such as *kenjitogyo-nogi, daijosai*, etc. Thus, the Japanese Emperor system has maintained inseparable relations with Shintoism until today.

Since ancient times the Imperial Palace has had in itself three shrines: Kashikodokoro (the Highest place) dedicated to the spirit of Amaterasu-omikami, Koreiden (temple of imperial spirits) dedicated to the spirits of successive emperors, and Shinden dedicated to the myriads of gods of heaven and earth. Among the waka poems the present Emperor Kinjo made in 1975, one said "every morning I pray to the gods dedicated in the shrines in my garden for their keeping peace in the world." Here "the shrines" indicate the three shrines in the Imperial Palace.

The Japanese imperial system is based on an ancient mythological oracle that the supreme goddess Amaterasu-omikami gave her grandson Niniginomikoto to grant eternity to the imperial throne, when she sent him to govern ancient Japan from *takamagahara* (the heavens). According to the book *Nihonshoki*, the oracle said that "this reed-plain-1500-autumns-fair-rice-ear land is the region which my descendants shall be lords of. Do thou, my August Grandchild, proceed thither and govern it. Go! And may prosperity attend thy dynasty, and may it, like heaven and earth, endure forever." The immovable regime, in which the descendants of Amaterasu-omikami were to preside over the sovereignty of Japan, was thus established.

At the time of Niniginomikoto's descent to the earth, the sun goddess Amate-rasu-omikami gave him three treasures (i.e. the eight-hand mirror, the curved jewel of *yasaka* gem, and the sword *xusanagi*) as the symbols of the throne. These three treasures, symbolizing the three holy virtues of "wisdom," "benevolence," and "courage," with which every emperor should be endowed, have been respectfully inherited by successive emperors. Among the three, the eight-hand mirror (*yatanokagami*) has been especially valued by the emperors, for it has been considered to represent the spirit of the supreme goddess Amaterasu-omikami, as shown in the oracle to worship the divine mirror: "when thou lookest upon this mirror, let it be as if thou wert looking on me." Here we can find the reason our ancestors respected the will of successive emperors as the will of the supreme sun goddess, and let them be sovereigns over the whole nation.

The *tennoism* (imperial system) of Japan is a result or manifestation of the gods' will, which is more than the people's will of caprice, interest, and times. It is a manifestation of the truth of heaven and earth as its principle. Consequently, *tennoism*, as a result of divine will, is not only an upholder but also a manifestation itself of the human way of truth. This fact has been proved many times through the achievements of successive emperors, especially during times of national crises.

Let me illustrate this point with one example. The present Kinjo Emperor who proclaimed at the end of World War II, "As I do not care what will happen to myself, we shall make the intolerable tolerable in surrendering to the Allies." Then the Emperor met by himself with General Douglas MacArthur, the supreme commander of the allies, on September 27, 1945, saying, "As I shall bear all the responsibility for this war by myself, so I would like you to give my nation no further suffering."

This example indicates the special quality of the Japanese emperor system. It requires sacrificial dedication by the emperors. Here it should be noted that such a special quality is derived from Shintoism.

Shintoism as a Treasure of the World

Mr. J.W.T. Mason, an American journalist who stayed in Japan before World War II and studied Shintoism deeply, wrote in the preface of his work, *The Meaning of Shinto* (1935) as follows: "Shinto is simple in its outward forms but has profound inward significances. It is the one enduring national treasure. But, Shinto must not be buried in a museum of the mind. Shinto can be Japan's major contribution to world culture, but Japan does not yet know how to offer the contribution. Shinto has a message for the world." He concluded with honoring Shintoism as a treasure of the world that Japan can be proud of.

Thus far I have emphasized only the characteristics of Shintoism viewed from the study of comparative religion, especially the differences between Shintoist gods and the Christian God. Then, do they have nothing in common at all? I think the two are common in many points, for the New Testament says that not merely Jesus Christ but all human beings are children of God, and that all things came out of God and are endowed with the spirit of God:

> For all who are led by the Spirit of God are sons of God. And if children, then heirs, heirs of God and fellow heirs with Christ, provided we suffer with him in order that ye may also be glorified with him. (Romans 8:14,17).

> Do you not know that you are God's temple and that God's Spirit dwells in you? (I Corinthians 3:16).

> And because you are sons, God has sent the Spirit of his Son into our hearts, crying, "Abba! Father!" So through God you are no longer a slave but a son, and if a son then an heir (Galatians 4:6-7).

> For from him and through him and to him are all things. To him be glory for ever. Amen (Romans 11:36).

> That they should seek God, in the hope that they might feel after him and find him. Yet he is not far from each one of us, for in him we live and move and, have our being as even some of your poets have said "For we are indeed his offspring" (Acts 17:27-28).

> All who keep his commandments abide in him, and he in them. And by this we know that he abides in us, by the Spirit which he has given us (I John 3:24).

This indicates that oriental religions represented by Shintoism and Buddhism have many points of contact with western religions as represented by Christianity.

Nothing is more foolish than for religious people who teach 'truth,' 'benevolence,' and 'mercy' to be hostile to each other and repeat bloody conflicts. In this age when the ecological crisis threatens the whole world, the realization of reconciliation and harmony as well as unity among the world religions today must be strongly hoped for: minor differences must be diminished for greater common interests.

To conclude this paper, I should like to thank the eight hundred myriads of gods as well as God the absolute for giving me a chance to introduce Japanese Shintoism on this occasion of the Assembly of the World Religions, which is dedicated to the sacred cause of realizing world peace through harmony and unity among world religions.

11

Fences Around God

Avtar Singh

When I was young God always appeared to be full of power, everywhere, and knew everything. When I looked up in the sky, He appeared to me as spread limitlessly. My idea of the infinite was not well developed then but the deep receding blue sky suggested a limitless continuity. I prayed to God in the religious shrine, in my class room, in bed, sometimes even while playing. I remember submitting prayers to him at all places and all times. I must confess that I never doubted his power to accomplish for me whatever I needed or wanted. Some of my supplications now appear to me as naive and unnecessary. But then I was only a very young child and had certainly no inkling that I would become a student of religion and philosophy for nearly all my adult life.

I was living in India and finished my high school in 1947 the year that India got its independence and also its division. My memories of this period are hazy but some are certainly painful. Our house and family, like that of everyone else, experienced great tension. Some of our neighbors and friends migrated to the other side and some of our relatives arrived over there also. Many of my earlier beliefs about religion and interfaith relationships, according to friends, were not very mature. Religion was often held responsible for the carnage when, in fact, the real cause was a desire to possess what belonged to others. Evening prayers in our house became disturbed and irregular. The tension was very intense and too close. The fence around God appeared to be growing in height.

The post-partition Punjab state in India witnessed a growth in religious activity. Many of the older shrines associated with the lives of saints and founders of religion were repaired and renovated. Religious congregations grew in numbers and people noticed a general atmosphere of piety. The Sikhs have always been an intensely religious people. A Sikh man becomes conscious of his turbaned identity quite early in life. The religious places of all other religions also witnessed a spurt in the religious concern of the believers. There occurred an enhanced emphasis on the need to maintain identity and purity in following the directives of the religious tradition. Prior to partition identity codes were not prominent. After, they came to be underscored and stressed more boldly. The growing fence between religions bore the notice "no trespassing!"

Somewhere the subconscious mind of people picked up the new idea of a God who was powerful but worked behind the tall fence and in secrecy. I often heard the phrase "we don't know" instead of the earlier answer "God knows." People were transposing their own ignorance onto God the omniscient. There was, and still is, a great need to raise the level of intellectual effort to comprehend the true nature of God and to communicate it as convincingly as possible. This process needs to be pursued with gentleness and love. It helps to remove ignorance and false prejudice. There is an urgent need to understand intellectually the spiritual teachings of one's own religion as clearly as possible. This awakening should then be followed by an effort to know other faiths as thoroughly as possible. My general experience is that ignorance places undesirable fences around God.

After 1947, India experienced a growing interest in Indian philosophy and religions. A new generation of scholars trained in Western methods sought to apply a newly synthesized methodology and understanding to the analysis of the theology grounded in Indian religions. A growing Indian nationalism influenced the native interpretation of theology. The new political boundaries continued to affect the tenor of interfaith movements. Similarly, missionary work provoked distrust because of the past historical experience. Nontheologians have sought to interpret theology in socio-political terms. The richness of theology and its contribution to the interfaith movement was restricted to a narrow interpretation and was denied a fair hearing. In the face of religious conflict, a new panacea of social relationship was presented in the guise of secularism.

The supporters of secularism unfairly accuse and condemn theology for evils it does not have. Secularists proclaim that nonreligious interpersonal movements are far more fruitful and desirable. They maintain that theology and its implications are necessarily divisive and cause human agony resulting from conflict among various faiths. There are myriad similar accusations against religion and theology. The motivation for this campaign is obvious. Theologians sometimes accept false accusations against religion as perhaps not entirely false. Religious people and theologians seem to have started entertaining doubts that perhaps religious commitment prohibits harmonious interfaith movements. But is that so?

Does the interfaith movement deny the possibility of different faiths? Is it inevitable that persons participating in the interfaith movement will have to deny the theology envisaged in their own faiths? It is my submission that, when theology is truly God-oriented, it is bound to encourage the feelings of respect and mutual attraction of all persons although they may belong to different religious traditions. But when theology is wrongly conceived as man-dominated, it tends to acquire the characteristics of human weakness. Only an earth-bound and man-dominated theology may consider the interfaith movement to be in conflict with theology.

There are three principle ways in which we may look at the theological implications of the interfaith movement. First, we should notice that much is being said about theology by its opponents. A genuine criticism functions as a word of caution. It informs us of what we should avoid in our journey for the truth. But there is also much motivated and distorted criticism of religion and theology. The springs of such criticism are often sociopolitical ideologies. A genuine theologian can see through this easily and should dismiss it promptly. Second, sometimes exclusiveness may be a genuine effort to maintain the purity of faith. The theologian in this case may be an honest person and this is a healthy attitude. It is perhaps possible to persuade this kind of theologian that the interfaith movement, by widening one's religious view, adds to the purity of one's life of faith. An expanding view is closer to the truth of God's nature. The truth is the highest form of purity. The interfaith movement is a journey towards the largeness of the sacred heart. The divine invites all, and shuns none! So an honest and genuine skeptic of the interfaith movement may be won over for the holy togetherness.

There is a third possible perspective about the theological implications of the interfaith movement. The persons holding this view are enthusiastic for the joining of heads, hearts, and hands in sharing and reinforcing each other's faith. It generates in them an ability to abjure the smallness of conflicts and to cultivate a large-hearted kindness. It may range from the preliminary desire to avoid the hurting comment to the point of surrendering one's all for the uplift of others. Moral values may become indissolubly intertwined with an intense desire for the spiritual welfare of others. For persons at this level of spiritual life, the Sikh prophets have said "*koi na dise bahara iio*" (none is seen as an outsider). What they give to others is far more than they keep for themselves. The courage that comes from holding such an enthusiastic view can enable believers to overcome the hurdles that come their way. Their theology is God-oriented.

You might wonder why we have talked of false charges against the theological implications of the interfaith movement. You may also perhaps try to guess the purpose of my earlier biographical narration. The biographical episodes show how the notion of God, can be partly influenced by the social and political events in a person's life. I also wanted to draw attention to the process of raising a fence around God. In this process we first abstract and then concretize the abstract. It is a life long habit of singling out the small from the large and the seemingly unmanageable whole which overflows the narrow limits of human perceptions. This process of looking at the whole from a limited angle of vision is natural, and in ordinary circumstances the only one available to us. An important point to remember, however, is that a person who respects his own tradition has the potential of coming to respect the traditions of other faiths. Here I offer an important implication of theology. If God is one and if he alone is the creator, then all that are created by him have a right to be respected. All faiths derive their light from the one light and all lights are the instruments of removing darkness. Thus all lights are welcome! Once we accept this as faith in God, the interfaith movement will be seen as conducive to our efforts to realize God. If we become aware of the possible effect of the disturbing experiences of life on man's views of 'our own faith,' and 'another's faith' it may be easy to see that it is a relation of faith to faith and therefore a relation among brothers.

There is a great need for the coming together of people of different faiths to demonstrate the goodness that naturally flows from such meetings. It is our reasoning here that any theology grounded in the experience of God will show the social necessity and the spiritual conduciveness of interfaith dialogue. A superficial and unanalyzed acceptance of all that has happened in our life without looking for the deeper, spiritual significance often results in lives lived without the realization of the real and true being of God. Negative judgments of the theological implications of the interfaith movement are an unwarranted and a backward step.

There is another noteworthy religious teaching which has an important lesson for the interfaith movement. We have learned from the testimony of the prophets that God is love. It may, therefore, be accepted that God is realized through love. We have also taught in Sikhism that "*jin prem kio tin hi prabhu paya*"(Those who love realize him). As God is love, the theological implication of the interfaith movement is that of a path leading to the grace of God's love. Any contribution of people in this direction is a step towards God. An effort to bring together the seekers of God's love is in itself an indication of the love for God. We may remember two important aspects of the theological implications in this regard. Negatively, human insensitivity from indifference to extreme hatred and cruelty is a denial of God. Positively, God being love, theology teaches us to be likewise to others. Kindness and altruism are not merely moral acts but also spiritual steps toward God. It is the human expression of what a person seeks from God. The ability to help others is derived from God's grace. The ascending levels of interfaith represent ascending levels of receiving God's grace. An uninhibited and uninterrupted contribution towards interfaith trust and interfaith dialogue is the shining of divine light and love.

We are now in a position to face a question. If theology holds that God is omniscient, omnipresent, and omnipotent, then should we not accept the privilege of God to cause as many revelations as he pleased, anywhere he chooses, and in any form he likes? The faiths of humanity are expressive of His unfettered freedom and omnipotence. Our finitude and our limitations are our finitude and our limitations. God is infinite and limitless. He is free to inspire anyone and free to grant his vision to anyone, anywhere. The humility that arises from an understanding of the theology of God's limitless power awakens in our hearts the desire and respect for an interfaith movement.

The interfaith inspiration is then an additive factor in God's limitless expression. It is the bonding together of people of faith. The ethic that will follow from this realization will enrich and sustain the spiritual life of all people.

Theology is not merely an intellectual act of separating theoretical articulation from the experience of God. A proper theology is always based in the experience of God. And this experience liberates us from the narrow and the lower and unites us with the wider and the higher. Interfaith dialogue is thus an attempt to dismantle the fence around God. Theology can render great help in this joyous movement towards the divine ideal. This may lead us to the real happiness which comes from the true perception of theology and what it can offer for the ethical life.

In conclusion, the interfaith movement for understanding and harmony is a potent instrument for removing the weeds of ignorance and demolishing the fences around God. Beyond is God, and the human understanding of him known as theology.

Part III
Resources at the Frontier

12

Islam in Dialogue with People of Faith—Insights from the Islamic Tradition

Badru D. Kateregga

Islam means total submission to the commands and will of Allah the only true God. Islam is not merely a religion in the popular western sense of the word, i.e. confined to rituals in a private domain, but a total way of life, *al-diin*. Islam is an Arabic word which connotes submission, surrender, and obedience. It has also its roots in the words *slim* and *salam* which mean peace. Therefore, Islam is a religion of peace; it is a way of life for the individual person to live in peace in every aspect of life. Hence any person who follows the path of peace, the religion of Islam, is called a Muslim.

Islam is a universal religion, the message of God meant for all human beings. It enjoys a unique distinction of having no association with any particular person or people.[1] Islam, as a matter of fact, is an attributive title, whoever possesses this attribute regardless of his race, community nation, or clan, is indeed a Muslim.

Islamic View of Other Religions
Islam relates to people of faith at least on two levels; first, as humans and second as people who have received the revealed scriptures, i.e. Jews, Christians, and others.

At the first level, being the final revelation, and in its self-understanding, intended to be the religion for all humans, Islam had to relate itself to the religions of mankind, and through them to humanity.

Islam and the Natural Religion

Islam affirms the existence of primordial, natural religion, a genuine 'religio naturalis' which is a gift of God to all humans.[2] This natural religion is called *diin al fitrah* or the religion of creation. All humans are endowed with it without exception. God called this natural religion "His own religion" (*Qur'an* 2:132) and commanded all humans to honor and belong to it. God says in the *Qur'an* "Turn your face to the primordial religion in which God created all humans. That is the immutable pattern of God that is the standard religion..." (*Qur'an* 30:30). Islam has identified this natural religion as the endowment of reason and understanding of the critical faculties. The *Qur'an* further testifies: "Only those with knowledge will reason out and understand it" (*Qur'an* 29:43). Islam has declared the human senses as avenues of knowledge (*Qur'an* 90:8-10). Writing and language are also other tools of knowledge. All these are 'perfections' which God created and bestowed to the end that humans make themselves felicitous by their use. The use of all these faculties or perfections commanded by God, must lead to the religion of God.

The content of natural religion is universally imperative. The Muslim view is that all humans ought to fulfill it since they have been equipped at birth with all that is required to know it. It is simple to know for its first component is the recognition that God is indeed God—that no one else is God. God is other than his creation and the relationship between creator and creature cannot be other than worship and service. Allah says in the *Qur'an*: "I have not created humans or *jinn* but to serve me" (*Qur'an* 51:56). It is the observance of his patterns which are knowable by reason with which he equipped all human beings. Therefore, no human being can be justified in his *kufr* or un-Godliness. No human may be excused for relapsing into *shirk* (polytheism). It is everybody's responsibility to recognize and acknowledge God as God. It is everybody's business, prerogative, and supreme duty to do so. To this effect, Islam is worried by those religions or theories which discriminate between humans at birth, deeming some capable and others incapable by nature of knowing the one God. No one should be absolved or declared incapable of his supreme duty of acknowledging and worshipping the one God. That would be tantamount to robbing him of his capacity for natural religion as absolutely normative for all humans.

Islam and the Revealed Religions

The universalism of Islam is further buttressed by Islam's understanding of history. Islam affirms that God did not leave mankind entirely to its own resources in the matter of acknowledging him as God and Creator. In his mercy, he sent prophets to convey to them his divine message that they owe religion to God alone. These prophets were raised from among almost every people. The *Qur'an* witnesses:

> And verily we have raised in every nation a messenger proclaiming: Serve Allah and shun false gods. (*Qur'an* 16:36).

Again the *Qur'an* states:

> We sent no messenger but with revelation that there is no god but God (*Qur'an* 21:25).

> So, no matter how humans may have denied their humanity by refusing to perceive the truth of God, they were duly informed and warned by a messenger whom God had sent to them to teach them the truth in their own tongue and idiom (*Qur'an* 14:4).

In this respect Islam recognizes the Jews and Christians as blessed recipients of God's revelations through prophecy apart from being possessors of *diin al fitrah* the natural religion. Islam identifies itself with Judaism and Christianity. It regards the God of Judaism and Christianity as its own God, their prophets as its own prophets and their revelations and scriptures as its own revelations and scripture. Allah tells the Muslims: "Say [to the Jews and Christians], We [Muslims] believe in that which was revealed to us, as well as that which was revealed to you. Our God and your God is one and the same. We all submit to Him." (*Qur'an* 29:46). In another verse Allah again tells the Muslims: "Say [Muslims]: We believe in God, in what He revealed to us, to Ibrahim, Isma'al, Ishaq, Ya'qub, and the tribes, to Moses, Jesus and all the revelations of the prophets without discriminating between them. To God we submit" (*Qur'an* 2:136). So Islam holds Judaism and Christianity to be one religious fraternity. This unity obviously makes Muslims

regard the Jews and Christians as their brothers in faith, in submission to the One God of all. The *Qur'an* refers to Christians
and Jews as the *Ahl al Kitab*, People of the Book. It encourages
Muslims to live amicably with People of the Book, to eat their
food and even marry their women. "The food of those who
received the scripture is lawful for you. And your food is lawful
for them and so are the virtuous women of those who received
the scripture before you" (*Qur'an* 5:5).

There are indeed disagreements between the three traditions but they occur under the canopy of faith in God and
belonging to His religion.[3] The disagreements and even the
common ground of the three traditions provide a wonderful
opportunity for interreligious dialogue. Now that I have mentioned dialogue, let me review the resources within the Islamic
heritage which can help to promote interreligious dialogue.

Islam and Interreligious Dialogue

Most of the resources which could help to promote dialogue
between Islam and members of other faiths are heavily em-
bedded within the tradition and mission of Islam itself. One of
the central themes of the Holy *Qur'an* is the call to the universal
brotherhood of man. The *Qur'an* declares in many of its verses
that all men are brothers to one another since they are children
of the same father and mother. In this sense they are relatives
and members of the same family. The *Qur'an* teaches: "O,
mankind! We created you from a single (pair) of a male and
female and made you into nations and tribes that ye may know
each other (not that ye may despise each other). Verily the most
honored of you in the sight of God is (he who is) the most
righteous of you." (*Qur'an* 49:13). In many instances the *Qur'an*
addresses all humanity as children of Adam: "O! children of
Adam let not Satan seduce you" (*Qur'an* 7:27). The Islamic emphasis on the universal brotherhood of man is a good resource
for dialogue.

Islam lays great importance on society's commitment to justice. In the *Qur'an* Allah states: "O you who believe, stand out
firmly for God as witnesses to fair dealing and let not the hatred
of others to you swerve to wrong and depart from justice. Be
just, that is next to piety." (*Qur'an* 5:8). Justice should be observed in all human interactions. Islam demands that justice in
exercise of authority be absolute. Discrimination is totally condemned, be it on grounds of religion, race, color, kinship or
hostility.

Islam gave to humanity 1405 years ago an ideal code for human rights. The proclamation of the dignity of man in Islam is based on the fact that all people are equal without any difference—except on the ground of piety.[4] As for the dignity of man the *Qur'an* proclaims: "We have honored the sons of Adam." The holy prophet emphasizes that there is no distinction in dignity and fundamental rights between one person and another. All mankind comes from the same origin and we are all asked to submit to the will of the almighty who is revered in all truth, to help one another for the good of all on the basis of unrestricted equality.

Human rights in Islam are strongly rooted in the belief that God alone is the lawgiver and the origin of human rights. Being of divine origin, no leader or government or parliament can restrain, abrogate or violate human rights granted by God. It is sad that many governments including Islamic ones, are ignoring if not grossly violating such rights. Human rights which are part and parcel of the Islamic heritage constitute fertile ground for interfaith dialogue.

Perhaps the greatest characteristic which renders Islam open for dialogue with people of faith is its love for peace. Peace is embodied in all Islamic principles. Peace exists in manifestation of its salutations. "Assalaam Alaikum," meaning "May God's Peace be Upon You," is the Muslim greeting. This is to inculcate the idea of peace in the minds of Muslims and to remind them of it constantly.[5] The *Qur'an* witnesses: "And their greeting in Paradise shall be Peace" (*Qur'an* 10:10).

I am quite sure that any discussion of peace in Islam is disturbing to many who are used to looking at Muslims as always belligerent. To a lay observer, peace in Islam will no doubt be in contrast with events in the Muslim world, be it the assassination of President Sadat by Islamic Integrists, the war of attrition in the Gulf between Iran and Iraq, the persecution of Muslim brothers in Syria and Sudan, the dismemberment of Lebanon, the war in Chad; the list could go on.

However, one important point to appreciate is that most of these events have little or nothing to do with Islam. One should understand Islam in light of the original teachings of the *Qur'an* and *Sunnah* (traditions) of the Prophet Muhammad (Peace be upon him). As already observed, Islam is the religion of peace by definition and content. Peace issues from God. For that reason when man diverts from God, he will never experience real peace with himself and with others. Consequently, that is why peace solely in a secular framework does not work in vain for it is only relative.

Islam will never aggress against non-Muslims who make peace with it or are even indifferent to it.[6] Islam does not force people to accept it because it is a faith that must come from deep conviction of an individual. The *Qur'an* confirms this by saying: "There is no compulsion in religion" (*Qur'an* 2:256). Islam strives for peace rather than seeking war. It does not permit the killing of a human being merely because he or she fails to believe in Islam. Resort to war on part of Muslims against non-Muslims is therefore not permitted on the basis of religious difference. The appropriate question normally asked by non-Muslims is: Why do Muslims wage wars of *jihad*? The word *jihad* has been mistranslated into "holy war," an expression picked up by western media and unfortunately perpetuated by certain Islamic agencies. It is referred to in the Arabic text as *jihad fi sabi Lillah*. Jihad is derived from the Arabic word *jihad* meaning ability, exertion or effort. *Jihad fi sabi Lillah* therefore, means efforts on God's way, effort to spread Islam, and defend it against its aggressors, effort towards a determined objective, i.e., against the visible enemy, against the devil, or against oneself.[7] In that case, *jihad* is not an offensive means of spreading Islam, rather it is permitted as a defensive measure to protect Muslims and their system of life if there is aggression. Therefore, war is not the mission of Islam nor the normal course for the *ummah* (community). Peace is the rule and essence of Islam and war the exception.

The world today is passing through a state of turmoil and unrest. It is torn by strife, wars, disharmony, killing, arson, the nuclear threat, and a general lack of peace, etc. In several of these global issues religion has had its hand. However, religion has a positive role that it can play to make this world a better place to live in. In the words of Dom Helder Pessoa Camara, archbishop of Olinda-Rcife in Brazil (a recipient of the Miwano Peace Prize): "Religions, inspite of historical differences, must now seek to unite all men."[8] In this current turbulent world where peace seems to have left humanity there are common terms that a Muslim can advocate from his heritage which the ear of a Jew, a Hindu, a Christian, a Buddhist, a Sikh, a Zoroastrian, a Jain, a Shintoist, a Bahai, an atheist and every human being can hear. The common terms to mention but a few, are: justice, peace, goodwill, and understanding, which have always been central to the Islamic tradition.

Since the Islamic heritage possesses the necessary resources to promote interreligious dialogue one might wonder what conceptions would guide an Islamic interreligious encounter.

In this case, the *Qur'an* and *Sunnah* (the basic sources of Islamic knowledge) would provide a wonderful guide.

Islam has never in its history opposed dialogue or inter-religious dialogue. Allah says: "Call unto the way of thy Lord with wisdom and fair exhortation and argue with them with sweet reasonableness" (*Qur'an* 16:125). This passage, the basis of dialogue, lays down principles of religious teachings which are good for all times. We must invite all to the way of God with wisdom and discretion. Our preaching must be reasonable, non-dogmatic, non-offensive, gentle and attractive. Islam enjoys the traditional attitude of tolerance which presents a good image for interreligious dialogue. Allah's command that "There is no compulsion in religion" (*Qur'an* 2:256) is to govern the relationships between Muslims and non-Muslims alike. Within the world *ummah* everyone should be free to convince and to be convinced of the truth.[9] When the first Muslim state was established in Madinah, Prophet Muhammad assured the Jews that they would not be oppressed nor would there be any Muslim communal agitation against them. "To the Jews their religion and to Muslims theirs," he declared. Since the Prophet Muhammad (Peace be upon him) laid down these fundamental principles, the land of Islam became the safe refuge for Jews whenever they were persecuted. The principles of religious tolerance and respect for human rights have always been enshrined in the hearts of sincere Muslims. Muslims gave an historical example when they entered Jerusalem for the first time in 637 A.D. A pact was signed by Caliph Umar and the Patriarch of Jerusalem Sophronius. By this famous agreement, the Caliph granted the Christians security for their lives, their property, their churches and crosses. The same pact forbade Muslim occupation or plunder of Christian churches, the reduction of their number or narrowing of their areas.

From the beginning, Islam offered the universal community as the basis of human association instead of the nation, people, or ethnic group. In the first written constitution which the prophet gave to the new Islamic state in Madinah, the *ummah* of Muslims was one Community and the *ummah* of Jews was another. Later the *ummah*(s) of Christians, Zoroastrians, Hindus and Buddhists joined the Islamic state.

The Islamic state itself was an *ummah* of a different order, an expanding world *ummah* designed eventually to include all humanity as its citizens. Each *ummah* is to coexist in peace, order the lives of its members according to its own religion, institutions and laws. All this is guaranteed by the Shari'ah, the God given law.[10]

Lessons for the Future

Through our brief survey of the Islamic heritage, it is clear, that Islam has a lot to offer (theologically and historically) in this relatively new area of interreligious dialogue. The *Qur'an* and *Sunnah* provide explicit teachings and examples of how Muslims should relate with people of faith and all human beings including self declared atheists. My experience with scriptures of other traditions is that they have disappointingly little to say about Islam. Yet Muslims have had contact and relations with people of faith across the continents and over the centuries. In some cases as history will bear out, Muslims have tried to implement the proper teachings of Islam regarding relationships with people of other traditions. In other cases Muslims have gone contrary to the teachings of Islam in their encounter with people of other faiths. This bitter lesson of the past, which is not only a prerogative of Islam, but of almost all existing traditions, does not auger well for the future. However, despite good or bad relationships between Muslims and other people of faith in the past there is hope for better relations in the future, especially through interreligious dialogue. Muslims and members of other traditions are becoming increasingly aware that they all recognize God as creator, that they share the same humanity, a common spirituality and are bound together by interdependence and brotherhood. All are concerned with basic human existence, dignity, and opportunity. They share the common threats of pollution, scarcity of food and energy, armed and ideological conflicts. All are concerned about the moral decay and injustice facing humanity. The common plight which humanity currently faces provides the urgent need and relevant forum for the meeting of members of different religious traditions in dialogue. All efforts and contributions in this direction are highly commendable. The time has come for religion to play a more positive role in seeking to unite all men in building a free just, moral, and peaceful society. There is every need for different religious traditions to meet in dialogue, to discuss, and advance with practical solutions for the sake of humanity.

Perhaps I have been talking about dialogue all along without explaining the term. What is dialogue? Dialogue is not a debate. To use Professor Swidler's words: "Dialogue is a conversation on a common subject between two or more persons with differing views the primary purpose of which is for each participant to learn from the other so that he can change and grow."[11] In dialogue each partner must listen to the other as openly and sympathetically as he or she can in an attempt to understand the other's position as precisely and as it were, as much from within as possible. Dialogue demands that there is a readiness to see others in a new light; no longer as enemies to be overcome, disciples to be indoctrinated or candidates to be won over, but in all sincerity as companions with whom to share in all fraternal equality what is best in our common existence.[12] It is through dialogue that cross-traditional tolerance, respect, and spiritual awareness can be developed. This is possible because dialogue demands that we treat each other as believers and become aware of the values which inspire each other in daily life as individuals and as members of society.

Perhaps in this century, to achieve our objective, i.e. developing cross-traditional tolerance, respect, and spiritual awareness, we need to push dialogue to a further level, the interreligious level. Interreligious dialogue is a different kind of dialogue where partners come as persons somehow identified with a religious community, that is, as Muslims, Hindus, Christians, etc. Interreligious dialogue is a relatively new venture. It operates in three areas and under three phases. The areas are: the practical, where we collaborate to help humanity; the cognitive, where we seek understanding and truth; and the spiritual, where we attempt to experience the partner's religion "from within." The three phases correspond to the three areas. In the first phase, we unlearn misinformation about each other, and begin to know each other as we truly are. In the second phase we begin to discern values in the partner's tradition that we may wish to appropriate into our own tradition. If we are serious, persistent, and sensitive enough in dialogue we may at times enter phase three. In this phase, we together begin to explore new areas of reality of meaning and truth of which neither had even been aware before.

Conclusion

Our brief study of the Islamic heritage and tradition has shown that Islam relates to people of faith at both the human and scriptural levels. Islam possesses the necessary resources to promote interreligious dialogue. These include among others, a commitment to justice and the universal brotherhood of man, the call to serve humanity, respect for human rights, tolerance, love for peace, etc. The *Qur'an* and *Sunnah* of the Prophet Muhammad (Peace be upon him), and the history of the Muslim *ummah* have and will always provide guidelines for the course of interreligious dialogue. It has to be emphasized that neither at the beginning nor in the future will Islam ever oppose dialogue either at the individual or interreligious level. Muslims are genuinely concerned that although they live with believers of other traditions as neighbors, yet they seldom witness or listen to one another in matters concerning faith or other global issues. The issues which divide Muslims and followers of other traditions should not in this age build walls of hostility as has been the case for many centuries. The very nature of the issues demands patience, listening, and witness—in short, an interreligious dialogue. Dialogue is the key for cross-tradition tolerance, respect, and spiritual awareness. Dialogue, once patiently pursued, can become an instrument of new "revelation" a further "unveiling" of reality on which we must act. For interreligious dialogue to be meaningful and effective, believers of all traditions should endeavor to sponsor or host meetings of interreligious encounter and not only leave it as a monopoly of Christians. Dialogue is a two way street, a game of equal partners.

Notes

1. A.A. Maududi, *Towards Understanding Islam* (Nairobi: Islamic Foundation, 1973), 1.
2. See M. Abdul al Ra'uf, "Judaism and Christianity in the Perspective of Islam," in *Trialogue of the Abrahamic Faiths*, ed. Raji al Faruqi (Washington: International Institute of Islamic Thought, 1983), 22.
3. *Trialogue of the Abrahamic Faiths*, 27.
4. A.S. Kanenally, "Meaning of Peace in its Religious Dimension," in *Universal Peace And Its Principles*, (Nairobi: Islamic Foundation, 1984), 13.
5. Abdul-Kadir Hubaiti, "Peace a Central Theme of Islam," in *Universal Peace and Its Principles*, 19.
6. B.D. Kateregga and D.W. Shenk, *Islam and Christianity: A Muslim and a Christian in Dialogue* (Grand Rapids: W.B. Eerdmans Publishing Co., 1981), 78.
7. Ibid., 76.
8. D.H.P. Camara, in *Religion for Peace*: A Newsletter of the World Conference on Religion and Peace, New York, (Aug. 1983), 1.
9. I. Raj al Faruqi, "The Nation-State and Social order in the Perspective of Islam," in *Trialogue of Abrahamic Faiths*, 58.
10. Ibid.
11. Leonard Swidler, "Dialogue Decalogue," *Journal of Ecumenical Studies*, vol. 20, no. 1 (Philadelphia: Temple University, 1983), 1- 4.
12. See Sigvard Von Sicard. "Christian-Muslim Co-operation in Africa," in *Bulletin on Islam and Christian-Muslim Relations in Africa* (Birmingham: Selly Oak Colleges, 1983), vol. 1, no. 1, 3.

13

A Korean Buddhist View on Interreligious Dialogue— Won-Hyo's Ideal on Peace and Union

Ki-Young Rhi

Time of Dispute

Being himself a great monk-scholar of Mahayana Buddhism, Won-Hyo (617- 686) follows faithfully the ideal of Mahayana. He starts all his philosophical speculations and religious understandings from the global idea of the harmonious universe professed in the greatest *Mahayanasutra*, the *Avatamsaka* (*Hwa-Om-Kyong*) which mainly insists on the close mutual interrelationship of all the components of the universe without exception. This universe itself was proclaimed in this sutra as the manifestation and function of Buddha's body of law, the *dharmakaya*.

Won-Hyo understood that *dharmakaya* is the life, the mind, the seed or the egg from which the whole world develops and in which the whole world evolves and into which at the end of life the whole enters. Various and different terminologies are used by Won-Hyo to designate the essence (*dharmakaya*), the manifestations (*sambhogakaya*) and the action (*nirmanakaya*) of the Buddha's body: for example, one mind, one mindness, one vehicle (*Eka-yana*), the way, the source, the source of one mindness and so on.

He believes that all living beings (*sattva*) are actually the constituting parts of this Buddha's body, living temporarily in this world of transmigration (*samsara*) revealing their various imperfections which are the results of their own ignorance (*avidya*).

Like other Mahayana thinkers of East Asia, Won-Hyo also had a keen awareness of the serious contamination of the time he lived in, due to accumulated egocentric ways of thinking. He knew already the description of the *pascimakala* (the time of the end) given by several important Mahayana scriptures.

Increasing phenomena of dispute, dispute as social conflict, dispute in the name of religious denominations, for instance, were the salient features of this time of the end. The following five kinds of dirtinesses (*kasaya*), which are considered the results of accumulated wrong ways of thinking may have a certain significance even for today:

1. the dirtiness of the time;
2. the dirtiness of the living beings;
3. the dirtiness of the views or the ways of thinking;
4. the dirtiness of the human passions, and finally,
5. the dirtiness of the life-length.

Religion as the Way of Life to Dispel the Dispute

Won-hyo understood the essence of Buddha's teaching (*Buddhasasana*) as the way of life to dispel dispute. In other words, the point of Buddha's teaching is to realize the perfect peace and union which is the ultimate reality of the universe (the one mindness or the true nature of this phenomenal world, *dharmadhatu*). Explaining the main theme of the *Maha-parinirvana-sutra*, Won-Hyo says:

> The sutra, bringing together the different assertions of the scriptures, integrates them into the one taste of the ocean. It harmonizes also the diverse disputes of many thinkers, developing the most universal spirit of the Buddha. In this way the sutra provides the possibility to all kinds of noisy living beings to go back all together to the final goal. The final goal is the non-dual real nature, to which all the living beings rush after long sleep and dream. It is indeed the great enlightenment.

Won-Hyo's words make clear his conviction that the final goal of religion is the transformation of common life, full of dispute and quarrel, into a life of peaceful union and harmonious integration. The text cited above alludes to the belief that the so-called "final goal," the great enlightenment, is quite similar to the Vedantic conception of the realization of non-duality (advaita). The same idea was expressed in many places in Won-Hyo's writings. I cite here another text from Won-Hyo's treatise on the Sukhavatlvyuha.

> Sometimes if one becomes a victim of the five kinds of dirtiness because of the winds of passion, he floats and sinks in the waves of suffering, continuing to flow on the dirty stream endlessly. Sometimes if one can cut down the four kinds of stream, thanks to the roots of goodness, then one never retreats but finally arrives at the other shore, stopping every kind of disturbance forever.

> But even these two, flowing and stopping, are also the great dream. At the very moment of the perfect enlightenment, there is no HERE and THERE. The distinction between the dirty land and the pure land comes from the ignorant view through which one cannot see the one-mind. There is no separate existence of samsara and nirvana.

> Nevertheless, it is impossible for those who do not accumulate through their efforts the merits to go back and understand this origin, this great enlightenment. And it is not possible also to those who continue the long dreaming to open their eyes and see that.

Perhaps the following texts from his Treatise on the Vajrasamadhisutra will help us better comprehend Won-Hyo's view.

> All the dharmas (phenomena) are only the one-mind. All the sattvas (living beings) are nothing but the One Original Enlightenment.

> All the sattvas who are to be saved by the Tathagata (arrived at the perfect state as it should be) are nothing but the flow of the one mind.

Once asked by a disciple what gate a beginner should take to enter into the way of spiritual exercise, Won-Hyo answered as follows:

There are no separate *dharmas* from the one mind. The six bad ways of life, going up and down the waves, flow only because of ignorance (*avidya*) that makes one fail to understand the one mindness.

Though there are the waves of the six bad ways of life, they cannot go out of the source of the one mind. For the six bad ways of life move and appear only in this mind and by this mind. One can make the vow to save all those *sattvas* of the six bad ways of life.

Since these *sattvas* of the six bad ways of life cannot escape from the one mind, it is quite natural to have for them great compassion, regarding them absolutely as like as themselves.

There are the two gates: one is the gate of the "eternal silence," and another is the gate of the "birth and death"; according to the first gate of the one mind, practice the *samatha* exercise, and according to the second gate of the same one mind, raise your spiritual exercise of *vipasana*. When you are able to live with these two, you will become an able man for the meritorious life. (*The Treatise on the Awakening of Faith in the Mahayana.*)

Il-Sung (Eke-Yana) as the Ultimate Reality

Il-Sung (Eka-Yana) literally means one vehicle, which one has to ride in order to go back to one's own self. *Il-Sung* means at the same time that one reality which is already realized in oneself, the true self. This is a *yana* (vehicle), but this does not mean any particular doctrine or ideology such as the Mahayana or Hinayana. The principal Mahayana *sutras* and *sastras* (treatises) such as the *Saddharma-pundarika-sutra*, the *Vimalakirti-nirdesa*, the *Lankavatara-sutra*, the *Parinirvana-sutra*, the *Avatamsaka-sutra* and the *Mahayana-sraddhotpada-sastra* use this term as well as the term *mahayana* to mean the same. It designates the very source of life both for individual living beings and also for the universal life. From the psychological point of view, it is called the mind, but from the biological point of view the term the embryo or the germ of life was used. This is also the synonym of the *dharmakaya* (Buddha's body of law or essential body which does not mean a common human body) or the *dharmadhatu* (metaphysically it means the true reality, but it means also all the phenomenal world of that reality). *Il-Sung* is called the *Tathagata garbha*, the embryo or the germ of *Tathagata*, for it is another aspect of all living beings (*sattva*). In his *Treatise*, Won-

Hyo declared that the main theme of the *Saddharma-pundarika-sutra* (The Lotus of the True Law) is to clarify the meaning and the importance of this term *Il-Sung* (*Eka-Yana*). The following comments on this term professed by Won-Hyo might give quite significant guidelines for our present discussion on inter-religious dialogue. Won-Hyo declares that the *Il-Sung* has to be considered from two angles: Who are the riders of this vehicle? What is it that in fact we ride? To these two questions Won-Hyo replies as follows:

On the question who might be the riders of this vehicle we might say there are three categories of living beings:

(1) those who live their spiritual lives under the banners of the following triple *Yanas: Sravaka-Yana, Pratyekabuddha-Yana,* and *Bodhisattva-Yana*;

(2) the following four kinds of *Sravakayana* practitioners: practitioners whose minds are definitively fixed, practitioners whose minds are affected by extreme arrogance, practitioners whose intentions are weak and retrogressive, practitioners who are taking this Sravakahood just for the altruistic purpose to convert them into the true *dharma* (*sad-dharma*);

(3) the following four kinds of common living beings (*sattva*): those who are to be born in moisture, those who are to be born from the egg, those who are to be born from the matrix, those who are to be born from the mysterious spiritual operations.

Then what is it in fact that we ride? According to my own understanding there are the following four aspects of this *Il-sung* (the *Eka-Yana*):

(1) *Li* (reason or law as the invisible eternal principle) is verily the one *dharmadhatu*. Sometimes this is called also the *dharmakaya* (the body of law) or the *Tathagata-garbha* (the embryo of *Tathagata*).

(2) *Kyo* (teachings or instructions given in various modes and conceptions) is so to speak all the teachings and instructions taught by the Buddhas of all the times and of all the places during their life-time from the enlightenment to the death.

(3) *In* (cause) has two aspects. First it is the Buddha's nature that everybody has. It is from this nature that every living being is able to manifest the triple bodies of Buddha (*dharmakaya, sambhogakaya* and *nirmanakaya*). Second is the good spiritual disposition through which every living being tends to do meritorious activities, whatever the present

status of the person might be, whether holy men or
common people, Buddhists or non-Buddhists.

(4) *Kwa* (effect, fruit). As we saw before, *Il-Sung* is the
enlightened mind which is at the same time the cause and
the effect. When it is considered as already given at birth, it
might be called enlightenment *a priori*; but when it is
considered as the effect acquired during the life-time, it
might be called enlightenment *a posteriori*. The first
corresponds with the *dharmakaya* and the second with the
sambhogakaya or the *nirmanakaya*.

How to Arrive at This Ultimate Reality, Il-Sung?

To this question which seems to me very crucial for us who
are seeking success in interreligious dialogue, the best answer I
found is a brief resume of the Treatise on the *Vajrasamahi-sutra*
written by Won-Hyo himself.

> If there are constant flows and vicious circles of false im-
> aginings from beginningless time, it is because of the ten-
> dency of living beings to separate the forms and names
> and become attached to them.

> This is the reason why, if one wants to go back to the
> source of this stream, one should separate himself from
> the false characters the *dharmas* which exist only tem-
> porarily. So in the first chapter, the sutra emphasizes the
> need of deep meditation about formlessness as the fun-
> damental character of the world.

> But if there still remains any subjective intention to look
> for any objective things, he cannot recognize the en-
> lightenment *a priori*, bestowed with him from the eternity.
> So the sutra explains in the second chapter the necessity of
> the elimination of the subjective ego-consciousness.

The similar content of these first two stages is illustrated also
in another place, as follows:

> When a Bodhisattva who has cultivated the highest intui-
> tive knowledge, attempts to look for any particular nature
> and form of things, he does not seize anything subjective
> or objective such as *atman* (self) or *anatman* (not-self), *nitya*
> (permanence) or *anitya* (impermanence), *utpada* (ap-
> pearance) or *anutpada* (disappearance), *bhava* (being) or
> *adhava* (non-being).

At that moment, the Bodhisattva personally realizes the sameness of things, understanding the true reality of all the dharmas. He becomes completely free from the false views, entering into the reality which is beyond duality and opposition, neither beginning nor ending, neither birth nor death, neither being nor non-being. The ultimate reality surpasses all the ways of words and phrases, and it goes beyond all the realms of mental activities. (Won-Hyo, *The Essentials of the Mahaprajnaparamita-sutra*.)

From this, we can understand that the means to arrive at this final goal that Won-Hyo had in mind was indeed the spiritual concentration which aims at the complete integration of subject/object dichotomy. Won-Hyo illustrates the same view in his commentary on a sutra which treats the fundamental actions of Bodhisattva, *Bo-sal-bon-op-kyong*.

The ways without any particular denomination are not the "non-ways."
The gates without any particular denomination are not the "non-gates."
Since there are no "non-gates," everything and all things are the gates through which one can enter into the final goal:
Since there are no "non-ways," everyplace and every situation are the ways through which one can go back to the source.
This way which leads to the source is hard to follow for its secrecy;
This gate which leads to the final goal is hard to enter for its extreme broadness.

The text cited above shows Won-Hyo's attitude toward someone who has attachment to particular names and forms of religion as unique and absolute.

He emphasized the crucial importance of the *dhyana* (spiritual concentration); but the text proves that he was not holding any conformist attitude toward *dhyana*. He thought rather that everywhere and everytime where there is daily life, *dhyana* should be done and might be done.

We were taking perhaps too long to explain Won-Hyo's summary of the first two chapters of the *Vajrasamadhisutra*. Let us continue to read the rest of the summary.

The third chapter of the *Vajrasamadhi-sutra* treats the original enlightenment, the so-called enlightenment *a priori* and its powerful function. It clarifies that as soon as one achieves the double efforts for emancipation from both the objective realities and the subjective ego-consciousness as well, he can immediately meet with the original one-mindness that is the enlightenment *a priori*.

The title of the fourth chapter is "On the Move from the False to the Real." It explains the powerful functions of enlightenment a priori which enables living beings to move from the false to the real.

The fifth chapter treats the true nature of this one mindness which is the emptiness. It clarifies that the emptiness is the result of the successful practices of the first two elementary spiritual exercises.

The last chapter, the sixth, entitled as "On the *Tathagatagarbha* (The Germ of the *Tathagata*)" reveals the meaning of the final state, the perfect realization of the one taste, the perfection of the human beings in accordance with true nature. The sutra concludes that in this way nothing arbitrary has been done and thanks to it, one becomes able to do everything valuable without conflicts.

Thus in Won-Hyo we have charted for us a way to peace. His way unfolds against the backdrop of the "harmonious universe" and it is the way we seek.

14

Ghandi's Experiments in Interreligious Dialogue

K.L. Seshagiri Rao

Human civilization, reflecting the vicissitudes of a checkered history, has till today, marched indifferently, at times advancing spiritual and moral values and at times depreciating and neglecting them. Most human progress is at best piecemeal; it does not exhibit any predetermined dialectic inevitability. Whenever there has been an advance in moral and spiritual values, it has resulted mostly from the driving force of a religious personality embodying a comprehensive and integrated way of life.

In the past, religions have seemed by no means an unmixed blessing. "On the one hand, they have contributed greatly toward peace and progress, building hospitals and charitable institutions, promoting art and literature, and conferring many other blessings on humanity; on the other hand, in the name of religion, people have waged wars, persecuted their fellow beings, and destroyed monuments of human culture."[1] How is it that religions which preach love and human brotherhood and peace could have given rise to conflicts generating hatred in their relationships with other communities? That there have been such conflicts cannot be denied. Nevertheless, it is not the religions that are responsible for the hatred and cruelty, it is human bigotry and narrowness.

As far as one can see, the human community will continue to be religiously pluralistic. But traditional theologies, developed in religious isolation, have already become inadequate if not obsolete. They do not permit members of the different religious traditions to live side by side in friendly cooperation. They raise walls of separation between large sections of human beings and mitigate against human unity. In an ever shrinking world, our religious attitudes have to come to terms with this fact, and avoid further pointless and tragic conflict.

About the middle of the present century, Arnold Toynbee predicted that a thousand years from now, when historians look back on the twentieth century, they will be very little interested in the conflicts between communism and capitalism, but they will see it as a period in which Eastern and Western religions interpenetrated one another and took the first steps towards building a genuine world civilization. Each religious tradition, in as much as it has nourished certain valuable insights (although neglecting some others), will have a significant contribution to make toward the emerging global civilization.

Gandhi

Gandhi lived and died vindicating moral and spiritual values against the forces of materialism, parochialism, and violence. He believed that if man is to grow in peace and understanding, he must meet other human beings with fearlessness and friendliness irrespective of religious or national affiliations. As he pointed out, dialogue is essential for progress. The different communities and their leaders need not only to communicate and cooperate to make the world become a better place to live in, but they need also an open environment in which to pursue truth. Growth in spiritual life, he held, will develop in man the capacity for humanity, charity, and tolerance and enable him to build a new civilization based on justice and moral regeneration.

Gandhi was in the thick of religious dialogue from the early years of his life. Among his father's friends were a good many Muslims, Parsis (Zoroastrians), and Jains as well as Hindus; they gathered frequently in his house for religious discussions. And the young Gandhi eagerly listened to their conversation. This experience impressed on his mind the problem of religious diversity, and the need to forge unity among the followers of different religions.

His religious quest was further stimulated by his Christian friends in England and South Africa. In London, he spent a large part of his time in religious discussion. The literature of the Theosophists introduced him to the movement for the unity of religions. Sir Edwin Arnold's English version of the *Bhagavad Gita*, The Song Celestial, stirred him so deeply that for the rest of his life it became his constant guide. He also read *The Light of Asia* and *The Sayings of Zarathustra* with great interest. He was moved by the teachings of the New Testament, especially the Sermon on the Mount. The verse, "But I say unto you that ye resist not evil; but whosoever shall smite thee on the right cheek, turn to him the other also" went straight to his heart. The personality of Jesus held a fascination for him all his life.

Gandhi also read Carlyle's *Heroes and Hero-Worship*, and learned from it of Muhammad's "greatness, bravery, and austere living." Washington Irving's *Life of Mahomet and His Successors* raised the prophet in his estimation. The prophet's austere life and profound teachings influenced him a great deal. C. F. Andrews observes: "Gandhi's profound admiration for the character of Prophet Muhammad as a man of faith and action, and also for his son-in-law Ali, as a man of tender love and suffering, deeply affected him. He was impressed to a remarkable degree by the nobility of the early caliphate and the fervent faith of the first followers of the prophet. The bare simplicity with which they lived, their chivalrous devotion to the poor, their intense belief in God's overruling majesty, all these things had a great effect on him."[2]

Theoretical Dialogue

The Mahatma pursued religious dialogue on two levels: theoretical and practical. At the theoretical level, his objective was sympathetic understanding of the living world religions. Ignorance about the faiths of other men, he realized, gives rise to prejudices and misrepresentations resulting in a certain unwillingness to accept the integrity of the followers of other traditions. People quarrel about religion only when they lose sight of the human dimension of all religions. It is lack of sensitive understanding of others' faith that has often led the practitioners of religions to mutual recrimination and bloodshed.

Religious believers generally have insufficient opportunities for and interest in knowing about the values and insights of the various world religions; indeed there is a pervasive ignorance of the creative principles of all faiths, including one's own. Whatever the reason for such a state of affairs in the past, Gandhi felt that it could not be allowed to continue. Modern men and women need to expand their religious consciousness by understanding in depth the spiritual truths revealed in religions other than their own.

Gandhi believed that education without the study of the religions is incomplete. Religious study is not only a legitimate intellectual pursuit but a vital aspect of human culture and civilization. It relates to the wellsprings of individual and social life, and deals with the central questions of human life and destiny. One neglects the study of religions at the risk of failing to understand humanity and history. Reminiscing about his early life, Gandhi expressed much regret at the lack of facilities to study religion at his school. He discussed this predicament in his *Autobiography* (p. 120) : "I am Hindu by faith, and yet I do not know much about Hinduism, and I know much less of other religions. In fact, I do not know what is and what should be my belief, I intend to make a careful study of my own religion, and as far as I can, of other religions as well." This he did later on, devoting a good measure of his time to the study of comparative religion, which exercised a profound influence on his life. He became convinced that the study of the different religions would contribute to a healthy religious pluralism.

Gandhi would not make individual comparisons between religions qualitatively. Indeed he saw no use in such endeavour. To him the main point was not how palatable or unpalatable one religion was to the followers of another religion but the fact of its profound influence on its own followers. "As we wish the followers of other religions to appreciate us, so ought we to seek with all our hearts to appreciate them. Surely, this is the Golden Rule."[3] Gandhi was humble and eager to learn from other traditions and their followers. He believed that there was good in every tradition, and went straight to their best, purest, and noblest elements with a view to benefiting from them in his own life.

His study of the religions revealed that every religious tradition had its period of growth and decline and that no historical religion was perfect. He saw that each religious tradition has needed purging of old abuses at one time or another, and that each religion has had its band of reformers and saints. He considered it misguided, therefore, for any tradition to fasten on itself or on others the crudities of a bygone age. Recognizing that each great religion contained numerous elements, tendencies, and movements, he refused to characterize a religion on the basis of a single sect or movement.

Gandhi's approach was rather to encourage the purification of religions than to seek their replacement. He believed that a knowledge of other religions makes Hindus better Hindus, Muslims better Muslims, Christians better Christians, and all humans better members of the world community. Interreligious dialogue, he saw, offers help in refining and developing neglected dimensions of each religious tradition. The insights of different religions belong to all peoples. The truths revealed to the Christians should become precious to the followers of other faiths, and vice-versa. Religious dialogue also sensitizes people of different backgrounds to one another. No religion should, therefore, bar its followers from studying other religions or supplementing their own spiritual knowledge and discipline.

Gandhi was generous in acknowledging his deep debt to other faiths. But he insisted that while we should throw open our windows for fresh breezes from different directions, we should refuse to be swept off our feet. He developed a capacity for assimilating insights of other traditions and thus enriching his own. In a revealing conversation, Gandhi told Mrs. Henry Polak in South Africa: "I did once seriously think of embracing the Christian faith. The gentle figure of Christ, so patient, so kind, so loving, so full of forgiveness that he taught his followers not to retaliate when abused or struck, but to turn the other cheek—I thought it was a beautiful example of a perfect man." "But you did not embrace Christianity, did you?", she asked. "No," replied Gandhi thoughtfully. "I studied your scriptures for some time and thought earnestly about them...but eventually I came to the conclusion that there was no need for me to join your creed to be a believer in the beauty of the teaching of Jesus or try to follow his example." And he added: "If a man reaches the heart of his own religion, he has reached the heart of others too. There is only one God, but there are many paths to Him."[4]

Practical Dialogue

Religious dialogue for Gandhi, was not just a theoretical or academic matter; it had an existential dimension. He put more emphasis on the practical aspects of religion and inward life than on beliefs and dogmas. Because of this he was able to cooperate with the adherents of other religions in realizing the higher ideals of life. As a result, members of different races and faiths worked and struggled together in his movements for freedom and justice on behalf of the oppressed sections of society in South Africa and in India. The Indian National Congress, which spearheaded the nonviolent freedom struggle under the leadership of Gandhi, included Parsis (Zoroastrians), Hindus, Muslims, Christians, Buddhists, and followers of other religions. He did not think that any theological consensus was a

131

prerequisite for working together for human justice and freedom. Participants in his movement were reminded, however that all religions emphasized man's responsibility for other human beings and were urged to follow the highest vision of their respective faiths.

Gandhi's ashrams both in South Africa and in India were outstanding examples of harmonious cooperation. They were the "moral laboratories where his experiments with truth and nonviolence were conducted in the living of daily life; there were no dividing lines of class, nationality, or creed. The inmates of his ashrams belonged to different religions and races and lived a life of voluntary poverty, simplicity, purity, and service. In the community life of the ashrams, Gandhi gave first place to culture of the heart and training of the spirit. "To develop the spirit is to develop character and to enable one to work towards a knowledge of God and self-realization," he said.

Gandhi helped and encouraged the inmates of his ashrams to keep their respective religious observances. For example, he took care to see that the Muslim youngsters in the ashram community offered their names (prayer) and observed their Ramadam fast. He also encouraged the Hindu members to observe *pradosha* (fast until evening), and the Christians their Lent. The result of the experiment was that all the inmates became convinced of the value of fasting and the practice of self-denial. It led to support in the observance of their respective religious customs and festivals. It also demonstrated the unity of the ashram community despite the members' differences in beliefs and practices. When the South African courts, practicing religious discrimination, refused to recognize marriages performed according to non-Christian rites, the entire ashram community— Hindus, Christians, Parsis, etc.—took it as a serious affront to the sanctity of Indian married life and struggled nonviolently, under Gandhi's leadership, until the South African government repealed the discriminatory religious treatment.

To his ashram in Ahmedabad, Gandhi invited an "untouchable" family. The acceptance of such a family caused a good deal of opposition. Many of his followers became disgruntled; they did not want to live with the "untouchables" and some left. Even his wife objected at first. Monetary support to the ashram from the public stopped. But Gandhi would not give in, since it was a matter of religious principle with him. He was prepared to move into the untouchable quarters of the city and, like an untouchable, live by manual labor. An unknown person came up with help, and in a short period the opposition died down; even the orthodox changed their minds. And Gandhi adopted the daughter of an untouchable family, Lakshmi, as his own daughter.

Gandhi was frankly a religious Hindu, and a *sanatani* or orthodox Hindu at that. He was relentless, however, in his criticism of the excrescences that had accumulated in Hinduism through the ages. He exposed the evils in the Hindu social and religious structure and discarded whatever offended his moral sense. He was equally active in campaigning publicly for their removal. He worked for the transformation of Hindu society and for the setting of new moral standards, and this, eventually changed the lives of millions of people. He worked for the redemption of the outcasts, the emancipation of women, basic education, cottage industries, prohibition, and like causes.

Gandhi's interreligious dialogue resulted in: (1) mutual learning; (2) sensitive awareness of other religions; (3) deepening of this awareness into respect; (4) a progressive reinterpretation of his own life and traditions; and (5) mutual cooperation for the common objectives of truth and justice.

The most remarkable aspect of Gandhi's life and work is his dedication to the search for truth. "Truth became my sole objective," he said. "It began to grow in magnitude every day and my definition of it has been ever widening."[5] Even when Gandhi appeared to be engaged in struggles which were not purely religious in character or in movements connected with social reform and justice, his dominant motive was still religious. "Man's ultimate aim is the realization of God, and all his activities, social, and religious have to be guided by the ultimate aim of the vision of God. The immediate service of all human beings becomes a necessary part of the endeavor, simply because the only way to find God is to see Him in His creation and be one with it. This can be done only by service to all. I am part and parcel of the whole and I cannot find him apart from the rest of humanity.... If I could persuade myself that I could find Him in a Himalayan cave, I would proceed there immediately; but I know that I cannot find Him apart from humanity."[6]

Gandhi started with the conviction that God is truth, later he declared that truth is God. For him, truth meant more than mere truthfulness; it signified eternal being. It included what is true in knowledge, what is right in conduct, and what is just and fair in human relations. Life is an experiment in which human beings ought to discover the ever more comprehensive truth. The different ways through which human beings pursued truth interested him exceedingly. He did not stop at seeking and discovering truth: he proceeded to establish it in terms of justice and fair play to all. He stressed, therefore, that the only means of attaining truth in life is *ahimsa*, non-violence, which is nothing less than the "liability to love the meanest of creation as oneself." It is in this unique way that Gandhi brought home to everyone the religious spirit—not in heavy theological language, but in the language of daily life and truthful living.

Gandhi's purpose in dialogue was not elimination of religious differences, but appreciation of one another's faith and practice, leading to cooperation in the moral and social spheres. He sought to understand both the similarities and the differences. He was impressed by the fact that moral and spiritual values are stressed by all religions. The "Golden Rule" in one form or another and the injunction to transcend the ego are present in all of them. All preach that man's relation to man is more important than his relation to material things. All teach that service to the poor, the sick, the helpless, and the oppressed is service to God. In the eternal struggle of good and evil, all religions are called upon to take sides with the good and raise humanity to a higher moral level. In this sense, the success of any religion is the success of all religions. It is only natural to expect, therefore, that different religions should cooperate with one another in dealing with these problems.

Gandhi was aware, on the other hand, of the characteristic differences between the great religions arising from historical and cultural backgrounds. They do not all have the same beliefs and doctrines; nor do they prescribe the same rituals or prayers, or subscribe to the same kind of myths. He believed that any attempt to root out these differences not only is bound to fail but is a form of sacrilege. Since differences are important, and in some cases unbridgeable, he discouraged uncritical syncretism. Actually, he welcomed the enrichment that comes with religious diversity. He wanted people from all religions to maintain their special symbols of identity. The need was not a new religion, but respectful dialogue among the adherents of different religions.

Gandhi did not look upon eclecticism with favor either. He did not approve of the abdication of one's own religion and its heritage. On the contrary, he advocated firm adherence to one's own religion. The eclectic does not go deeply into any religious tradition, and therefore lacks depth; his approach is superficial and he fails to grasp the distinctive message of any religious message of any religious tradition, even his own. According to him to call a person "eclectic" was to say that he had no faith. He advocated religious harmony, and not a blending of all religions into a uniformity of faith and practice.

Gandhi's focus in religious dialogue, therefore, was not myth, but the moral and spiritual resources of the different religious traditions. He was aware that religious practices often emphasized and developed sectarian trends and loyalties. He cautioned that it was dangerous to mankind as a whole today to overemphasize the parochial. He urged all people to look at things from a larger context and from a human perspective. For if the universal elements are released from their narrow settings, religions would become progressive and unifying forces in the world.

His Lasting Importance

In India, the problem of interreligious relations has engaged the attention of thinking persons for over three thousand years. In his own day, Gandhi was confronted with strained relations between Hindus and Muslims. Hatred and suspicion had poisoned the atmosphere. Bloody religious riots were frequent. The growing tension between the two communities distressed Gandhi a great deal. He deplored these riots, and believed that both Hindus and Muslims could and should live and work together for the common good. He pleaded and prayed and fasted for religious harmony. In fact, during the last decades of his life, his major preoccupation was harmony between Hindus and Muslims. He was a Hindu who advocated the rights of the Muslims. He pleaded with the Hindu majority to treat the minority with justice and fairness. He went from place to place, meeting Hindus and Muslims and proclaiming the fatherhood of God and the brotherhood of man. He said to the people: "God is one. Allah and Rama are His names." In the midst of pervasive darkness, Gandhi served as a beacon light. He sought to heal the wounds that people, in their religious frenzy, were inflicting upon themselves. He worked miracles. Lord Mountbatten, the last viceroy of India, described the situation in this way: "While the 55,000-man boundary force in the Punjab was swamped by riots, the one-man boundary force brought peace to Bengal."[7] A fanatic Hindu, however, believing that Gandhi was disloyal to Hinduism, assassinated him. Even in his death he achieved something remarkable; his martyrdom shamed his people out of hysteria of hatred and fratricide, and helped the country consolidate its constructive and democratic forces.

Gandhi wanted harmony and friendship to be established not merely between the Hindus and Muslims of India, but among the adherents of all the great religions of the world. "Hindu-Muslim unity means not only unity between Hindus and Muslims but between all those who believe India to be their home no matter to what faith they belong." The problem of the mutual relationship of religions is worldwide today. What is going on in Ireland, the Middle East, Cyprus, the Indian subcontinent, and elsewhere, in the name of religion is most distressing and depressing. The exaltation of terrorism in the name of religion is tragic. In the words of Gandhi, "To revile another's religion, to make reckless statements, utter untruth, to break the heads of innocent men, to desecrate temples or mosques is a denial of God."[8]

Gandhi's interreligious dialogue authentically represents the Indian attitude of respect for all religions. The idea that "truth is one: sages call it by different names" has been alive in Hinduism since the time of the Rgveda. Because of his great concern for truth, Gandhi was inwardly receptive to the currents of truth coming from other religions. To ignore any of them meant to ignore God's infinite richness, and impoverish humanity spiritually. He wanted all religions to revive their pristine past and develop their traditions. "I ask no Hindu or Mussalman to surrender an iota of his religious principle. Only let him be sure that it is religion. But I do ask of every Hindu and Mussalman not to fight for an earthly gain."[9]

Gandhi advocated harmony among the world's religions instead of playing down the importance of any of them. The sciences, which study the natural world, do not claim "any monopoly of wisdom for their own particular branch of study nor quarrel about the superiority of one science over the others."[10] In a similar way, Gandhi held, each religion must bring its individual contribution to humanity's understanding of the spiritual world and not quarrel about the superiority of one religion over another. For God's love embraces the whole world. He believed that all the world religions are God-given and that they serve the people to whom they are revealed. They are allies engaged in the common cause of the moral and spiritual uplift of humanity. In the context of the emerging world community, all the great religions are useful, necessary, and complementary to one another as revealing different facets of the one truth.

The problems that threaten the world community are not merely political or economic; they arise as well from certain basic religious and spiritual attitudes. If the faith and integrity of other persons are not respected, genuine communication and consequent world community will be at best a dream. Arnold Toynbee, after surveying the history of the entire human race, has made the following significant observation: "At this supremely dangerous moment in human history, the only way of salvation for mankind is the Indian way—Emperor Ashoka's and Mahatma Gandhi's principle of nonviolence and Shri Ramakrishna's testimony to the harmony of all religions. Here we have an attitude and spirit that can make it possible for the human race to grow into a single family—and, in the Atomic Age, this is the only alternative to destroying ourselves."[11]

Notes

1. Nikkilanda Swami, *Hinduism: Its Meaning for the Liberation of the Spirit* (New York: Harper, 1983), 185.
2. C.F. Andrews, *Mahatma Gandhi's Ideas* (London: George Allen & Unwin, 1931), 62.
3. K.L. Seshagiri Rao, *Mahatma Gandhi and C.F. Andrews* (Patiala: Punjabi University Press, 1978), 43.
4. See Krishna Kripalani, *Gandhi: A Life* (Calcutta: Calcutta Press, 1978), 25.
5. M.K. Gandhi, *Autobiography* (Boston: Beacon Press, 1983), 34.
6. Harijan 29. 8. 1936.
7. *Gandhi: A Life*, 185.
8. *Mahatma Gandhi's Ideas*, 308.
9. Ibid., 308.
10. R.B. Lal, *The Gita in the Light of Modern Science* (Bombay: Somaiya Publications, 1971), 9.
11. See *Bhavan's Journal*, vol. 28, no. 2 (Bombay), 27.

15

Concerning the Heritage of God-Experience—Its Recovery and Some of Its Fundamental Elements

Swami Devananda

I am writing within the general theme of "Recovering Our Classical Spiritual Heritage" with specific reference to inter-religious dialogue facilitated through a return to roots and a retrieval of traditional values. I was asked to do so from within "my own tradition," to discover within that tradition the heritage that must be recovered. Initially I must clarify which tradition is "my tradition."

As my spiritual life has always centered on and in Christ and it is through Christ that I have encountered and continue to encounter the ultimate, it would not be remiss for me to claim the Christian tradition as my own. But I would be less than honest with myself if I were to accept this claim as an exclusive one, as if my discipleship to Christ restricted me in my identification with any tradition where the experience of the ultimate is served and realized. Rather, I have found the opposite to be the case. For if, as Christ's disciple I accept, as he said, that he is "the way, the truth, and the life," then it inevitably follows that wherever there is found the living and life-giving experience of the real, wherever a way has been made for God and a door opened onto the divine, Christ is present. And present not merely as a passive witness, but as one with the source and giver of the experience: as the very light which gives sight to the eyes, enabling them to look upon the face of the ineffable and be stricken by the vision. For he is "the light which enlightens everyone who comes into the world."

Christ identified himself with all humankind, its whole history and range of movement toward the divine. And in his identification with the figure of Melchizedek, he was and is established as a priest forever, but not after the order of Aaron and the Levitical priesthood. Melchizedek, who we are told in Hebrews chapter seven was not born and did not die, stands forth as a priest of the cosmic covenant. This is the covenant eternally established with all humanity and both its sign and its mystery are read from the cosmos and from deep within the human heart. It was to this cosmic covenant and tradition that Christ joined himself as priest, recovering within himself the whole weight of the great search and awesome oblation of all its members.

It is the reality of this covenant that I experience and give witness to, recognizing the intimacy that exists between it and my own faith in Christ. And in these I continually discover Christ in a way which broadens and deepens my own experience of him. To quote the words of my own spiritual teacher, Father Bede Griffiths in his book *Return to the Center*, "I have to be a Hindu, a Buddhist, a Jain, a Parsee, a Sikh, a Muslim, and a Jew, as well as a Christian if I am to know the truth and to find the point of reconciliation in all religion."

So I find my tradition expansive enough to embrace all of the forms the cosmic covenant has taken. I find the ultimate revealing itself in all of them; as well as in the Christian revelation and the covenant with Israel which served as such remarkable leaven for the development of the Christian faith.

On Mount Tabor when Christ appeared before his disciples in transfigured glory, the fulfillment of the law and the prophets, his disciples wished to erect a tabernacle for him and his two companions. But he forbade them, as if to teach them thereby that no ediface, not even one constructed to house the very divine, could ever fully contain him or enclose him, nor the *dharma* he served or the words he spoke. So I remain open to all traditions, but I am aware that the transcendent reality communicating itself in and through the traditions remains infinitely beyond them. It is a richness never exhausted and a mystery never fully comprehended.

No tradition is absolute in itself. Even as each has its strengths, accordingly each has its limitations, being conditioned by time, place and circumstances. Nevertheless these limitations do not diminish the brightness and beauty of their original intent and impulse, but render them capable of being complemented and expanded through their communion with one another. Thus, each stands in need of continual renewal and in a way that is relevant, continuing to serve humankind's encounter with the supreme reality. And thus the process of recovery cannot take place in isolation. The truth in each religious tradition calls upon every other tradition's truth to purify its very nature as truth, to exceed its historical limits, and to strip itself of external forms and cumulative strictures of thought if and where these betray its essential insights or obstruct truth's realization at the human level.

The relative isolation within which the great traditions developed is now no longer possible. Thus all religions are equally challenged to serve the integration of the human person and to witness to the dignity and unity of life, and all traditions must discover this point of unity, of reconciliation, within themselves. At the human level, what is the use of our uniqueness or individuality if by it we only serve to isolate ourselves and become incapable of embracing the other? By so doing, we deny not only the other but ourselves and deny the urge for union, for oneness, which exists at the very heart of life itself.

It was the apprehension of this point of unity, of reconciliation, and the search for it that led me eventually to India and to the ashram of my guru. This same apprehension led me to respect and love a tradition which represents one of the most profound expressions of the eternal wisdom, Hinduism. I am and have long been, deeply influenced by the Hindu tradition, and find my faith well served by my dialogue with that tradition. I cannot conceive of my own Christian vocation without this element of dialogue, herein each tradition represents a part of the grander tradition of humankind's encounter with the real.

One element of the Hindu religious experience which I find particularly illuminating to my own subjective development is the insistence upon the encounter with the absolute, the primacy of the experience of God. This is an element which had not seemed as emphatic in the Christian milieu of my formative years. Yet it is this experience, this direct experiential knowledge of God which Christ came to share; his own knowledge of the Father and his experience as Son. His last prayer for his disciples as recorded in the seventeenth chapter of John's gospel bears this out, herein he extends his own glory as Son, his very oneness with the Father, to those who "believe" in him. And further it would seem that it is to this knowledge, this glory and experience, that he calls every person. It is this direct knowledge to which his supreme sacrifice opens a way, and which the Christian tradition itself exists but to serve. The roots of all religious traditions are to be found in an encounter, an experience at once of a supreme reality and absolute mystery.

This absolute mystery transcends the knowing of mind and body and yet upon it both mind and body are founded, by virtue of it they have being. This mystery is the ground of being and consciousness, but is itself not properly a being or an object of consciousness. It cannot be said to be a being in that it is the very ground from which all beings stand out, as the word "exist" (*ex-sistere*) signifies. But it does not stand out. It is not properly an object of consciousness in that it cannot be thought, cannot be reflected upon inasmuch as thought is a reflection on being. But after having said this I must admit the paradox that, according to the traditions, all real happiness depends on knowing this unknowable, or depends upon our relationship to it. This "knowing" is the foundation upon which all of them rest. It is as well, the fulfillment of all striving. It is that which upon being known, all else is known.

Buddha, Mahavir, Zoroaster, Mohammed, Guru Nanak, the Hindu *rishis* and sages, the Hebrew prophets, and Christ all had an experience of this "knowing" and through their lives, their words and teachings, the communities founded under their inspiration, as well as through their simple presence, strove to point toward this experience. All were intent upon confronting us with the mystery and inviting us to embrace it in such a way that it could be "known." Not ultimately defined or comprehended, as it remains always beyond the range of sense and mind, but known, experienced, "in an identity of subject and object, being and knowing," beyond thought. A "pure awareness of beings" in which the eye by which I see God and God sees me is realized and experienced as the same eye; a single vision in which God is realized in the pure act as its ground.

Each tradition seeks to offer a culture of practice and a belief which disposes us to this "knowing" and which facilitates this "seeing" in us. And it is precisely the culture of this "knowing" which is the highest and purest expression of any given tradition. This is the heritage which must be recovered, this heritage of "knowing," of encounter with and experience of God. And if this can be recovered, then will also be discovered that point at which the true reconciliation of religions can take place.

This great and all-engaging mystery reaches to the depths and transforms our vision and our lives. The experience of it rends us from a habitual half-sleep and casts upon us a radiance both fiery and soothing, a radiance which incites wakefulness and attentiveness to the real. This mystery, and our attentiveness to it, is the alpha and the omega of all spiritual life and endeavor. Indeed, there is no moment of our lives that we are apart from its all-pervading presence: no moment that is not bright with its splendor.

It is in loving response to this presence and our experience of it and to the call which, urges us ever toward it that all the various life disciplines and practices recommended by the traditions are engaged. All *sadhanas*, practices, and *tapasyas*, all disciplines, are at once both the fruit of our experience of the supreme and the necessary rain which causes its seed to grow and to flower in our lives. Even as a plant does not accomplish its own growth but grows only in communion with sun and rain and whatever other nourishing forces are necessary to it, so also our spiritual life and its growth is determined by the mystery. We may prepare the ground and water the seed with such practices and disciplines as may be appropriate but only God gives the increase. Our spiritual practice will bear the fruit of greater "knowing" and "seeing" when it is the faithful servant of the mystery and when its roots fix deep into the mystery's heart.

What are some of the foundational elements of this heritage and its culture of practice? In the Hindu and Christian traditions, as well as in all the great traditions we find the practice of renunciation to be a prime element. *Sannyas*, as it is called in the Hindu tradition, is the casting aside or laying down of attachment to the world and its possessions. It is an affirmative abandoning of oneself and all that one has to God, which is also the poverty of the Sermon on the Mount. This renunciation which is still an affirmation, recognizes that everything comes from God and belongs to God. We can only at every moment receive all that we are and all that we have from the hands of God. Renunciation rests on the faculty of discrimination, of *viveka*, which according to the Vedanta is the essential prerequisite for spiritual life. We are to discriminate the unreal from the real, the temporal from the eternal, the changing from the changeless. We adopt and exercise a theology of differences as regards appearance and the reality, lest we mistake the rope for a serpent or a stone for bread, each of which may duly claim our regard, but which are hardly interchangeable.

The renunciate, recognizing the transitory nature of life, sees that it is truly impossible to attach ourselves to anything, regardless of the desire to do so. For the very thing we seek to attach ourselves to or possess is itself continually passing away, eluding our grasp, and finally disappearing. The flow of life continues despite our best efforts to suspend it and the very current which first brings to us the object of our desire will without doubt in time wrench it from our grasp. It is inevitable. Nothing remains and so to cling to anything is to suffer the illusion of possession, without ever having truly possessed, the possession itself being impossible. That which we love, desire, or cling to will always be taken from us as long as the object of that love, desire, or clinging exists within time or is defined by temporal notions, as long as it remains merely an object.

In the act of renunciation one strives not so much to be unrelated to the world or the things of the world but rather to enter into an appropriate relationship with existence, recognizing the fundamental law that "this, too, shall pass away." It is not that the world is not valued, it is simply no longer related to obsessively. And so the *sannyasi* or renunciate exhibits a certain naturalness and ease relative to all this. He or she is not engaged in some sort of unnatural pursuit, treating the world and its objects as something to be avoided at all costs or as being inherently obstructive of the intuition of the divine. Rather in acknowledging the world and the fundamental truths by which it exists and respecting all, the *sannyasi* attains a certain freedom. The renunciate sees that change and death are fundamental laws of life and that to cling, to form, or attempt to fix it in possession only leads to a fixation on denial or rebellion against the laws of existence.

The words of Christ in the New Testament resound with this principle of renunciation, Christ himself being the supreme renunciate who receives all that he has and is from the Father and who offers all, unstintingly, in return to the Father. His words embody the very power of his own self-offering and yet he holds nothing as his own, glorying only in the return of all to its source, the ultimate consummation of love. For Christ, renunciation is an absolute dependence on and trust in a loving God, a casting of oneself and one's destiny utterly upon God. He advises us to take no thought of tomorrow, what we shall eat or drink or wear, but to trust in a God who knows all of our needs, in whom we live and move and have our being. In all things he taught and demonstrated the renunciation of self-will and concern, inviting all to make their unceasing prayer "not my will but Thy will be done."

If we imagine that the call to such renunciation applies only to monks or *sannyasis*, or professional renunciates in hermitages or convents far from the communion of ordinary people and their world, we have only to note the audience to which these words of Christ were addressed. They were addressed to ordinary men and women living in the midst of the world and its allurements, beset with its sorrows, and struggling to survive. For such people withdrawal from the actual concourse of the world was hardly an alternative or a possibility to be seriously entertained. This is also the grand vision of renunciation to be found in the *Gita*, stressing a dispossession not so much in fact as in consciousness, thereby opening the way of *mukti*, liberation, to all through the cultivation and practice of an enlightened detachment. The typical renunciate of the *Gita* is the *tyagi*, the one who far from withdrawing from the world of beings and action abides at the very heart of it, involved yet not attached to the fruit of involvement or action. The *tyagi* engages every act as a sacrifice, and thus remains free in the midst of action by not clinging to its result.

Ramana Maharshi reminds us that the true renunciation is "not the discarding of external things but of the ego." Just as Jesus said, "he who loves his life loses it, and he who hates his life in this world will keep it for eternal life." The renunciation ultimately required is of the sense of "I" and "mine," of the self-will and self-love that separates us from one another and from God. "So long as the 'I' of the renouncer remains unchanged," notes Swami Abhishiktananda (Fr. Henri Le Saux) "he has not renounced anything at all." Men and women are not self-contained, independent entities and as long as we harbor the illusion that we are, we will be prey to a continual and fundamental frustration of being. St. Augustine has said that we will know no rest until we find it in God. We will continue to experience this frustration of being as long as we obstinately refuse to obey the law of our own nature, denying the gesture of self-transcendence. Or we may fulfill the law, transcending our own self-possession in a movement of total self-giving, and so realize our own true being in the One who is being itself.

The renunciate, then, is precisely the one who endeavors to fulfill this law on all levels, being espoused to the values of poverty, chastity, and obedience, or of appropriate relationship to the world, the flesh, and the self. At first is renounced one's own obsessive relationship to the material world, the world of things and possessions. One then makes use of it and its elements in a non-attached manner, with full respect for it as the creation of an infinite power and aware always of the presence of that power within it. Thus the renunciate is not disposed to manipulate the creation according to private whim. If a person's treasure does not rest in things nor security in accumulation, it is axiomatic that such a one will strive to lead a life of simplicity, free of the sense of ownership. Such is the man or woman of equal vision who sees a bar of gold and a clod of earth with the same fundamental dispassion and who grants to each the same relative respect, being attached to neither but making appropriate use of each. He or she may own nothing in the world and yet be the richest of all. Or, again, may be surrounded by material goods, favored with their abundance, and yet remain a beggar. The renunciate is not disturbed by possessions or their lack, ever mindful that true wealth is to be found in any and all cases in God alone. This is the one who having heard with his or her whole being the words "Seek ye first the kingdom of God and His righteousness" is so stricken by them that the assurance "and all these things shall be added unto you" utterly escapes notice. Having heard the summons to the beyond the truly poor in spirit respond with loving abandon, not at all caring for such problems of "addition." This is the poverty which Christ extolled.

Not seeking to find ultimate fulfillment in the life of the body, its passions, appetites, desires, the renunciate exercises a certain detachment from the flesh. Not an unholy abhorrence for it, but neither a wanton indulgence of it. Thus the legitimate needs of the body, both physical and psychological, are allowed to present themselves and subsequently be met without the interference of one's own unreasonable demands. Recognizing that the body is destined for the resurrection, recognizing its dignity, that it is "meant for the Lord" the renunciate does not make it a playground for insatiableness or obsessive-compulsive tendencies. Whether celibate or not, in any case, the body is offered to God and so discovered in worth in relationship to its ground.

This standard is acceptable for the renunciate who is married or single, living in community or as an eremite, and may apply to all who comport themselves whether singly or together, as a "living sacrifice, holy and acceptable to God." Wherever passion or desire are not made an absolute or exaggerated value but surrendered with dignity and detachment, the spirit of chastity is present.

The one who lives a life of renunciation needs always to cultivate a certain humor regarding his or her own needs, inclinations, and mortality. Without this it is easy to fall into a deadly earnestness, contorting the being and eventually floundering in an over-indulged self-concern. The self-concern which takes itself too seriously may appear as a kind of counterfeit sanctity, but it is actually in opposition to the injunction to have a single eye which is always pointed God-ward. Until ultimately we become so free of self-reference that the day will come when we will be incapable of "locating" ourselves save in this very act of vision. This is the most radical detachment of all: detachment from self.

The renunciate consciously surrenders to the *dharma*, the universal law, recognizing that he or she is not autonomous and may only make a choice between submission to the life principle or to those forces which seek to frustrate the life principle. If one has not consciously submitted to the law of the spirit, then one falls into subjection to the powers of the unconscious, the "powers of this world" as St. Paul calls them. They are the destructive forces in nature and the disintegrating forces within the human psyche.

Every great tradition has recognized that there are at work in the world cosmic powers and intelligences. These are the angels of the Judeo-Christian tradition, the archons and daemons, the *devas* of Hinduism, the *asuras* of Zoroastrianism. They are at work in the ordering of nature, the evolution of the universe and of humanity, in the organization of all living things. But every tradition has also recognized that not all of these forces are consciously submissive to the universal good, but may turn and center upon themselves seeking to become their own law, rebelling against the *dharma*, and denying their own source in God. These powers of which every tradition speaks thus may become forces of dissembling and disorder, no longer committed to the good of all. But through the principle of obedience, the renunciate enters into proper relationship with the cosmic powers, fulfilling the lawful intent of being, in surrender to God. Cooperating thereby with the divine life "present in the earth, the heavens, and that which is beyond" the renunciate lives from the principle of that life within, being established in Brahman rather than in self or in the powers of nature. This is obedience.

There exists a pluralist consensus about another essential element of spiritual heritage which is to be recovered: meditation. Meditation is also an essential component of the life of renunciation, being itself a kind of renunciation. The renunciate is by his very nature also the contemplative, as renunciation does not exist without contemplation. The divine remains beyond the reach of sense and mind, dwelling in "unapproachable darkness," and yet life remains insipid and meaningless as long as this unapproachable is not approached. We are born to know God and yet the faculties of knowing which are common to us are incapable of grasping God, as God is not a common object of perception. How then is God to be known? It is here that meditation is essential: the act by which one seeks to go beyond the senses and the mind, beyond thoughts and feelings, and enter into the "darkness" in which God dwells and which God is. It is a renunciation of one kind of attention, in which attention is wrested from its attachment to form and is allowed to remain attentive but formless in God who is without form, being pure spirit. Swami Gnanananda, a great Hindu sage and the guru of Fr. Henri Le Saux, explained meditation or *dhyana* as: "Return within to the place where there is nothing and take care that nothing comes in. Penetrate to the depth of yourself, to the place where thought no longer exists and take care that no thought raises its head! There where nothing exists is fullness! Here where nothing is seen is the vision of being there; here where nothing appears any longer is the sudden appearance of the self! *Dhyana*, it is this!"

What meditation is not is the binding of attention to an object of perception or a concept of being. It is rather the release of all attention into being itself. Truly for the contemplative there is no object of contemplation but only the awareness of the divine presence, which cannot in fact be objectified. Transcending the binding force of attention, the contemplative attains to a stillness, a silence, in which God becomes obvious.

Every being by the fact of its existence is already engaged in this meditation. For existence is nothing less than the meditation of the presence through the body and its faculties. Everything that has being is already and always present to the divine. The contemplative is simply one in whom this presence has become conscious; who celebrates this presence by a gesture in which the body, mind, and soul are integrated in a profound silence and offered in sacrifice to God. In the Hindu tradition this principle of sacrifice is a fundamental one and it effectively adheres in all experience as a foundational practice.

In the practice of poverty, the binding force that relates us obsessively to "the world" is unmasked and may then be transcended in sacrifice. In chastity and obedience the same force which relates us obsessively to "the flesh" and "the self" respectively likewise becomes obvious and is undone. And in contemplation, the force itself which relates us obsessively to all three is transcended in sacrifice and our being rests in a simple intuition of the divine prior to the dispersion of attention. Meditation is the gathering to a point of the scattered forces of our attention. We, then, having integrated our being under the *aegis* of a unified attention, offer it as a single sacrifice to the divine. This is the sum of the sacrifice that is called for. The sacrifice of the being as a whole to the ultimate. And meditation is a supreme gesture of this sacrifice.

To live a contemplative life is to recognize that we are always present to the supreme, the mystery of being, and to be always attentive to this mystery in the midst of all our activities. It is to realize that the "search for God" is itself a misnomer; for God is, in the words of Swami Abhishiktananda, "an essentially present illumination." To search for God is like "searching for the sun at midday." So we must leave a desperate search for the ultimate experience and begin to live our own presence to God in all simplicity and gratitude, becoming more and more consciously attentive to the divine mystery, God's presence to us and in us, and allowing it to transfigure us completely, thus realizing within ourselves that fullness to which we are destined.

In conclusion, let me voice my belief that it is only in the recovery in the culture of this attention to the mystery, this heritage of encounter with the ultimate, that religion will be able to justify its existence. If religion fails to provide a culture in which this encounter is encouraged in living demonstration then it will have ceased to serve that reality of which it is a sign, thus rebelling against the spirit and source of its own existence and becoming a force of strife and division rather than of harmony and integration. Religious culture has the choices, then of cooperating in its own destruction by a kind of collective spiritual apostasy against the unity of its own source, or of finding its fulfillment and completion in a self-transcending relationship with that reality before whose full glory it must always pale, and into which it must finally disappear on that day when what is now seen through a glass darkly shall be realized in an eternal face to face.

Notes

Abhishiktananda, Swami, *Guru and Disciple* (London: SPCK, 1974).

----------, *The Further Shore* (Dehli: ISPCK, 1975.)

----------, *The Secret of Arunachala* (Dehli: ISPCK, 1979).

Griffiths, Bede, *Return to the Center* (Springfield, Ill.: Templegate, 1977).

----------, *The Cosmic Revelation*, (Springfield, Ill.: Templegate, 1983).

----------, *The Golden String* (London: Fount Paperbacks, 1979).

----------, *The Marriage of East and West*, (Springfield, Ill.: Templegate, 1982).

Mascaro, Juan, *The Upanishads* (New York: Penguin Books, Ltd, 1983).

----------, *The Bhagavad Gita* (New York: Penguin Books, Ltd; 1984.)

----------, *The Dhammapada* (New York: Penguin Books, Ltd, 1983).

Ramdas, Swami, *Hints to Aspirants* (Kanhangad: Anandashram, 1981).

Vattakuzy, Emmanuel, *Indian Christian Sannyasa and Swami Abhishik-tananda* (Bangalore: TPI, 1981).

16

Beyond Agreeing to Disagree—A Future Direction in Interfaith Dialogue

James Kodera

Much has happened since the World's Parliament of Religions in Chicago in 1893. The change is of vital importance not only to put into proper perspective the nature of interfaith dialogue, but also of exploring the possibility of closer relations among the people of God in his created order that is always one. The late nineteenth century wrought hallmarks of modernity, particularly rationalism and empiricism and the resultant skepticism and secularism that inevitably altered the role and character of religion in human life. After slavery effectively ended in the American south, a new capitalism that flourished in Northern mill towns ushered in urbanization as a pattern of life, foretelling the days of prosperity to come and yet oblivious to, if not concealing, its inherent oppression and injustice upon which the commonwealth was to be established. These challenges may have assaulted the foundations of the traditional church, but they also brought opportunities for reexamining its call, revitalizing its mission, and rejuvenating its life as a whole. The flourishing of Protestant movements in America grows directly out of these and other challenges of the late nineteenth

century. One need not turn to the ancient Chinese seer to realize the essential inner connection, though it may seem
paradoxical, between crisis and opportunity. Crisis begets opportunity, not only to succumb to but also to rise above the challenges of one's own time and place. Such a dialectic view of history resonates with human experience everywhere, just as
much as the interfaith dialogues since the first World's Parliament of Religions reflect the changing circumstances of
religions, the present struggling and aspirations among people
of good will, whether Christian or Jew, Hindu or Moslem, Buddhist or Confucian, are the ingredients with which to shape not
only the global human communities that are coming ever closer
together but also the nature of the relationship—shall we say
collaboration, or erosion thereof?—between humanity and its
Creator, who can be shared but not monopolized by one interest group alone.

Before turning to my main subject of exploring a possible
direction in future interfaith dialogues, I should like to glance
at some features of interfaith dialogues since the late nineteenth
century. Parenthetically, I mention that I am persuaded of the
wisdom of differentiating "faith" and "religion" as does Wilfred
Cantwell Smith in his *The Meaning and End of Religion: A New Approach to the Religious Traditions of Mankind.*[1] As Smith argues,
religion" is indeed a paradoxical juxtaposition of "faith" and
"cumulative tradition, or a personal conviction and a social, cultural, and earthly phenomenon. Surely, a genuine dialogue by
people who are of keen mind to recognize the need for a
dialogue and those who are generous at heart to exhort its
desirability for the good of all deals more with faith than
religion, for faith is always in the present and therefore
dynamic, while religion is a phenomenon inherited from the
past. It may be said that religion is the context in which faith is
formed and sustained, while religion is the context itself. Faith
is, therefore, much less constrained by the dictates of the past.

People of the "East" and the "West"—the terms are always
misleading but still expressive of the two cultural orbits of the
global human community—surely knew of each other at their
earliest stages of flourishing. Hellenistic art opened an avenue
for the northern Indians of Gandhara to express the fullness of
Buddhist religious aspirations for extrahuman attainment and
yet fundamentally human potential. Ever since the disciple
Thomas went to India, as legend has it, the Gospel of the
Nazarene Jesus was known to the Indians, perhaps as parallel to
the devotionalism so fertile in south India. Marco Polo gave the
western world a marvel when he reported on his daring jour-

ney to China in the thirteenth century. Until the fourteenth century, the East in many ways excelled the West. One can hardly forget the pilgrimage of Hsuan Tsang of T'ang China who reached the land of the Buddha, India, that was "West" par excellence to the Chinese. While these encounters brought the East and the West closer together, marking an important stage in human history, it was a period of mutual admiration and adaptation. The conflict between the East and the West has its beginning with the zealous expansionism of the Christian West into the "heathen East" in the sixteenth century. When challenged from within by the Protestant reformers, the Church of Rome sought to expand its sphere of influence and control beyond the confines of Europe into the continents of Africa, Asia and South America. Added incentive came from the colonial interests of the West that put to practical use the compass and the gun powder that the Chinese had invented centuries earlier. The colonialists and the missionaries, in fact, sailed far and wide in tandem so that the distinction was not readily apparent to those whom they sought to conquer by the gun or by the Bible. Inspite of the indiginization policy of the Jesuits and of the good intentions of many a bearer of the Gospel, Christening of the East was met with suspicion and hostility.[2] The aftermath was a costly one to both the East and the West, as dramatized by the twenty-six Martyrs of Nagasaki of 1597.

The close alliance between the Jesuit missionaries and the colonialists abated as the center of power shifted from the Catholic nations of the Iberian peninsula to the Protestant nations further north. Propelled by the Great Awakening that flourished from New England across the plains of North America, the Christian message quickly found its way to Hawaii and to Asia in the nineteenth century. Though not with military prowess, the Protestant missionaries from America who crossed the Pacific well into the present century were no less zealous in their evangelizing of the world. In the strong belief that being Christian was synonymous with being civilized, there was little sympathy for the indigenous people, whether the American Indians, Hawaiian Islanders, or Asians. Just as many converted to Christianity in the sixteenth century to gain worldly advantage over their contenders in their own countries, as we know from the feudal lords in war-torn Japan—recently fictionalized in the popular novel *Shogun* by James Clavell—young men and women who aspired to superior western learning and civilization turned to the Christianity preached by the Protestant missionaries. In both instances, there were unquestionably those who were genuinely touched by the redeeming love of Christ, but there is little doubt that ulterior motives brought a powerful force behind the success of the missionaries activities. The shifting of the center of the modern western world from Europe to North America in the late nineteenth century into the twentieth obviously endowed the American missionaries with the authority and prestige and assured the success of their campaign, no less hegemonic than their European Roman Catholic predecessors. Whether Catholic or Protestant, European or American, the sixteenth or the nineteenth century, the missionaries on the whole never called into question the claim that there could be no salvation without Christ.

The first notable occasion when non-Christian faiths received serious attention involves the philosophy of Schopenhauer. He exhorted his students to turn East, seeking illustrations for his "blind will" that he argued was the undergirding force in human history. The historic Buddha's teaching that possessive desire unfolds itself through the unfailing law of causality (pratityasamutpada) poignantly resonated with the web of life experience with a tragic pattern inextricably woven into its entirety. It is no surprise that among Schopenhauer's students we find the first bona fide specialists in the West of Eastern spiritual legacies, as witnessed by the voluminous Great Books of the East series, edited by Max Mueller. It is only in the late nineteenth century that the West came to take seriously the legitimacy and dignity of the spiritual heritage of the East, whether of India, China or Japan. Artifacts of exquisite refinement that were brought to the eastern shores of North America throughout the period of the China Trade must have hinted at the spiritual depth of the East, no inferior to that of the West. Thus the West realized that Christianity may not be the sine qua non prerequisite for civilization, and salvation. I find the beginning of interfaith dialogue in the humbling and sobering, but also maturing realization that the global human community was in fact much more pluralistic than had been recognized and that the Christian West had no monopoly on human civilization.

The task with which the West was thus confronted was how the Christians were to relate to those who espoused different faiths regarding the nature and destiny of history, the source of good and evil, and above all a path to ultimate redemption. The advent of the study of religion, freed from the a priori credenda of ecclesiastical authorities, had much to do with the pluralism to which they were awakened and the comparative issues that arose in the late nineteenth century. Ernst Troeltsch, one of the

154

architects of modern scientific study of religion, exemplifies the change in attitude toward non-Christian religions in the early twentieth century. Having defended the absoluteness of Christianity in 1900, he comes to espouse a radically relativistic view of all religions, including Christianity, in his 1923 article.[3] Troeltsch's relativism, however, is not irreconcilable with the idea of the absolute in that he affirms it as a common goal pursued by all religions, and not just by Christianity, in its evolutionary process. For him, each religion is a manifestation of the struggling and aspiring of the human spirit, unfolding within a particular cultural framework. Karl Barth's theology rises as a reaction to Troeltsch's evolutionary relativism and a reaffirmation of Jesus Christ as God's full self-revelation.[4] Barth declines to equate naively Christianity exclusively with one true religion, for Christianity, too, is under the same judgment as any other religion. And yet, to the extent that the Christian church lives by the grace of God as revealed in the person of Jesus, it is nonetheless the locus of the right and true religion. The Lausanne Covenant of 1974 carries neo-orthodoxy one step further by proclaiming the utter uniqueness and universality of Christ as known through the Bible, both the Old and New Testaments, and by exhorting Christians for world evangelizing in these critical times. Thus, the Lausanne Covenant restores once again the urgency of evangelism, after Troeltsch and his liberal followers called into question the naiveté of missionary ventures.

The nature of interfaith relationships has now taken on new directions. On the one hand, there is a flourishing of fundamentalist, evangelical Christians who, in the spirit of the Lausanne Covenant, seek once again to Christianize the whole world, transcending denominational lines which they, rightly, regard as a barrier with crippling effects on the shared life of all Christians. Their uncompromising attitude toward both the secular world and other religions has provided a seed both for the strength that stems from exclusivism, if bordering on prejudice, and also for the weakness of parochialism that refuses to acknowledge the integrity of those who view differently life and death, history and salvation. Their sense of urgency is in no small measure related to the rise of non-Christians, particularly the Muslims, in the ever complex whirlpool of geo-political realities of today's world, and to the challenges posed to the erstwhile dominance of Christianity, sometimes more narrowly white, Western (Westernized?) Christianity. The impassioned claim of the "Moral Majority" that America was founded as a "Christian nation" is a direct response to the gradual erosion of America's prestige in the world. The steady rise of orthodox Judaism, particularly in America, is unquestionably related directly to the holocaust, one of the most violent assaults on any ethno-religious group in human history. On the other hand, there are also those who are deeply repentant of the wrongdoings of the past, including the futility of the missionary zeal, questionable amalgamation of Christianity with western culture and power, and an insidious sexism and racism.

Today, the spectrum of interfaith relationships runs from evangelical fundamentalism on the right to various shades of liberalism on the left. The exclusivism of the religious right, whether Christian or Islamic, is remarkably energetic in their zealous undertaking aimed at encompassing the whole world in the orbit of their control. Regarding others either inferior, misguided or merely as potential converts, the inevitability of clash between these absolutistic truth claims is apparent as they continue their fervent expansionism. The intolerance inherent in their faith, which leaves little room for doubt or dissension, may be a source for their organizational strength, offering a communal structure and theological stand never to betray the faithful, but it may also serve as the catalyst for its own downfall. A careful distinction between righteousness and self-righteousness, between freedom and control, between moral courage and fanaticism, between service and servitude would do much to rectify the inner weakness of their outward strength. At the more liberal end of the spectrum are those who have seen men and women of good will and love who were not of their own faith. They have seen people transformed by teachings other than Christian, moved to acts of love and justice, and witnessing the highest level of human dignity and character. In the twentieth century, Mohandas Gandhi, the Mahatma, moved the whole world by the strength of his love for the oppressed whom he taught to resist oppression without retaliating against the oppressors and thereby to rise above the hateful oppression and to win liberation. Gandhi's own philosophy of nonviolence was nurtured as much by the Sermon on the Mount and Tolstoi as by the *Bhagavad Gita* but he remained faithful to the best of the Hindu tradition in which he was born. Martin Luther King, Jr. was inspired by Gandhi, but he remained a Christian. Simone Weil's aspiration to live the life of the afflicted had Christian roots, but she refused to be an insider of the Christian church in order to remain a Jew and to share the affliction of those whom the church neglected, particularly the Jewish inmates in concentration camps. In the past three decades, the wisdom of Eastern religions have provided solace to men and women in search of spiritual fulfillment and of social responsibility. It cannot be forgotten that the Vietnam War served for them as a poignant reminder of the futility of war and patriotism, disguised as "peace with honor."

Never before as during the Vietnam War and its aftermath did the study of Eastern religions flourish among people of inquisitive minds and souls. Beholding the moral and spiritual waste-land, poets and social activists alike turned to the East, as did T.S. Eliot, no longer as an object of aesthetic and intellectual curiosity like their forbearers a century and two ago but now as a corrective and salvation for the decay of the West. Just as much as the technology of the West was once eagerly sought as the salvation for the East, the West thirsted for the timeless wisdom of the East. In their pilgrimage, some like Richard Alpert, Allen Ginsburg and Alan Watts, relinquished the West in favor of the newly discovered East. But many remained loyal to the best hope of the West that once again can come alive through inspirations from the East. They were in a distinguished company that included, besides Eliot, Max Mueller, Hermann Hesse, Christopher Isherwood and Ezra Pound. More recently, a new vision was born in the field of theoretical physics for a confluence between Eastern philosophy and Western science, as exemplified by *The Tao of Physics* by Capra. Whatever the arena of their concern, wherever, the locus of their homage, they build bridges between the East and the West, between the past and the future. Thanks to their struggling yet hopeful endeavor, motivated not only by their inner thirst but also by good will for others and for the world with which they seem to relate authentically, both the West and the East enhance themselves and each other.

Among the theologically minded, there have been those who sought to follow with utmost sincerity and humility more than one different but equally valid path to the one truth that can only be shared. John Dykstra Eusden's recent book, *Zen and Christian: The Journey Between*[5] exemplifies the generosity characteristic of the congenial mind that sees no problem in practicing, beyond acknowledging cognitively, a tradition other than one's own in order to remain faithful to it, but also recognizes a key to growing more deeply into one's own tradition through another. Meanwhile, a quest continues for a common faith, shared by many traditions, whether such an encompassing theology lies ahead in the evolutionary process, as believed Troeltsch, or is already manifest as "perennial philosophy." Roy C. Amore's *Two Masters, One Message* is a recent attempt at finding a common teaching in Theravada Buddhist *sutras* and the New Testament.[6] The Roman Catholics' contributions range from Raimundo Panikkar's *The Unknown Christ of Hinduism* to studies on Zen Buddhism by Jesuits Heinrich Dumoulin, William Johnston, and K. Kadowaki.[7] Panikkar's work applies Karl Rahner's idea of the "anonymous Christian," an idea promulgated in the spirit of the Second Vatican Council which exhibited an attitude of accommodation not present within the Church of Rome before the council.[8] Compared with the genuine respect that the Jesuits named above hold for Zen Buddhism, the idea of the "anonymous Christian" strikes the Hindu as a mere backhanded compliment. But the most widely debated recent work that takes religious pluralism seriously is Wilfred Cantwell Smith's *Toward a World Theology: Faith and Comparative History of Religion.*[9] Smith uses a dialogical method, exchanging and sharing "common tales," in pursuit of a unity, an interrelation in the "religious history, and not religion," of the humankind.[10] There is a problem with Smith's proposal in his assumption that we humans come to a dialogue with an already fixed faith stance, while in reality we constantly remold a position that we have held before. Thus dialogue is not simply a meeting of the minds entrenched in a particular tradition but rather of the minds that seek to be transformed by the other in the course of the dialogue. Faith is formed and reformed constantly. Though not necessarily the same as the evolutionary view of faith, the realization of the ever open-ended nature of faith, of human life itself, that is, the relativity of life understood as process, would quicken the dialogical method that Smith advocates. At the end of the dialogue, one rooted, for example, in the Calvinist tradition of the Presbyterian Church, as is Smith, would no longer be the same as one was at the beginning, while the same inner transformation is evoked by the relational dynamic of the dialogue. One emerges more than, grander than a mere Presbyterian, for a process of transformation, which is always mutual, has taken place among those who gathered ready not only to tell one's own religious history to the other but also to listen and thereby to be transformed by the other's religious history.

We live today in a world that is becoming figuratively smaller than yesteryear due to improved transportation and communication. We also live in a world that is at the same time also larger because our sphere of activity has been markedly expanded. The nineteenth century missionary from the eastern United States took half a year to Asia on a clipper ship, while a businessman today needs only thirteen hours from New York to Tokyo flying over the north pole. As opportunities have increased, so have challenges, difficulties, and dangers. We now face for the first time in human history on this planet the possibility of total extinction by the nuclear holocaust. In spite of the signs of apocalypse looming larger day by day, competition in a finite world is abating. For, as the population increases dizzingly, the arable land is decreasing just as fast, particularly in those parts of the world most hungry and often most populated. The ideological race between two visions of democracy, of equal ownership and of equal opportunity, continues as if people were of secondary importance to ideology. It appears self-evident that human beings can no longer afford the divisiveness that threatens all parties, but strain and strife among people of different religious heritage continue to escalate. There is equal zeal in offense and defense, among the Shiite Moslems and the Jews, the Sikhs and the Hindus, the Tamils and the Sinhalese, the Catholics and the Protestants, the Marxists and the Capitalists. At the same time, however, people of good will, inspired by faith and by a quality inherent in human nature both recognized by sociobiologists as necessary for the survival of the human species are coming together not only to reconcile the divisions of the past but also to work together for a common purpose that ultimately must address the survival of the human race and the preservation of the dignity of life in every human being, no matter what the religious conviction.

The dialogical mode of interfaith communication, even with maximum willingness to overlook the differences, appears powerless, however, to deal with the fear and anger that remain among those who follow not the theologian or the seer but the gang leader. Mobocracy outrules any other leadership in a world dictated by raw human passions. The dialogical approach is flawed ultimately by its own medium, words, without which there could be no dialogue. Words are given to clarify and to enable interpersonal communication, but we also know from our own human experience that they also distort and conceal our thoughts and intentions and deceive others. Theologians who rely on the power of their own words cannot heal the wounds. They can serve as prophets who speak on behalf of one who sends them, namely "God," but even the most eloquent of theological discourses on God fails ultimately to convey the reality of the living God, of God's love. In the history of interfaith relationship we may be now at the point of wanting to agree with one another, but disagreement persists within each tradition, and much more between them. When words are used, where thinking intervenes, opposites are at the basis of cogitation. Agreement always implies disagreement. The delicate balance sustained by amicable agreement is quickly broken by disagreement that is either suppressed or emerging. What then is the resolution of the dilemma inherent in the human activity of cogitation, of using words? How can we remove the thick walls of disagreement, suspicion, and silent animosity, erected inspite of the good intentions of some? How can we utter words that do not obscure the living reality of God, that remain and evoke the healing power of God?

Our conclusion is that interfaith dialogues go beyond the level of verbal discourse to include contemplation, not upon ourselves but upon one to whom many of our traditions attribute the beginning of our being, one to which we all turn as the source of all that which defies human explanation. All faiths emanate from that which is known by different names. All traditions return to its source in order to straighten once again the paths made crooked by human ingenuity. In the *Rig Veda*, the One is he whom the sages call by different names (*Rig Veda*, 164). By their own nature, words divide. In so far as any assertion bears intelligibility only when contrasted with its opposite, there is always disunity lurking behind unity, disagreement behind agreement. The dialectical nature of human cogitation always assumes opposition. The only resolution of the opposition then lies in returning to the beginning of the of dialectic, to the source that unfolded the first stage of the dialectic, to the wordless that begot the first word. Just as the reality of God is not the same as the idea about God, theology must in the end bow to the ineffable, empirical terrain where the "spirit" moves more powerfully and eloquently than any of the words that follow. Chuang Tzu, the Chinese Taoist six centuries before Jesus of Nazareth, once remarked, "I wish I could meet a man of no words so that I can have a word with him." How then can one speak the unspeakable without committing the fallacy inherent in speaking? How can we return to the wordless source out of which are derived all words, and yet without uttering a word? Contemplation restores the sanctity of silence to the verbal discourse that theology is. Contemplation, when shared empirically, resolves differences without postulating yet another set of opposites. Contemplation frees us, frees future interfaith dialogues from the tyranny of cogitation. It does not mean that we must not talk at all. The earnest suggestion made here is that we remain rooted in the silent wholeness that allows articulation, in the infinite source out of which emanate all finite particulars, in the "word" itself behind the Word made flesh. The ineffable spirit, too, must be articulated for it to enter into human consciousness, but most direct difference is symbolic language. All words are abstract representations of the lived world and therefore are figurative. The ineffable, the infinite can be evoked most effectively with the most subtle, the most elusive, the least tactile, lest one equates the representation with the represented. This is why the richest liturgical language is always verse, and not prose; terse, and not verbose. Abstract art is to the trained eye more concrete than detailed work. There is nothing more explicit than suggestion. As Chuang Tzu remarked, the purpose of words is to convey ideas; when the ideas are conveyed, the word is better left behind.

Notes

1. Wilfred Cantwell Smith, *The Meaning and End of Religion: A New Approach to the Religious Traditions of Mankind* (New York: Macmillan, 1963).
2. See Jonathan D. Spence, *The Memory Palace of Mattco Ricci* (New York: Viking, 1984).
3. Ernst Troeltsch, "The Place of Christianity Among the World Religions," in *Christianity and Other Religions*, ed. John Hick and Brian Hebblethwaite (Philadelphia: Fortress, 1981), 11-31.
4. See "The Revelation of God as the Abolition of Religion" in *Church Dogmatics*, vol. 1 (Edinburgh: T&T Clark, 1961).
5. John Dykstra Eusden, *Zen and Christian: The Journey Between* (New York: Crossroad, 1981)
6. Roy C. Amore, *Two Masters, One Message* (Nashville, 1973).
7. Raimundo Panikkar, *The Unknown Christ of Hinduism* (Maryknoll: Orbis, 1964).
8. Karl Rahner, *Shriften zur Theologie VI* (Einseideln, 1965).
9. Wilfred Cantwell Smith, *Towards a World Theology: Faith and Comparative History of Religion* (Philadelphia: Fortress, 1981), 4.
10. Ibid., 4.

17

Jainism—Its Resources for Interreligious Dialogue

Gokul Chandra Jain

My objective is to present some important resources of Jainism for interreligious dialogue. It is a humble attempt to point out certain classical spiritual resources of the religion essential to passing on the religious heritage to the present and coming generations. While doing so it is essential to look into the history, philosophy and ethical code of conduct of the religious system. It is rather difficult to do full justice to the religion within a brief paper like this, however efforts will be made to draw attention to the fundamentals which are helpful for interreligious dialogue.

Jainism is an English rendering of *Jaina Dharma* or *Jina Dharma*. It is a religion, a philosophical system, a way of life practiced and preached by *Jina* (literally: conqueror of self), a perfect human being. Jainism is a fully developed and well-established religious system. Its philosophy rests on sound foundations, and its followers are well organized as a community. The system is indigenous to India. It retains some extremely primitive conceptions and happens to be the oldest living representative of the *sramana* current in ancient Indian culture. It is non-Vedic in origin and probably non-Aryan too. It is neither a revealed religion against Vedic sacrifices nor, as held by some scholars, an offshoot of Brahmanism or Buddhism.

Vardhamana Mahavira, popularly known as the founder of Jainism, was born in 599 B.C. He was the senior contemporary of Gautama the Buddha, the founder of Buddhism. According to the history of Jainism, Mahavira was the twenty-fourth Tirthankara and reformer of the doctrine established by Risabha the first Tirthankara of the *sramana* tradition. It is interesting to note that this statement is confirmed by literature, as well as by epigraphical record. All the twenty-four Tirthankaras were born as human children and gradually developed themselves into perfect human beings, literally known as Jina. They preached for the welfare of society, urging a society based on high moral values providing equal freedom and opportunity to develop each member of the community as a Jina or Tirthankara.

The history of Indian religions reveals that Jainism influenced for centuries the development of human civilization and culture. The heritage of Jainism in the form of literature, art and social culture is abundant. Jaina literature written in ancient classical languages is available. The artistic heritage in the form of sculpture, images, temples and in various other forms is found all over India. These heritages help us to understand the resources of this tradition for interreligious dialogue.

Concept of Reality

According to Jainism the universe consists of two main substances, soul and non-soul or living and non-living, each having a different nature and existence. Each soul possesses an infinite capacity of knowledge (wisdom) as its intrinsic nature. The non-soul has different forms from smallest to biggest. Thus Jaina philosophy is dualistic believing in the separate existence of soul and non-soul or matter. The nature of each substance is uncreated and eternal. It is characterized by appearance and disappearance in the midst of permanence. Every object of reality embodies in itself an affirmative and a negative aspect synthesized and held together by its own complex nature.

Jainism holds that all living beings from the smallest creature to the human being, have their inherent power of soul crippled by association with karmic matter and as a result they are undergoing births and deaths and various other experiences. The living and non-living being (in the form of karmic matter) coming into contact with each other forge certain energies which bring about birth, death, and other experiences of life. This process could be stopped and energies already forged destroyed by a course of discipline.

The living substance or soul is active. Its activity is threefold: activity of the body, activity of the organ of speech, and activity of the mind. Every activity leaves behind traces of aftereffects in physical and psychic forms. Every action, word, or thought produces besides its visible aspects, invisible and transcendent effects. It produces under certain conditions, potential energies which forge the visible effects. These effects may be good or bad according to the activity.

The human being is the highest developed form of living being. Jaina thinkers give full importance to the development of one's personality with one's own efforts. Every member of the society must follow the code of conduct prescribed for him. Jainism believes in the doctrine of karma and rebirth in addition to the ultimate development as Jina. Every one is responsible for his own karma or activity of body, speech, and mind. Thus Jainism gives full responsibility to every one to engage in good activities. In this respect Jainism does not accept any agent who possesses the power of creator, preserver, or destroyer. Every one is responsible for his own deeds and actions. Jaina thinkers clearly indicate that the function of souls is to help one another. Help is rendered by the living for one another, mutual help between the master and the servant, the teacher and the taught. The master renders help to the servants by giving money and they serve their master by doing good and protecting him from evil. The preceptor teaches what is good here and in the next world and makes his disciples follow his teaching. And the disciples benefit their preceptor by their devoted service.

The Theory of Ahimsa

Jainism stresses *ahimsa* which is popularly translated as nonviolence. But actually *ahimsa* means more than nonviolence. Ahimsa is directly related with existence. If one wants to exist he must allow others to exist. Thus *ahimsa* is basically respecting every being to live and allowing all living beings to work together without discrimination of caste, creed, color, and gender. It is also not confined to any particular place and particular age. The theory of *ahimsa* is to love every living being, to be friendly with others and to have sympathy for every being in distress. Anitagati, a Jaina Acharya, writes:

Satvesu maitri gunisu promodama
Klistesu jivesu krpa pattam
Madhyatha bhavam viprita vrttoi sada mamatma Vidadhatu Deva.

O Lord make myself such that I may have love for all
beings,
Joy in the meritorious, unstinted sympathy for the distressed,
And tolerance towards the perversely inclined.

Ahimsa is not only a metaphysical doctrine, a philosophical
postulate or an ethical dogma. It is the primary principle of life,
the very essence of human conduct. It is moreover, a mental attitude, a definite outlook towards life, and an ever guiding factor in one's relations and dealings with other human beings,
and with all living beings. It is not merely physical nonviolence,
but it upholds the sanctity of life and implies a wholesome
respect for life in all forms.

In its positive aspect *ahimsa* denotes humanness, humani-
tarianism, kindness, tenderness, mercy, sympathy, love, and
the spirit of coexistence, i.e., to live and help others to live. An
ahimsite person is full of compassion and understanding for
others and is always ready to help and serve the needy and the
suffering at the cost of his own personal comfort, convenience,
or gain.

In its negative aspect, *ahimsa* means abstinence from inflicting
mental or physical pain, or from hurting, injuring or severing
the life forces of any living being, human and subhuman, by
thought, word or deed, either one's own or those of another.
Nor should one approve violent acts committed by others. In
short it is abstinence from such violence as is deliberate, willful
or wanton, whether it is caused due to rashness or negligence,
or for some selfish motive, gain, enjoyment, amusement, or
sport, or on account of envy, jealousy, hatred or enmity.

The Theory of Non-Absolutism

The theory of non-absolutism, technically known as
anekanavada, is the philosophical foundation which provides a
wide sphere for interreligious dialogue. The theory is also
known as the relativity of knowledge. According to this theory
Jainism honors others' view points because all human beings
are limited in this ability to know a thing in its absolute form. A
thing is neither real nor unreal, neither eternal nor non-eter-
nal, neither static nor dynamic, neither small nor big in the absolute sense, but has dual nature. Therefore, none can claim
that this is right and that is not right because on the one hand
reality is complex, on the other hand there is a limitation to our
knowledge so long as one does not attain omniscience. To know

is to relate, therefore our knowledge is essentially relative and limited in the sphere of application of knowledge or in the extent of knowledge. Our thought is relative. The whole reality in its completeness cannot be grasped by partial thought. The same is true of our speech. What we say is also relative and conditioned. No saying can be claimed as absolute. This theory of non-absolutism provides the philosophical foundation for understanding others' view points and for honoring others' thoughts by giving due weight to them. Thus the Jaina theory of non-absolutism gives a wide sphere for interreligious dialogue.

To conclude it can be said that Jainism as a religious system provides many meeting points for interreligious dialogue and convey to the modern world the message of peace and understanding for social good.

Notes

H.O. Bhattacharya, *Reals in the Jaina Metaphysics*, (Delhi, 1966).

A. Ghosh, ed. *Jaina Art and Architecture* (New Delhi, 1974).

Gokul Chandra Jain, "Yoga and Society: The Jaina View," *Vaishali Institute Research Bulletin*, no. 47 (Vaishali, 1983).

H.L. Jain, *Jainsim: Its History, Philosophy and Religion* (Calcutta: The Cultural Heritage of India).

J.P. Jain, *Genesis and Spirit of Jaina Art* (New Delhi, 1974).

----------, *Religion and Culture of the Jains* (Delhi, 1971).

Jyoti Prasad Jain, "Impact of Ahimsa on Human Affairs," *Vaishali Institute Bulletin*, no. 4 (Vaishali, 1983).

S.A. Jain, *Reality (Vira Sasana Sangha)*, (Calcutta, 1960).

Balchandra Sidahantashastri, *Dhyanasataka (Vira Seva Mandir)* (New Delhi, 1976).

A.N. Upadhya, *The Ethical Background* (New Delhi, 1974).

167

18

Towards a Theology of Harmony

Djohan Effendi

It is an honorable task for the exponents of every religion to explore liberal views of other religions and faiths based on and developed from their own religious resources to anticipate the future. The idea of one religion dominating and conquering the followers of different religions and faiths, even in the name of sacred mission, is a thing of the past. It must be replaced by the notion of living together and sharing with each other to enrich the spiritual life of humankind and to strengthen the ethical foundation of our world.

Unity and Plurality

Islam emphasizes, not only the unity of God as its basic tenet and creed but also the unity of humankind. "Humankind is a single nation" the *Qur'an* states (2:213). Commenting on this verse Muhammad Ali wrote in his commentary:

> The oneness of humanity is a truth on which the *Qur'an* lays the greatest stress. They are sometimes told that they have all been "created of a single soul" (4:1); again that they are all descended from the same parents (49:13); still again that they are as it were dwellers in one home, having the same earth as a resting-place and the same

169

heaven as a canopy (2:22). It thus lays down the principle of the oneness of humanity in the clearest words.[1]

Besides, Islam recognizes that humankind, by nature, lives in plurality. The *Qur'an* says:

> O men! Behold, we have created you all out of a male and a female, have made you into nations and tribes, so that you might come to know one another. Verily, the noblest of you in sight of God is the one who is most deeply conscious of Him (49:13).

It must be noted that this recognition, nevertheless, does not eliminate the principle of the unity of humankind and the oneness of humanity. Ghulam Farid, in his work, said:

> The verse, in fact, constitutes the Magna Carta of human fraternity and equality. It lays the axe at false and foolish notions of superiority, born of racial arrogance or national conceit. Having been created from a male and a female as human beings all men have been declared equal in the sight of God. The worth of a man is not to be judged by the pigment of his skin, the amount of wealth he possesses, or by his rank or social status, descent or pedigree, but by his moral greatness and by the way in which he discharges his obligations to God and man. The whole human race is but one family. Division into tribes, nations and races is meant to give them better knowledge of one another, in order that they might benefit from one another's national characteristics and good qualities.[2]

It must be underlined that the recognition of Islam concerning the plurality of humankind includes the plurality of ways of life. Here is a quotation from the *Qur'an*:

> Unto every one of you have we appointed (different) laws and ways of life. And if God so willed, He could surely have made you all a single community; but (He willed it otherwise) in order to test you by means of what he has vouchsafed unto you. Vie, then, with one another in doing good works (5:48).

Indeed the *Qur'an* itself does not deny the existence of good men in other religions, and states that God will reward their sincere belief and good deeds. The *Qur'an* says:

> Verily, those who attain to faith (in this writ), as well as those who follow the Jewish faith, and the Christians, and the Sabians—all who believe in God and the last day and

do righteous deeds—shall have their reward with their Sustainer; and no fear need they have, and neither shall they grieve (2:62). As a monotheistic religion Islam resists all kinds of polytheism. However, it forbids the Muslims to abuse gods of other people who do not believe in God the only one. The *Qur'an* says:

And abuse not those whom they call upon besides Allah, lest, exceeding the limits they abuse Allah through ignorance (6: 109).

It is obvious that Islam demands that Muslims avoid steps that bring about conflict and enmities among the people of different religions and faiths. Giving an explanation for this verse Muhammad Asad said:

This prohibition of reviling anything that other people hold sacred—even in contravention of the principle of God is oneness—is expressed in the plural and is, addressed to all believers. Thus, while Muslims are expected to argue against the false beliefs of others, they are not allowed to abuse the objects of those beliefs and hurt thereby the feelings of their erring fellow men.[3]

Belief in All Prophets

One of the principles of the Islamic creed is belief in prophets sent by God to deliver His message. According to the *Qur'an*, there is no nation in the world to whom a prophet has not come. Here are some verses:

There is not a people but a warner has gone among them (35:24).

For every nation there is a messenger (10:47).

Thou art only a warner and for every people a guide (13:7).

The *Qur'an* mentions a number of prophets' names but it states that these are not all. We are told that there have been prophets besides those prophets whose names the *Qur'an* mentions. "And we sent messengers; We have mentioned that prophets have appeared in all nations." It goes further and renders it necessary that a Muslim should believe in all those prophets. Here are a few of the quotations:

We believe in Allah and in that which has been revealed to us, and in that which was revealed to Abraham, and Ishmael, and Jacob and the tribes, and in that which was given to Moses, Jesus, and in that which was given to the prophets from their Lord, we do not make any distinction between any of them and to Him we do submit (2:136).

The Messenger believes in what has been revealed to him from his Lord, and (so do) the believers. They all believe in Allah and His angels and His Books and His messengers. We make no difference between any of His messengers (2:285).

Commenting on the expression "We make no difference between any of His messengers" Yusaf Ali wrote:

It is not for us to make any distinction between one and another of God's apostles; we must honor them all equally, though we know that God in His wisdom sent them with different kinds of mission and gave them different degrees of rank.[4]

In connection with the principle of belief in all prophets Fazlur Rahman said:

True different prophets have come to different people and nations at different times, but their messages are universal and identical. All these messages emanate from a single source: the "Mother of the Book" (43:4; 13:39) and "The Hidden Book"(56:78). Since these messages are universal and identical, it is incumbent on all people to believe in all divine messengers. This is why Muhammad felt himself obligated to believe in the prophethood of Noah, Abraham, Moses, and Jesus, for God's religion is indivisible and prophethood is also indivisible. Indeed, the Prophet is made to declare in the *Qur'an* that not only does he believe in the Torah and the Gospel but "I believe in whatever book God may have revealed" (42:15). This is because God's guidance is universal and not restricted to any nation or nations: "And there is no nation wherein a warner has not come" (35:24) and "For every people a guide has been provided" (13:7). The word "Book" is, in fact, often used in the *Qur'an* not with reference to any specific revealed book but as a generic term denoting the totality of divine revelations (see 2:213, for example).[5]

The *Qur'an* further condemns those who believe in some prophets and disbelieve in others, and judges them as disbelievers (4:150- 151). It says:

> Those who disbelieve in Allah and His messengers, and desire to make any distinction between Allah and His messengers and say: We believe in some and disbelieve in others, and desire to take a course in between—these are truly disbelievers (4:150, 151).

Explaining this verse Muhammad Ali said: "In Islam the rejection of any or all God's apostles constitutes almost as grave a sin as a denial of God Himself."[6]

It is obvious that a belief in all the prophets of the world is an essential principle of the religion of Islam.

The Freedom of Religion

Islam as it is taught by the *Qur'an* asserts the freedom of religion. "There is no compulsion in religion" (2:256) is a conviction in the clearest words. In fact, there are a number of statements in the *Qur'an* that show that religiosity is a person's own concern, and that he is given the free choice of accepting one religion and rejecting another. Here are some quotations:

> The truth is from your Lord, so let him who wishes believe and let him who wishes disbelieve (18:29).

> We have shown him the way, he may be thankful or unthankful (76:3).

> Clear proofs have indeed come to you from the Lord; so whoever sees, it is for their own good, and whoever blinds, it is to his own harm. And I am not a keeper over you (6:105).

> And if thy Lord is pleased, all those who are in the world would have believed, all of them. Wilt thou then force men till they are believers? (10:99)"

It must be held by all Muslims that the freedom of religion is very principal and essential for religious life. In this case there is no bargaining. It is a question of basic human rights.

Conclusion

Enjoined by the *Qur'an* to believe in all prophets, and not to exercise compulsion in matters of religion, the Muslims have to, persistently in all times and in all climes, regard people of different religions and faiths as their brothers in the spirit of religious tolerance and human brotherhood.

Theologically, for the Muslims, it is their religious obligation to develop understanding and to respect others. In this way interreligious relationships are established. In addition to the Koranic injunction "...so that you might come to know one another" (49:13) and "Vie with one another in doing good works" (5:48), they have this expression: "And help one another in righteousness and piety, and help not another in sin and aggression" (5:2) in the spirit. From this point of view, dialogue and cooperation between the people of different religions and faiths in various levels and various aspects must be developed from time to time and from region to region.

Notes

1. Maulana Muhammad Ali, *The Holy Qur'an* (Lahore: Ahmadiyya Anjuman Isha'at Islam, 1973), 89.
2. Malik Ghaulam Farid, *The Holy Qur'an* (Rabwah: The Oriental and Religious Publishing Corporation Ltd., 1969), 1106.
3. Muhammad Asad, *The Message of the Qur'an* (Gilbraltar: Dar Al-andalus, 1980), 188.
4. A. Yusaf Ali, *The Holy Qur'an* (Dehli: Kitab Publishing House, 1973), 116.
5. Fazlur Rahmar, *Major Themes of the Qur'an* (Chicago: Bibliotheca Islamica, 1980), 163-164.
6. *The Message of the Qur'an*, 133.

Part IV

Issues at the Frontier

19

The Need for Constant Dialogue Among the Leaders of the World's Religions

Wande Abimbola

The world today is the scene of constant social, economic and political strife causing war, suffering and misunderstanding among the different nations and peoples of the world. At the center of this global conflict and cold war is religious intolerance. In the Middle East, Africa and other parts of the world, religions have served as a divisive rather than a unifying element among peoples of the same nation. This is an intolerable situation which should not be allowed to continue. For if some leaders of the world's religions can come together in constant dialogue and in the pursuit of world peace, tomorrow's world will be more peaceful.

Conflict between the different religions of the world is caused largely by misunderstanding which can be removed by dialogue. To be sure, differences will forever exist between the varied religions of the world because some hold fast to beliefs which are diametrically opposed to the beliefs of other religions. No amount of dialogue will remove these basic differences in beliefs and practices which are thousands of years old. Dialogue should not in fact be directed at those elements which make one religion different from another. But dialogue should emphasize those areas which the religions of humankind share in common or hold identical points of view. It is our own strong notion that such points of convergence are enumerable when we look deeply into the belief processes of the rich religious traditions of humankind. If it is our interest, as religious leaders to encourage world peace, we should emphasize such moral attitudes to our fellows as love, faith, friendship, hope, perseverance, honesty, truth, patience, sacrifice, hard work, discipline, kindness, loyalty, etc., which form the basic fabric of the moral values of all the religions. There is no religion which is not based on some of these moral values. Some religions may emphasize one aspect more than another, but all religions certainly share these tenets, the propagation of which could transform the sinful world of today into an earthly paradise of tomorrow.

Rather than emphasize the common values mentioned above, the leaders of the two most propagated world religions—Christianity and Islam—have gone out of their way and out of the teachings of Jesus and Muhammad to propagate doctrines of destruction, genocide, war, hatred, and civil strife by emphasizing doctrines which undermine the existence of the other religions of the world. Nowhere has this doctrine of hatred, rather than love, been more prevalent than in black Africa where hundreds of Christians and Islamic missionaries spend millions of dollars every year threatening the ordinary folk of that continent with hell fire, stealing their icons, destroying their temples, and waging a relentless physical and psychological warfare against their priests and their adherents. Such evangelism must be put to rest in the name of the Creator of this earth and the universe. Centuries of this type of evangelism have not succeeded in wiping out the traditional values of black Africa. The billions of dollars spent in the propagation of these false doctrines have therefore been wasted. Much more can be achieved in Africa and elsewhere if the leaders of Islam and Christianity will stand up and say, "This is our religion, this is what it does to a person who believes in it. Try it and it will make you happy, make you to be at peace with your neighbors as well as win for you eternal life."

What will anybody gain if traditional religions of black Africa, their values, their images, and their beliefs are destroyed and replaced with Christian and Islamic values? It does not necessarily make Africans more friendly to the Western and Islamic world. Rather, it will create nations of black Africans who have been alienated from their own traditional values and who are therefore dispossessed, embittered, and ready to fight against their oppressors.

The only way to avoid this type of conflict is to begin today a process of dialogue among the religions of the world. We should create a global forum where we all can meet, exchange ideas and plan for greater understanding between the nations and peoples of the world. When such a forum is planned and organized, those of us representing the voice of Africa will work tirelessly for its success for we have suffered much from religious bigotry and intolerance.

Before I end this short essay, I would like to quote a verse from Ogbedi, one of the chapters of the holy scriptures of Ifa, the sacred literature of the Yoruba. This verse tells of the dangers involved for all the inhabitants of the world, plants, animals, human beings, insects, birds, animate, inanimate creatures, if we fail to live together as good neighbors, and if each individual preys on his neighbors and tries to annihilate his enemies. What we need is "collective work" to improve the lot of the inhabitants of this planet rather than continued propagation of narrow, selfish, and greedy objectives which will only further endanger world peace. The verse goes as follows:

Ogbedi, the rugged one. Ogbedi, the strong man. Wrap it up very well and prevent the rough edges from appearing outside. Prevent them from shooting out. A divination was performed for Mr. By-force, who went to ask the Grasshopper for collective farm work. He asked the Hen for the same obligation. He asked the Wolf, the Dog, the Hyena, the Hunter, the Walking Stick. He asked Fire for the same obligation. And he asked Rain. He called Drought, and invited Dew Drops last of them all.

On the appointed day, he said to them, "Alright, my friends, let us go. And they followed him. When he got to the farm, he lined them up against the overgrown farmland which he wanted to clear. He placed the Grasshopper at the edge of the farm. He placed the Hen next to him. He placed the Wolf next to the Hen. He placed the Dog next to the Wolf. He placed the Hyena next to the Dog. He placed the Hunter next to the Hyena. He placed the Viper next to the Hunter. He placed the Walking Stick next to the Viper. He placed Fire next to the Walking Stick. He placed Rain next to the Fire. He placed Drought next to Rain. And he placed Dew-Drops on the other edge of the farm. He placed Hen next to him.

After a while the Grasshopper yawned, and said in despair, "This collective work by Mr. By-force, what a strange thing it is, hunger has come." To which the Hen replied, "What an insult!" The Hen struck the Grasshopper suddenly. The Wolf pounced on the Hen. The Dog pounced on the Wolf. The Hyena pounced on the Dog. The Hunter shifted position, and shot the Hyena. But as the Hunter moved backwards, the Viper bit him suddenly. Before the Viper himself moved away, the Walking Stick struck him with full force. Fire came out of the Walking Stick's bottom end. Before long, Rain started to fall, and it put out the Fire immediately. The result was that the Drought started. As all of them killed one another all over the place. There remained only Dew-Drops. If it ran this way, it would run that way. Mr. By-force himself stood at a distance looking at them. Dew-Drops exclaimed, " What a terrible thing! Will all of us perish like this, as a result of war and all the bad things? What will I do now?"

Dew-Drops was moving from one place to the other. After some time he started his ancestors' traditional rites. He started to drop and drop persistently. All those who had been half dead started to get up one by one. The result was that after evil had been turned into good, after Dew had dropped all over the ground, and after things became pleasant again, they all spent money to celebrate their escape from danger. They spent money to feast their friends. They were saying, "Dew-Drops, come and make repairs. Dew-Drops come and make amends. Don't you see how things by force have spoiled the world of today. Dew-Drops, come make repairs."

Like Dew-Drops in the story, all the leaders of the world's religions should mend our shattered earth ravaged by religious intolerance and warfare, and thus usher in a new era of peace, cooperation, and dialogue for humankind. We will never see the universe in the same way even if we are all Christians or Muslims. We will never share exactly the same beliefs about life and death. Neither will we order our lives according to the same values and practices. A world in which all the inhabitants are Catholics or Muslims or Ifa priests or Hindus will be a very dull, uninteresting and boring world. Religious diversity can be turned into a thing of beauty if only we can emphasize those things we share in common rather than those areas where we differ. No single religion can dominate this world even if nations spend all their resources in propagating their own particular faiths. We are all here, and through constant discussion, through working hard together for the collective good rather than continuing in the senseless belief that our own traditions are more valid than those of others, can we create a new era of peace. Only our creator knows those who are serving him best.

20

Dialogue in the School Classroom

W. Owen Cole

The choice of subject has not been an easy one for me to make. My first inclination was to consider the areas Sikhs and Christians might explore in interfaith dialogue, as much because of my indebtedness to the many Sikh friends I have and the respect I have for the Sikh religion as my own academic interest. However, my primary, longest standing, most burning, and ultimate concern is for religious education in school, and especially in those parts of Britain where Muslim, Sikh, black Christian, Hindu, and children who belong to no faith community are sitting side by side and sharing an educational experience for eleven years at least, and perhaps fourteen. It is the religious interaction of these children, long before they ever enter our colleges and universities which interests me and causes me anxiety; children like my own daughters, who for the whole of their time in Leeds were members of a minority white school population dominated by white teachers, some of them Christian but a few Jewish, teaching a traditional ethnocentric, or, at best, Eurocentric curriculum. To a large degree their racial attitudes, the religious beliefs of such children, and their concepts of religious studies have been formed long before they reach higher education, where many of us, especially those like myself who prepare intending teachers whose interests and major studies may be in science or history rather than religious studies, meet a wide range of students.

Before proceeding further I had better explain the British scene regarding religious education in schools. The history of British education has been one of close association with the churches. Until 1870 almost every child receiving an elementary education was the beneficiary of one denomination or another. Even in 1938 the number of such schools, Quaker, Methodist, Roman Catholic, but mainly Anglican was put at 10,753 out of 21,116, some 52 percent of the total. In 1944 a new education act became law. Partly because the Church of England decided to hand over many of its schools to the state, being unable to maintain them, but also because a war, seen by many Britons as a Christian crusade, was coming to a satisfactory end, it was agreed that religion should be built into the curriculum, through lessons in religious education, and into the general life of the school through a daily act of worship in which everyone was required to participate. There was a conscience clause, mainly intended to meet the reservations of Roman Catholics, but available for others to use, such as Jews, which allowed them to withdraw from lessons and from worship, but the main result was the emergence of religious education as a subject in all schools. Here, however, I must interject an element of realism. During this period I attended three secondary and grammar schools and had no religious education in any of them. Despite the law it was slow to emerge and in some schools even today it has made little progress, whereas there were some non-church schools before 1944 in which it was taught.

The content of religious education was mostly biblical, the reason being that the process was one of nurturing and confirming children in the British faith, Christianity, but without bias towards any denomination. The Bible, being common to all was to be taught in a way partial to none. There was usually some attention given to heroes such as Livingstone, or Father Damien, perhaps the story of how Christianity came to Britain and thence to the world, some theology for able sixth formers, and occasionally world religions were taught, though teachers were expected to demonstrate the superiority of Christianity over all others.

It was into this situation that I came when, in 1954, I began to train as a school teacher. To my surprise I discovered that there was a subject called religious education. I elected to teach it as my second subject, history being my first, and enjoyed it, in primary schools initially, and then in a comprehensive school. Looking back to those days I recognize that my purpose was to enforce the Christian faith of those children who possessed one and to defend the credibility of belief against those who criticized and attacked it. Gradually, from this position I began to question this role and also the ability of many of my pupils to understand biblical concepts. By this time, about 1967, the use of the classroom for purposes of evangelism or even nurture, was being questioned, the religious content of religious education was being reduced to a kind of moral education based on caring and sharing, but lacking any academic content or respectability. Where the Bible survived the approach to teaching it was often arid and, from the pupil's standpoint, meaningless. The 'r' had gone, the 'e' stood for emptiness.

Into this situation stepped Ninian Smart, Geoffrey Parrinder, and John Hinnells. Four teachers, including John Hinnells, then of Newcastle University, who were working in that city, concluded that teaching the great religions of the world, not from the view of Christian approach, or the apologetic, but in their own right and for their own intrinsic worth, might be the way to put the 'r' back into religious education. The open, educational purpose and approach would provide the proper way of including the 'e'. A conference was held at Shap Wells Hotel in northern England, from which resulted the Shap Working Party on World Religions in education, which has done much to pioneer and stimulate this kind of religious education in schools. The year was 1969.

The previous year I had moved from Newcastle to Leeds to take up an appointment as head of religious studies in a college of education. Here I began teaching Hinduism, Islam and Sikhism. My daughters attended multiracial schools and I soon began to take an interest in the kind of religious education which might be taught in those schools. I found myself working in such schools and preparing my students to teach in them. It was patently clear that the usual diet of Bible stories was inadequate and inappropriate. In the white pupils an exclusively Christian syllabus would endorse a feeling of white superiority, even though there were black children from the Caribbean in the class. (Whoever heard of a black person who had done anything worthwhile? Certainly no one in British schools in those days.) My generation was taught in Sunday school to give their pennies to help the little black children overseas. Their poverty was known to be cultural as well as economic. To Asian children, Hindu, Muslim and Sikh, and also Jews, such exclusivity would convey the message that their culture had no worth. For the pupil it is the curriculum which conveys and confirms value. What children learn about in school is worth knowing about, what is not taught is unimportant. Hinduism,

Islam and Sikhism, as well as Judaism and Buddhism were not taught.

Since 1969 things have changed considerably. Yes, there are schools with Muslim children who never learn anything about Islam, and where no festivals other than Christian are recognized and celebrated. In some multicultural schools teachers mistakenly argue that rather than offend one religion by teaching it inaccurately, or by seeming to give it more attention than another it is better to omit religious education from the curriculum and not mention it at all. Not only is this defeatist but it seems to me educationally irresponsible, for the following reasons. First, for the Muslim child, for example, his or her religion is the most important thing which they bring to school. It is this which gives them identity and worth. To ignore it, and consequently treat them like any other child—which in effect probably means treating them as though they are English, post-Christian, middle class, is to do them no kindness, and to disrespect their culture, in effect if not in intent, and aims at assimilating them into British society by depriving them of their cultural distinctiveness. It does not encourage the white British child to respect his classmate, in fact, it can be argued that in this contracting world, international understanding, and empathy for other cultures and faiths are things that we should be fostering. Ignoring education about religion can scarcely be said to be doing that.

Religious education requires skills and strategies as well as content. One cannot teach the same things to five-year-olds as to those aged sixteen. Whatever is done in Sunday schools and similar classes in mosques or gurdwaras in Britain, those of us associated with the school classroom know that doctrinal education belongs to older years, not younger, and that the small child is ready for little that is explicitly religious at all. Nevertheless, through some awareness of the Buddha, Muhammad, Jesus, and similar figures, or through hearing about one another's festivals and sharing in some aspects of them, even five-year-olds can be established on the road to mutual respect as well as an interest in their classmates' way of life. Instead of appearing funny or strange their traditions can be fascinating and worth knowing about. There is no need to fear confusion, especially if the child belongs to a strong family culture. Of course, if his parents lack any real religious home the child's school experience may only endorse the child's rootlessness, they cannot be blamed for it. At this young age perhaps the aims which can be achieved are implicit respect and empathy and the arousing of interest.

Anyone who has studied religions at any depth knows that they do not all teach the same thing. Where there is not a doctrine of finality or exclusiveness, superiority may be implied. There are different teachings on matters of diet, whether there is one life or a number of rebirths, and how salvation is to be achieved. As children grow older an awareness of this reality is as essential as recognizing that there are different ways of looking at the reasons for World War I, the Northern Ireland crisis, the Punjab problem, or the trouble in Lebanon, to mention only a few current issues. In a mature democracy, or a multicultural society, it is essential that children be educated to accept and live with difference. So far we have done little to enable children to cope with difference. In Britain we have been slow and reluctant to introduce political education into the classroom with the consequence that children, still in a state of ignorance, like victorian girls going to their bridal bed, suddenly find themselves expected to cast their votes intelligently. With a similar lack of education we expect them to appear at eighteen free from racist attitudes. This will not be done unless, for example we openly recognize that Jews, Christians, and Muslims, have very different beliefs about Jesus, that these are sincerely held, and are perfectly honorable positions. It may be difficult for those who seek to protect their flocks, parents, rabbis, priests or imams, to be so open, but for the educator whose concern is for British society as a whole, and for accurate information, no other position is tolerable.

Dialogue in the school classroom in the way I am describing it is a new venture. Clearly it would not happen where all children were of one faith, or where only one religion was taught, or where the superiority of one religion was assumed even if others were referred to. However, even in multifaith classrooms where all the religions present, and perhaps others besides, are taught, dialogue may be very limited. Pushpa may explain the family shrine, Ahmed may tell his colleagues about worship in the mosque, but the differences which divide are ignored. For ease, or because the teacher is lacking in confidence, the approach is rather like that of the university—purely academic. If children want to argue and find out more they must do so in the playground.

The need for dialogue in school should need no arguing. Not only does this kind of discussion produce articulate young people, hopefully able to understand and respect the views of others, it should result in their being confident in their own religion in a reasonable way. Too often a firm faith depends either on not knowing anything about the beliefs and claims of other religions, or on holding distorted views of them. Certainly since the crusades it has been customary for Christians to malign Islam, so that I still receive students whose 'knowledge' of Islam amounts to knowing that all Muslims have four wives and worship Muhammad and that thieves are punished by having their hands amputated. If children who come to school as Muslims, Jews or whatever, are to study a variety of religions in the classroom not only must they hear their religion presented with respect and accuracy but they must also be helped to cope with the perplexities which arise when, for example, the Muslim pupil and the Christian learn that their scriptures disagree on matters of fact, the name of the son Abraham was prepared to sacrifice, the death of Jesus, being just two examples, as well as belief, for example in the status of Jesus. For the teacher to tell the child to discuss any faith problems with the imam or priest seems to me to be wrong and ill-advised, wrong because the teacher created the situation and so is responsible for dealing with it, ill-advised because we know that by and large priests and imams operate in ways which differ considerably from the school approach. The priest is quite likely to say, "It is really very simple, Muhammad got it wrong. He picked up his knowledge of Judaism and Christianity from peasants who gave him inaccurate information." The importance of the link of Ishmael with the Arab Semites is thus dismissed as an error.

Three revolutions have taken place in school religious education over the last fifteen years. From nurture into the Christian faith it has become educating children into an understanding of religion. From teaching the Bible its content has become the study of religion, drawing on a number of religions to provide the content of the study. From the teacher being an authority figure passing on her faith to the children she has become a partner in their learning process, helping them to engage with the religion they are studying. Often she is learning with them, helping them to find out, explore, discuss, think—not as one who has all the answers but as one skilled in the learning process and in enabling others to undertake and experience it. She is, therefore, perfectly fitted to take children along the path of dialogue, for even if she does not know why Abraham is prepared to sacrifice Ishmael, she knows where the information can be found—but even more important, she is aware that there is an important reason why it is Ishmael and not Isaac who figures in the story. If we can produce teachers who have accepted this revolution and are eager to participate in the religious education which has resulted from it, and we have children of many faiths in our classrooms, the opportunity for dialogue exists, ready to be explored. On most religions there are also books available for teachers and pupils to use in their studies.

As I approach the end of my paper I want to conclude by making a number of further points. First, I want to say that dialogue is far too important to be left to the likes of us, just as politics is too important to be left to the politicians. It is my life and yours that those people are affecting. Dialogue is too important to be left to the academics because of the decreasing size of the world we are living in. Whether a greater understanding of, and sensitivity to Iranian Islam might have resulted in no hostages being taken in Teheran I cannot say, but it certainly enabled a representative of the Archbishop of Canterbury to obtain the release of some Britons from Libya early in 1985. Second, returning to my own backyard, dialogue is essential if we are to create a harmonious multiracial Britain. Instead of waiting for a few Christians, Muslims, Jews, Hindus, Sikhs, Buddhists and Bahais, to come to our universities, or join inter-faith groups in Leeds, or Wolverhampton, we must go into the schools and use the opportunities which are at hand. Otherwise Britain will continue to be a racist nation.

Finally, I want to say that we in Britain are fortunate in our schools to have a forum where young people may learn dispassionately, and free from the zealot or evangelist, about religion, their own and that of the child in the next desk or at the same table. They do go on visits together to the mosque and gurdwara, the synagogue and the church, they do listen to the imam or the priest together, they do read the *Qur'an* and the *Gita* together. This is something which I am sure many of you must envy. My regret is that I can only teach and learn as an adult in this new Britain, I was not born into it. Sadly not everyone in Britain sees its emergence as a multiracial, multifaith society, as something good and enriching, but slowly people are coming to accept the reality—often positively. However, what I want to point out in closing is this, most adults never engage in dialogue, but in our schools, not just in Britain where religious studies feature in the curriculum, but in many other parts of Europe, America, Asia, and Africa, children do, in the playground if nowhere else. Let us remember them from the ivory towers of academia and help them and those who teach them. Dialogue is not merely an academic discipline.

Notes

In 1988 a new Education Reform Act was passed which contained clauses relating to Religious Education in England and Wales. It states that what is taught "shall reflect the fact that the religious traditions in Great Britain are in the main Christian while taking account of the teaching and practices of the other principal religions represented in Great Britain" (Chapter 40, Part 1, clause 8[3]). The approaches to R.E. outlined in this essay are unlikely to be affected by the Act and may even receive encouragement if the subject is taken more seriously.

21

Buddhist/Christian Dialogue—A Prolegomena

Thubten Losel

This essay attempts to bring into focus some key issues in the theistic/non-theistic ecumenical dialogue by using the Buddhist/Christian encounter as the basis of our discussion. It seems to me that the entire ecumenical movement has, in many ways, been overly rash and underly sincere. It is incumbent upon us to take a step back in order to analyze the motivations and indeed the very foundations and premises of our endeavor. Have we stopped to ask ourselves why we are engaged in this dialogue and what we foresee as its culmination? Have we questioned whether our mere participation requires a personal commitment from us and if so what that commitment might be? I believe that a truly ecumenical journey is unlike any other, that the profundity of and prerequisites for such a sojourn have been tremendously underestimated, and that if taken, it cannot but leave one transformed and a more dedicated and religious person.

Let us consider some of the misguided approaches to such an encounter so that perhaps in a *via negativa* we may come to an understanding of some of the principles of the dialogue.

The first model we shall consider might be called the naive wine-taster's approach to the ecumenical encounter. Here we find the claim that it is only by tasting, i.e. by intimately experiencing, each of the different religious traditions in a way that transcends their intellectual content, that one can truly engage in dialogue. The additional claim is often advanced that this supra-intellectual and experiential approach to the world's religions serves as verification of their identity. Diversity in this model is viewed as a deluded byproduct of discursive analysis, and that by transcending the latter in directly experiencing different religious traditions, their "one-ness" becomes evident.[1]

It is not surprising in an age where improved communication has made diversity evident and mental lethargy rampant that such a reductionistic approach should have gained such widespread acceptance. Needless to say, I consider this approach to be riddled with problems, the greatest of which I see as this: we find a premise which I think would be anathema to any religious tradition, namely that intellectual content is *transcended* by experience rather than *fulfilled* by it, that our tasting and living what the Buddha and Christ themselves experienced, instead of being the outcomes of their respective doctrinal formulations, are independent of doctrinal content. It is false to assume from the similarity of religious experiences *qua* experiences, the identity of the different religions *qua* religions. Nor does it help to plead ineffability, to claim that this presumed unity is beyond the scope of language, for we must remember that we are discussing the issue of interreligious *dialogue*, which by its very nature *is* linguistic. To claim that the purported unity can be neither understood nor expressed to another by means of language is to condemn the dialogue to failure from the start.

The next approach I call the approach of the blind partisan. It occurs when participants in the dialogue are so completely engrossed in their own viewpoint that it becomes impossible for them to recognize diversity. For example, so evident is it to some theists that God exists, that it becomes impossible to even imagine the fact that Buddhism has no notion of an omnipotent creator God. In essence, religion comes to be equated with theism, so that the idea of "non-theistic religion" becomes an impossibility.[2]

Needless to say, dialogue under these circumstances is an exercise in futility. It becomes, on the part of the chauvinist, an (oftentimes unconscious) attempt to impute his/her own views to others, and on the part of the other participant, a frustrating attempt to preserve and to accurately represent a unique tradition. It commits the partisan to enough study of, say, Buddhism, to be given a basis on which to make the imputation of a God credible, and yet not so much that the reality of Buddhist non-theism becomes evident. I would point out that extreme chauvinism of the kind described here is for the most part a subconscious syndrome in which the diseased is unaware of either the condition or of the actions that result from the condition.

The subtle chauvinist on the other hand is a different case. Here, despite recognizing the vast differences which do exist between, say, theistic and non-theistic religions, a variety of motivations act to make the individual *consciously* overlook these distinctions for the greater glory of some misguided syncretic goal. Here it is not a question of all of the fruits seeming to taste the same (Case 1), or of oranges being mistaken for tangerines (Case 2), but of some indigestible fruit salad, or what may be worse, pureé! There is no need to mention the impossibility of dialogue under these circumstances.

The three positions I have outlined above are extreme: the first because it over-emphasizes experience at the expense of rationality, the second because of its utter blindness to differences, and the third because of its extreme insincerity. The stance which I will discuss now I see to be eminently moderate and to be born out of the love that very openminded people have for other traditions. Despite these noble qualities, I believe it to be wrong, too, the reasons for which I will now explain.

The position is based on the premise that dialogue can occur only on the basis of a common substratum. It is claimed that the only way in which Christians and Buddhists can talk is if they share a common notion of an ultimate, that dialogue is predicated upon commonality. Hence the participants find themselves involved in a search for what in Buddhism can correspond to the Christian notion of God, and what in Christianity can correspond to the Buddhist notion of emptiness (skt. *sunyata,* tib. *stong nyid*). My objections to this approach have nothing to do with methodology, but simply with its lack of success. Practically speaking, the approach has little to show by way of results. There is simply nothing that can be pointed to in Buddhism that corresponds to a classical Christian notion of God. No plausible case can be made for positing the Buddha, karma, emptiness, the mind, or a god (skt. *deva,* tib. *lha*) as the equivalent of the God of Israel, and likewise for the notion of emptiness in Christianity. This is not to say that the traditional Christian notion of God could not be weakened to conform to the Buddhist idea of an enlightened being;[3] nor is it to say that the Buddhist concept of emptiness could not be radically modified to conform to the idea of *el vacio* as expressed by San Juan de la Cruz. Then however, all that the dialogue accomplishes is, quite literally, conformity, and we are led once again into the odious pureé of syncretism.

Now let us consider some counter measures to each of these four misguided approaches.

Reason. It seems to me that it is very important to realize that the medium in which the dialogue takes place is linguistic and conceptual in nature. As such it may very well be subject to limitations, but so be it. Never should this fact subvert our trust in reason, or lead us to the repudiation of it in favor of a rampant subjectivism based on experience.

Openmindedness. I am willing to live with the fact that my Christian brother or sister may believe deep down that when I worship the Buddha, I am actually worshipping his/her God.[4] I am not however willing to accept a blindness of the sort that does not allow them to see that this is not *my own belief.* We must be broadminded enough to admit the existence of differences on every level—not only between my own religion and the next, but between the way *I interpret* someone else's religion, and the way that *they themselves* do. The attitude that Buddhists are actually theists despite what they themselves claim is religious jingoism of the most intolerable kind, and just one step removed from nineteenth century Christian missionary zeal.[5]

Sincerity. It seems almost redundant to have to say that proper motivation should form the basis for interreligious dialogue, yet, sadly enough, it does seem necessary to make the point. In the more extreme cases there is the futile hope of converting the other party to one's own beliefs. In the more subtle, there exists a dissimilation of openmindedness which harbors megalomaniacal syncretistic goals. In this regard, let me say that I have never been able to appreciate the appeal of "all becoming one." "Many" seems so much more fascinating and beautiful to me.

Uniqueness. How absolutely amazing it is that, for those who opt to believe in God there exist hundreds of years of traditional theism to fall back on; and how wonderful that those who do not choose to do so, have options like Buddhism and Jainism. Diversity for me is not the stumbling block to dialogue, but the prerequisite for it. Were we to determine that Christians and Buddhists are in actuality expressing the same things, it could only signify the end of the dialogue. Only where there is difference, where there is tension, and where there is the possibility of confrontation and complementarity can there be born insight. Commonality is not the beginning of the dialogue but its end.

I have cited four misguided approaches to the interreligious dialogue and have suggested corresponding counter measures. What remains is for me to set forth some of the implications of this in a positive way. If the dialogue does not consist of a search for commonality, then what does it entail? For me it entails *the exploration of the practical implications of differences*. It is because of the tremendous historical, cultural, and doctrinal differences that exist between our traditions that they have developed into such beautifully unique systems of thought and practice. And it is this uniqueness, the fact that each tradition has its own special and distinct qualities, that serves as the basis for complementarity, which I see as the fruit of the dialogue.

In the eight years I have been a monk, I have sought to learn as much as possible about other monastic traditions, Buddhist, Christian, and Hindu alike. From the outset I took the cultural, historical, and doctrinal differences as givens, and in spite of this, the dialogue has been for me tremendously rewarding. I have come to understand how much my own tradition, the Tibetan Buddhist, has to learn. For example, how much the Christian monastic tradition has to show us regarding community life, how much Hindu monks can teach us about simplicity of living, how much the Theravada tradition can offer us a model of discipline, and how much the Japanese and Korean Zen traditions can show us regarding perseverance in meditation. These are things which I have come to appreciate, not in spite of differences but *because* of them. For me, the model to be followed is not one of searching for commonality, but of cultivating complementarity. Where one tradition falters, there should it turn to others for advice and counsel. This has been my own approach, and I can attest to its efficacy.

But is there no common factor, no underlying principle as the basis of the world's religions? Surely, even their ability to complement one another is indicative of some commonality. True, but the similarity has to do not with their respective conceptions of the ultimate, i.e. with God or with emptiness. It has to do with the existence of human suffering and humankind's ability to extricate itself from it. None of us desire misery and all of us want happiness; and these are the very issues upon which the world's religions focus. In an address to the International Buddhist Conference in New Delhi in 1978, His Holiness the Dalai Lama said:

> I believe in the need for human understanding and harmony for a wider reason, which is simply that we are all human beings. Geographical, cultural and physical differences are superficial. Even differences of faith and ideology are transcended when we begin to think of ourselves as human beings. We all want happiness and do not want suffering and every human being has the right to

pursue happiness. For in the final analysis, all of us basically have the same hopes and aspirations, and all of us belong to the same human family.[6]

So in a way, the dialogue *is* based on one identity, our common humanity. It is an identity that unfolds into the beauty of human differentiation and the subsequent possibility of communication, complementarity, and dialogue.

As I said at the outset, it was my intention in this paper to question some of the basic presuppositions on which the interreligious dialogue is based. Although the bulk of my criticism has been directed at theistic chauvinism, it could just as well apply in most cases to the Buddhists themselves. Indeed, if I have not faulted the Buddhists more, it is because I see a lack of commitment to the dialogue on their part, a kind of lethargy born from an attitude of self-righteousness. This, in fact, may be the single greatest hindrance to the Buddhist/Christian encounter, since it obstructs true participation from the very outset.

I mentioned above that I thought participation in the interreligious dialogue required a certain amount of commitment. The four countermeasures are manifestations of this. There must be a dedication to reason, to openmindedness, to sincerity and to preserving and cultivating the fruits of uniqueness. In addition I might add that there must be a firm commitment to the study of each other's traditions, not in a superficial way as the chauvinist does, but in a truly rigorous and extensive way. We must be committed to the transformation of our own tradition and to transforming ourselves in the light of the insight born from dialogue. But most importantly there must be a commitment to love, not the puerile kind that starts and ends with the lighting of a few candles, the holding of hands and the singing of a song, but of a deep and lasting kind that, like the live embers of an eternal fire, suffuse us with the steady warmth of mutual responsibility for, and dedication to one another. This is our heritage as living and thinking beings of infinite capacity.

Notes

1. The approach is typified by the famous nineteenth century Indian mystic, Ramakrishna Paramahansa. His stance, strengthened by the missionary zeal of his chief and very charismatic disciple, Vivekananda, and nurtured by latent Indian notions of *advaitic* unity have ripened into the "all-is-one"-ness that is so rampant in modern Hinduism.

2. To the uninformed, it may seem as though the Mahayana idea of the Buddha corresponds to the Christian notion of God, for they share the qualities of omniscience (skt. *sarvajña*, tib. *thams cad mkhyen pa*) and omnicompassion (skt. *mahakaruna*, tib. *snying rje chen po*). In Buddhism, however, the universe is considered to be cyclical and beginingless, thereby doing away with the need for a creator. In addition, omnipotence when combined with omnicompassion is viewed as contradictory to the presence of suffering in the universe, hence the Buddha is viewed as a potent but not omnipotent being. This position is characterized very well in a famous verse:

> The Conqueror does not wash away our sins with water
> He does not eliminate our suffering with his hands
> He does not transfer to us his own accomplishment
> Instead he liberates us by expounding the truth.

3. By the removal of his omnipotence, his ability to dispense salvific grace, his status as creator, etc.

4. Every religious system has its own models for interpreting the actions and doctrines of other religions. I would venture to guess that most Buddhists view classical Old Testament theism in much the same way that it was perceived by the Gnostics. Here, God, as He is portrayed in the literally interpreted Old Testament, is viewed as some sort of demiurge, or in Buddhist terms, as a mundane deity (skt. *laukikadevata*, tib. *jig rten pa'i lha*) still subject to the passions of anger and desire. But this should not blind Buddhists from seeing the fact that this is not the way that Christians and Jews themselves see their God and that has come a long way from the time of Moses.

5. The issue here is a very complex one, and its ramifications vast. It brings to mind the question of the possibility of salvation in other religious systems. In Buddhism, for example, the direct perception of the truth, i.e. of emptiness, is a necessary prerequisite for salvation, and neither labelling someone else's ultimate "emptiness" nor praying that it *be* emptiness is going to insure the salvation of that person unless the understanding of true emptiness actually exists. Even within Buddhism itself, it is said that only the Prasangika understanding of emptiness can act as the basis for salvation. Hence, no amount of insisting that God *is* emptiness is going to insure the salvation of Christians, from a Buddhist point of view, unless God actually is emptiness. Likewise, I would think that no amount of insisting that emptiness or Buddha is God is going to insure the salvation of Buddhists, from the Christian point of view, unless one of them actually *is* God.

6. Reprinted in *Dalai Lama: Europe 1982* (Pomaia, Italy: Foundation for the Preservation of the Mahayana Tradition, 1982).

22

The What and the How of Dialogue[1]

Paul Mojzes

Dialogue is a special form of encounter, in this case inter-religious in nature, which can take place between individuals or groups who hold different convictions. It is a distinctly human activity because dialogue does not take place between ideas, books, or even religions as abstractions but between concrete persons.

In order to reach a better understanding of what dialogue is, it is helpful to eliminate forms of encounter which are not dialogue. Dialogue is not:

> negotiation
> debate
> disputation
> parallel monologue
> practical cooperation
> proselytizing
> mutual accommodation
> merger
> involuntary exchange of ideas
> antagonistic confrontation, etc.

This is not to rule out the usefulness of some of the above mentioned encounters, but merely to rule them out as dialogues.

In the spectrum of human encounters, dialogue holds a middle ground. The spectrum includes (but is not restricted to) attitudes and practices of:

> antagonism
> indifference
> dialogue
> cooperation
> synthesis

Dialogue may take place between individuals and groups holding different convictions even if other members of their groups or they themselves, engage in other forms of encounter. Thus, for instance, dialogue and cooperation are not mutually exclusive; to the contrary they are compatible. Even antagonism and dialogue are not completely incompatible, in the sense that a dialogue between individuals or smaller groups who belong to groups or movements traditionally hostile to one another, may well lead to the gradual diminishing of such hostility. It is the presence of hostility and antagonism between religious groups which, indeed, mandate dialogue as a way to defuse behavior likely to escalate into destruction.

Conditions and Reasons for Dialogue

Certain external and internal conditions are necessary in order for dialogue to take place. External conditions are historical circumstances which either create a proper climate for the dialogue or make such a dialogue difficult or impossible. Internal conditions, on the other hand, are attitudes of the partners which either prevent the relationship from becoming dialogue or foster it.

A certain degree of freedom for both parties must exist for a dialogue to take place. One cannot be forced to dialogue, nor can one dialogue with "a knife at one's throat." Conditions of outright persecution preclude dialogue. So do conditions of hostile confrontation and propaganda. On the opposite side of the spectrum, the desire to fully conform to the other, based on a false sense of solidarity or unity, can also forestall dialogue.

The "objective" need for dialogue must also exist. Objective needs are those that are not the needs of one or the other partner, which could be labeled as "subjective." Both partners will experience some conditions to which response by one of them alone will not be sufficient to deal adequately with the situation. Recognition of mutual interdependence is a precondition of dialogue.

Of the internal conditions for dialogue the most important ones are to know one's own views well, to believe that truth is attainable, to have respect for the partner, and to consent to the notion that reality is greater than any one person or group can grasp and interpret.

To know one's own views well means to have convictions and to allow one's partner to have convictions. It is not a helpful situation when one or both parties are required to change the content of their own views in order to make dialogue possible. In the course of dialogue one's own views may change if one becomes convinced that the former view was wrong, but this should not lead to utter relativism. The partners also need to examine whether they are using the same terms or concepts for different realities, because this leads to confusion. Should partners enter the dialogue with the purpose of rethinking their conceptual framework, the consequences may be to confuse their own partner or to alienate themselves from their own milieu. However, some rethinking may be necessary if one takes the search for truth seriously.

Both partners in dialogue need to acknowledge that their aim is truth and that they are entering into dialogue for the sake of truth. A more comprehensive and accurate form of truth is being sought. They must agree that their aim is an objective validity of values which can be recognized. But truth in this sense is neither looking for an exact middle position nor a superficial syncretism. Complete skepticism of any truth-claim will not help the dialogue, nor will a claim that one must never, under any conditions, depart from one's own stated positions. Both partners need to acknowledge the rules of logical thinking as well.

Respect for the partners means the willingness to trust the partner. The authenticity and sincerity of the partner is presupposed. Respect for the partner demands that the partners listen to one another rather than prejudge or depend on third sources for information. The freedom of other humans must be implicitly or explicitly recognized.

Should any partners dogmatically assert that they possess the entire experiential truth and can interpret it infallibly and unchangeably, no dialogue can take place. Only the admission that something can be learned from a partner can enable us to

enter subjectively into dialogue. Both sides must be able to acknowledge this.

Motives and Purposes of Dialogue

One of the purposes of the dialogue is to deal theoretically
with certain problems which emerge from the struggles of
everyday life. This theoretical discussion should encourage
more effective common action. Otherwise the dialogue may
degenerate into mere quibbling or wasteful academic discussion.

The Yugoslav Marxist sociologist Oleg Mandic from Zagreb
suggested that the purpose of the dialogue is to help the
majority of the world who live in poverty, misery, and hunger.
This vast majority of people belong to some religious organization. Although this is a long process, he suggested that humane
people will struggle for the improvement through dialogue.

It is obvious that dialogue needs a goal. Purposeless dialogue
is hard to envision. The basic question is whether it has a worthy purpose. Under specific historic conditions different purposes may emerge as praiseworthy. The following purposes
may be listed: (1) attempts to better grasp the truth; (2) the
achievement of greater justice, human freedom, brotherhood
or sisterhood; and (3) action for the welfare of all or part of
humanity. The purpose of the dialogue should never be to endanger any group, e.g., Muslims, Jews, existentialists, or dissi-
dents. Only a method such as dialogue, which is infused with
humility, openness, selflessness, friendship, care, respect, and
responsibility (which can all be assumed under the term love),
when carried out in conjunction with the search for truth can
yield results consonant with the intended goal.

Dialogue can advance various goals including that of getting
to know the other, of enriching and completing their own
vision, of fighting the dogmatists in their own institutions, of
humanizing the world by changing it, and, finally, of making it
possible to engage in useful joint actions.

Finally, one must not forget the political motives or purposes
of the dialogue. This may be to gain a greater measure of
religious or political freedom, to obtain political support for
specific measures, especially those unpopular and not so easily
achievable without the support of the other, and so forth.
Sometimes such purposes are not primary and often they are
part of the "hidden agenda." When political motive emerges as
the primary purpose of the dialogue, the chances are that no
real dialogue will take place or that it will soon deteriorate. The

fate of the dialogue often depends on oscillating political contingencies.

A Provisional Definition of Dialogue

The following working definition of dialogue is proposed: dialogue is a way by which persons or groups of different persuasions respectfully and responsibly relate to one another in order to bring about mutual enrichment without removing essential differences between them. Dialogue is both a verbal and an attitudinal mutual approach which includes listening, sharing ideas, and working together despite the continued existence of real differences and tensions. Dialogue is a conscious process in which partners seek to give and take without recourse to force and intimidation. Mere cooperation for practical purposes, in which ideological or religious views are of no concern to the partners, is not dialogue. Dialogue comprises both theory and practice. Dialogue is an effort to surmount limits imposed by present social relations. It goes beyond mere influence by another view, even if that influence drastically alters or profoundly shapes one's own world view. Unless two or more distinct groups or persons are consciously involved as distinct protagonists in the give and take of theory and practice, something other than dialogue is taking place. Being aware of partnership in a joint enterprise is of crucial importance for the definition of dialogue.

Some people make no effort to explain what they mean by the word dialogue. Some use it vaguely, applying it to almost any meeting between religious groups, regardless of the attitudes and motives brought to the meeting. Thus for instance, a protocol meeting between a bishop and a bikkhu might be described by them as dialogue. Some more correctly identify dialogue as a specific type of encounter characterized by the equality and freedom of the participants, by a give-and-take situation, by an attempt to solve common theoretical and practical problems without aiming to misuse the partner or win a victory.

It is evident that there is a good deal of overlapping in discussions of the purpose, motives, and method of dialogue. It should be thus. Without some commonality no success could be expected, because the notions and expectations would be at complete variance. It is most helpful, however, to see not merely the points of overlapping but also the novel points introduced by the various contributors to dialogue. It is, in fact the composite impact which most enriches our understanding of dialogue. Taking a comprehensive view is most helpful. By applying the principle of coherence, it is possible to utilize the accumulated contributions of various dialogue partners, leaving out only those that are logically incompatible or deficient, and thus gain a very rich understanding of the purpose and nature of dialogue.

Dialogue is a method, a path, a way, by which one person or group relates to another. Views differ. Differences are not to be removed, but are to serve as mutual enrichment. Both partners must be open to insight gained in the joint endeavor. Tension, dissent, and even conflict are seen as part of the process. No attempt should be made to camouflage differences for the sake of the appearance of a superficial agreement. Partners in dialogue must seek to know one another directly by listening, by speaking, by working together.

Guidelines for More Successful Dialogue

The following guidelines might be offered to those seeking to engage in a successful dialogue, without claiming that every specific dialogue must meet all conditions or that the list is comprehensive:

1. Both partners must have a need for dialogue.
2. Have a preliminary knowledge of your partner and the position with which you are going to dialogue.
3. Have a clear understanding of your own position.
4. Be well informed about the topic being discussed and present it clearly.
5. Set concrete areas of discussion ahead of time.
6. It is more promising to discuss specific issues than general.
7. Do not stereotype. Be open to the presentation of your partner's viewpoint.
8. Interpret your partner's view in the best light. Look at the whole picture, and do not try to belittle his view.
9. Look at the weaknesses and strengths of both views.
10. Emphasize the things you have in common.
11. Listen to what your partner is saying. Strive for a clearer understanding of his or her position. Be willing continually to revise your understanding of the other's views.
12. There should be no hidden agendas, there should be no tactical or selfish motive for initiating the dialogue.

13. Be open to constructive criticism, and avoid destructive criticism. Be aware of your partner's sensitivities.
14. Each member of the dialogue should be self-critical and honest. This should not mean giving up dignity and self-respect.
15. Do not assume that conclusions reached are final. There will always be a need for continual dialogue regarding these views.
16. Each partner must accept responsibility for the good and the bad his or her group has done or is still doing.
17. Both the ideals and the realities of each group should be taken into account.
18. Face issues which cause conflict, but emphasize those things upon which partners agree. Antagonistic relations may then give way to cooperation.
19. Challenge one another to be faithful to your own search for truth.
20. Soul-searching and mutual enrichment should be part of the dialogue. Neither truth is absolute. Each partner needs the other in order to get a more complete picture of truth. Monopoly in thought leads to sluggishness in thinking and to perversion of truth.
21. Dialogue is impossible if either partner claims to have already solved the problem for all time to come.
22. Dialogue should present new appreciation for the value of both positions.
23. Dialogue occurs between persons or groups of persons, not between disembodied ideas.
24. Do not try to convert your partner, or the dialogue may turn again into a monologue. Differences must be maintained, although they should change from irreconcilable ones to a diversity of approaches for the common good.
25. Dialogue should enable easier cooperation.
26. Work toward accomplishing something for the better. Work at improving the situation.
27. Observe the dialectical nature of dialogue. Both views should be included in final conclusions, though not necessarily in equal measure. Both partners ought to move to new positions (not necessarily convergent ones) which would not have been possible without the dialogue.
28. Be aware that there are other people involved. The dialogue should be for the benefit of the whole community.

Dialogue should thus be a dialectical engagement rather than a path to convergence. No synthesis is to be expected. While some differences may be reconciled and while the partners may reach agreement, even unanimity, on some issues, the goal is not to create a hybrid of the future.

At best a good model would lead to partial convergence with continued dialectical engagement. One should not expect the process to be even progressively improving. There are likely to be ups and downs, setbacks in some locations, and unexpected gains in others.

In this understanding, dialogue is not a mere prelude to cooperation. Cooperation becomes part of the dialogue, because action can be viewed as the incarnate word (*logos*) through two (*dia*) partners. Hence dialogue should be the way of relating partners in the present and the future. It does not become superfluous after practical cooperation takes place. Rather it is the constant approach in a pluralistic world to living and finding happiness through struggle. If this be true, one cannot speak of the "death" of the dialogue, unless the partners decide to eliminate one another by warfare, or unless one or both of them should vanish as viable life styles. While some of these options are not entirely out of the question, one could venture an educated guess that both partners will survive the foreseeable future and, being unable to ignore one another, must encounter each other in dialogue. The less sophisticated approaches to dialogue will simply be transcended, as the partners seek out those dialogue options which experience proves to be the most suitable. Thus at best dialogue is the encounter of committed but self-critical religious parties for the sake of a better future of all humanity.

Notes

1. Portions of this essay are adapted and reprinted by permission from *Christian-Marxist Dialogue in Eastern Europe*, copyright © 1983 Augsburg Publishing House.

23

One Heart— Monastic Experience and Interreligious Dialogue

Pascaline Coff

People of every religious persuasion—be they Christian, Muslim, Jew, Hindu, Buddhist, Jain or other by reason of their human and religious vocation—are called to live dialogue in their daily lives. For dialogue is a manner of acting, an attitude and a spirit which guides one's conduct and communication and leads to communion. One's spirituality, then, is at the base, at the root of dialogue because spirituality embraces what is truly human and universal in a person. Hans Urs Balthasar defines spirituality as

> ...that basic practical or existential attitude of man which is the consequence and expression of the way in which he understands his religious—or more generally, his ethically committed existence; the way in which he acts and reacts habitually throughout his life according to his objective and ultimate insights and decisions.[1]

Women and men define themselves by virtue of their spiritual quality, and not their material, bodily or instinctive aspects. The spirit opens up in an unequivocal yet mysterious way the totality of being. It is an absolute totality since the spirit's claim to truth implies the absolute. Spirituality, therefore, can be summed up as the inward way, insofar as everything not this absolute center of the spirit is reduced to a merely relative position. But this is not enough. The spirit of woman and man wants to express itself in reality, wants to become the total content within everything relative. It is here that one becomes decisive and the power of the spirit prevails, pervades, permeates all. It is here that selfless service and real communication begin and continue.

With this understanding of spirituality we see dialogue as an anthropological necessity. We grow by encountering and sharing with others. It is only in meeting one another, serving one another, that we discover ourselves. No woman, no man is an island! The deeper the meeting, the more we find our true selves in communion with all the rest. Truth, bare reality, is better recognized, understood and lived by virtue of our encounters with one another. When these exchanges reach the level of the person, i.e. of consciousness and the mind, such relating becomes dialogue. When we freely choose to be in relation to the other, when the other is no longer an object but a subject with us, a source and deep center of self-awareness, then, and only then can a true meeting, a spiritual communion take place. Communication in depth is not communication but communion and this is the essence of dialogue, communion and love. Its fruits are peace and joy.

Religious Dialogue—The Christian Basis

Jesus Christ revealed to the world a God in dialogue: Father, Son, and Spirit—a divine Trinity in profoundest interrelation. God is truly the mystery of both communion and dialogue and has transmitted this manner of being to the Church. The Church in turn is bound by divine precept to love as Christ loved, i.e., to the very laying down of one's life for the other. Furthermore, the Church has as its end the eschatological Kingdom which consists in the fullness of participation in the life of the Trinity. Therefore, the Church, as offspring and instrument of this Kingdom must favor these values of unity, communion, and dialogue.[2]

Religion in itself is already a dialogue for the Christian, a dialogue first with God and also with women and men. Jesus was ceaselessly in communion with his Father and in his dialoguing with the people of his day was ceaselessly sharing or trying to share this profound communion. "Holy Father, protect by the power of thy name those whom thou has given me, that they may be one, as we are one" (John 17:11). "I am not myself the source of the words I speak to you; it is the Father who dwells in me doing his own work" (John 14:10). It has always been by exchanging experiences of God that growth in the divine mystery has transpired within human persons. And it is only from this center of one's being that true dialogue takes place. "The depths of a man can only by known by his own spirit, not by any other man" (I Corinthians 2:11). Both the giving and the receiving in dialogue must come from this inner depth where the spirit touches our spirit. Dialogue is based on and proceeds from a deep love and respect for the human person—then is it a true meeting and a mutual exchange—a self donation.

Qualities of Dialogue—Essential Conditions

Interrelating in profound love with one another demands an awakening, an openness, hospitality, a listening heart, knowledge of the other, full interior freedom, integrity, and unshakable dedication to one's own inner truth. Fear of losing one's identity or the tension between "identity and openness" often blocks communion and any real sharing. Once during an intermonastic gathering in the Hindu Ashram in Rishikesh, a pilgrimage center of the Hindus, a Christian partner in the dialogue shared such a fear. Swami Chidananda, President of the Ashram responded: "To the extent that you come out in openness, we Hindus will reach out to you in openness."[3]

Anyone who thinks they will be betraying their faith cannot and should not enter the dialogue. While many are fearful in the face of interreligious dialogue, Christians know from their own scriptures that "perfect love casts out all fear" (I John 4:18). The very thing that is feared does take place in true dialogue: there is a change of identity, a metanoia, a conversion which is an essential part of all dialogue. One of the greatest contemporary pioneers in this field calls this phenomenon "intrareligious" dialogue, an internal preparation for and a fruit of the actual dialogical process. As a preparation all prejudices, assumptions, competitions, superiority, and preconceptions as to aims and results are consumed within the heart:

> Any interreligious and interhuman dialogue, any exchange among cultures, has to be preceded by an intrareligious and intrahuman dialogue, an internal conversion with the person. The gulf between so many abysses—can

be bridged only if we realize the synthesis and the harmony within the microcosm of ourselves.[4]

Yet, interreligious dialogue is a preparation for, and a stepping stone to that intra-religious dialogue where living faith constantly demands from us a total renewal, a real, personal and ever-recurring metanoia.[5] Swami Abhishiktananda, another recent pioneer in intermonastic dialogue, referred to dialogue as a searchlight disturbing our false securities. It probes the present societies of women and men but first scans the heart of those taking part in it.[6] While neither partner is out to "convert" the other, the element of conversion in this sense of metanoia must be there in the heart of both. It is in this sense that we see the dialogical process as 'creating one heart.' Not that there is a syncretism, a watering down of what one believes, but a predisposition of unity and openness flowing from a sincere love for the other and for all that is sacred to them. Therefore, interreligious dialogue is an urgency. It is not only unavoidable today but is a religious imperative at every level as an indispensable element in the search for truth and the realization of justice. Dialogue is not a luxury among a scholastic few but is essential to everyone if we are to enter the twenty-first century in peace and love—with One Heart!

Notes

1. Hans Urs von Balthasar, "The Gospel as Norm and Test of All Spirituality in the Church," *Concilium*, vol. 9, trans. Theodore L. Weston (New York: Paulist Press, 1965), 7.

2. Marcello Zago, O.M.I., "Dialogue in the Mission of the Church", in *Secretariatus pro non-Christianis Bulletin*, (Rome: Citta del Vaticano, 1984), vol. XIX, no. 3, 267.

3. Quoted by Albert Nambiaparambil in "India: A Testing Ground for Interreligious Dialogue," *Secretariatus pro non-Christianis Bulletin*, (Rome: Citta del Vaticano, 1984), vol. XIX, no. 3, 348.

4. Raimundo Panikkar, *Myth, Faith & Hermeneutics* (New York: Paulist Press, 1979), 310.

5. Raimundo Panikkar, *The Intrareligious Dialogue* (New York: Paulist Press, 1978).

6. Swami Abhishiktananda, (Fr. Henri le Saux), "The Depth-Dimension of Religious Dialogue" in *Vidyajyoti*, New Delhi (May, 1981.), 52.

24

Interreligious Meeting—
An Approach to World Peace

Tsering Dhondup

My Religion: Buddhism

Before turning to the subject of my essay, I think it is important to give a brief introduction to my religion. I trust it will help the readers to understand my religious beliefs and conceptions. This will also allow me to explain my traditional heritage.

Buddhism was propounded by Gautama Buddha, an Indian prince, over 2,500 years ago. It was introduced into my country, Tibet, in the fifth century from India by the religious kings of Tibet and great Indian saints. Tibet is, perhaps, the only area of the world where a sociopolitical system is based on the teaching of Buddhism and where the maximum number of individuals were not only allowed but also encouraged to pursue and practice Buddhism. Therefore carrying out religious activities had become a part of life for the majority of people in Tibet.

We Buddhists believe in the theory of rebirth or life after death. As the seed of medicinal plants produce medicine and the seeds of poisonous plants produce poison, Buddhists believe that there are immediate sources of both the physical body and the invisible mind of every being. The immediate source of body must be the bodies of one's parents and the immediate source of the mind must be a mind that existed before or in continuity with a previous mind. This proves that there existed a past life and its continuity will lead to a next life. Hence, there is a common Buddhist proverb, "Look at your present circumstances to know what you have done in the past life, look at the attitude of your present mind to know what you will be doing in the next life."

The basic aim of all the religions is to control the mind. The mind is the cause and effect of every action that we take and from which we experience pleasant and unpleasant consequences. Buddhism stresses the importance of training the mind for gaining lasting peace or pleasure. An undisciplined mind harbors evil thoughts which stimulate evil action. The mind has to suffer the consequences of evil action. That is why some social scientists say that Buddhism is not a religion but a "science of mind."

Attitudes of Buddhists Towards the Followers of Other Religions

Lord Buddha, the founder of Buddhism, after giving three major sermons, once advised a group of his disciples, in the following words: "To judge the purity of gold, it is burnt, cut and rubbed. In the same way, carefully examine the teachings I gave you. If you find truth in them, follow them jealously; do not have hatred for other's, simply because it is not ours."

Practitioners or followers of Buddha do not have a sense of religious bigotry. They respect the views and ideas of non-Buddhists. Tibetan Buddhists hold that shorn of petty differences of approach and method followed by different religions, the aim of all religions is basically the same. His Holiness the Dalai Lama, the spiritual and temporal leader of Tibet, said in His Memoirs: "Just as a particular disease in the world is treated by various medical methods, so here are many religions to bring happiness to human beings and others. Different doctrines have been introduced by different exponents at different periods and in different ways. But I believe they all fundamentally aim at the same noble goal, in teaching moral precepts to mold the functions of mind, body and speech, they all teach us not to tell lies or bear false witness, or steal or take another's life and so on."[1]

212

Promotion of Interreligious Dialogue in the Buddhist Tradition

The ideal learned Buddhist teacher has to be an expert preacher to propagate the great teachings of Lord Buddha, as well as an eloquent debater and a writer. Through debates, one can put forward his point of view and argue with open mind to refute one's opponent's views. This must be done with an open mind. Debaters must share their thoughts and learn from the views of others. There are numerous legends of debate sessions held between learned Buddhists monks and great Hindu Jain and other scholars in the past. In those days, whoever lost the debate would even renounce his faith and embrace the faith of the victor. In citing this episode, I do not mean to advocate that all the religions of the world should hold debates to prove the superiority of one over the other. But I certainly would like to call upon the leaders of different religions to come closer and make sincere contact with each other. This would promote fraternity and a sense of brotherhood among the followers of different faiths.

His Holiness the Dalai Lama, in his travels to various countries of the world has taken the opportunity to meet with leaders of different religions and to discuss spiritual matters with them. In 1981, when His Holiness the Dalai Lama was in the United States, representatives of a Christian group contacted Him about the possibility of an exchange of Tibetan Buddhist and Christian monks. Thus, began a unique dialogue and understanding between the monks of these two faiths. Soon after, a group of young intellectual Buddhist monks visited various Christian monasteries in the West, taking part in all their activities. This enabled the participants to understand and appreciate each other. I think this is a right step towards achieving our common goal.

The Concepts That Should Guide Interreligious Cooperation

The happiness and well-being of individuals, groups, and societies is interlinked. While the development of modern science and technology has brought the world closer on one level, we still need to become aware of our inner links. Where the action of any person arises from hatred, ill-feeling, greed, and selfishness this causes not only restlessness and disaster for that person, but creates a chain of troubles for others too.

Today there is violence and conflict among warring nations and political blocks in the world, between the East and West, and between NATO and Warsaw pact countries. There is mistrust and an atmosphere of suspicion exists everywhere. More and more sophisticated machines and weapons of destruction are invented and developed. This has created further tensions and led to a dangerous situation. Thus the very survival of human life is at peril and our world has become a tragic place to live in.

But the world is ours and we are all members of the human family. We must work together to protect it and share it. In offering a solution for solving the human problems of today, His Holiness The Dalai Lama has said, "Of the many problems we face today, some are natural calamities and must be accepted and faced with equanimity. Others however, are of our own making, created by misunderstanding and can be corrected. One such type arises from the conflicts of ideologies, political or religious, when people fight each other for petty ends, losing sight of the basic humanity that binds us all together as a single human family. We must remember that the different religions, ideologies, and political systems of the world are meant for human beings to achieve happiness. We must not lose sight of this fundamental goal and at no time should we place means above ends; the supremacy of humanity over matter and ideology must always be maintained."[2]

The doctrines enunciated by all the great religious teachers contain the relevant cures for these human illnesses. The leaders of the world religions must cooperate with each other in promoting the spiritual values of the religions. In this way, we can establish a harmonious society where we can live in peace and bring happiness for all. The problems of the world can be solved.

The Basis for Developing Interreligious Tolerance and Respect

All the religions give us similar teachings and aim at the same goal. There have been, however, misunderstandings and differences of opinion among the followers of different religions due to the lack of contact. Unfortunately religions, which are primarily devoted to peace, have been made a cause for conflict between different communities. In human history blood has been shed in the name of religious differences and so-called holy wars. And weakness within the religious community has always been exploited by the politicians and people with selfish motives and thus our human family lives in division and disunity. But each individual has a universal responsibility to preserve peace and tranquility in the world. I think the leaders of the world religions can make a major contribution in developing interreligious tolerance, mutual respect, and understanding among their followers in particular and within the whole of humanity in general. His Holiness the Dalai Lama, while giving an outline of the Buddhism of Tibet, has called upon religious believers to end disunity among them, in the following words: "It would be better if disunity among the followers of different religions could come to an end. Unity among religions is not an impossible idea. It is possible and in the present state of the world, it is especially important. Mutual respect would be helpful to all believers and unity among them would also bring benefit to non-believers, for the unanimous flood of light would show them the way out of their ignorance. I strongly emphasize the urgent need of flawless unity among all religions. To this end, the followers of each religion should know something of other religions and that is why I want to try to explain a little of the Buddhism of Tibet."[3]

Peace is imperative in this tension ridden world. It is only through an acceptance of our interdependence, through a willingness to preserve the wonderful diversity of the earth, through a desire to understand the other's point of view that we can hope to achieve peace. Interreligious dialogue can help provide the forum for mutual understanding and cooperation.

In conclusion, I would like to make an earnest appeal to all to work for the peace and happiness of all human beings. Whether, we believe in religion or not, whether we live in the East or the West, we are human beings and we are hungering for a peaceful and happy life. Our differences of religion, political ideology, color, and creed should not become a barrier to human cooperation for achieving our common goal.

Notes

1. The Dalai Lama, *My Land My People* (New York: Potala, 1983), 237.
2. The Dalai Lama, *An Approach to World Peace* (London: Wisdom Publications, 1986), 5.
3. *My Land My People*, 237.

25

Postscript

M. Darrol Bryant and Frank Flinn

The Self, The Other and Interfaith Dialogue

As Ewert Cousins notes in the opening address in this volume, we are in an axial period. The wheel is turning and we do not know which spoke is going to be up and which down. We do know that the first major turn in the wheel, marked by the World's Parliament of Religions in 1893, brought about a fundamental shift in relations between people of different faiths. Durwood Foster's essay sheds much light on the expectations and accomplishments of the first axial period. For our part, we are sure to derive benefit from examining what the second shift might mean for us.

The following reflection on our present ecumenical situation is just one way of looking at what is going on. It draws upon the western experiences of the editors. Needless to say, there are other ways to read our situation, ways which reflect eastern experiences and the many nuances within each tradition. This reflection is our attempt to gain some perspective on the kaleidoscope of religious experience which the essays in this volume reveal. This attempt to gain *a* perspective in no way claims to be *the* perspective. The editors intend it as an invitation to all to meditate more deeply on what the great ecumenical encounters of our time mean to each of us.

When we sit down to reflect over our lives—thinking about what we have done, people we have associated with, our religious journey, who we are, etc.—each of us soon discovers that there are sides to ourselves which remain unknown and unfathomed. Inside each of us there abides an "other." For the most part, this "other" remains hidden and shadowy. We don't even know if it is truly an "other" voice we hear within.

On the other hand, when we meet another person in inter-faith dialogue, we know for sure we are encountering someone who is clearly and unambiguously other than we are. This encounter can produce either recognition or estrangement. In the happy event of mutual recognition and identification, the meeting in dialogue brings forth both the acceptance of the other and the recognition that this acceptance is integral to the recognition of the otherness within the self. Meeting "others," beyond differences and comparisons, is the catalyst whereby we encounter our own hidden and unmanifest selves.

What we have said so far is that, whether we begin with the self or the other, the journey brings us full circle if we are motivated by open-heartedness. Swami Vivekananda, as Anatanand Rambacham shows, plumbed the depths of the Hindu religious self and emerged into the clear light of ecumenical openness. Conversely, Odette Baumer-Despigne's journeys into the otherness of the Hindu tradition have rewakened in her the riches of her own Christian birth faith. Recognition of otherness in love is, at its deepest level, self-recognition. This holds true also for the discovery of the religious self.

The relationship between Mahatma Gandhi and the Rev. Dr. Martin Luther King, Jr., illustrates our point well. Although many have failed to see the Rev. King's theological profundity, no one has the least doubt that he belonged fully to the Christian tradition. Rev. King, like Gandhi before him, crossed the the religious divide that lies between Hindu and Christian. In this volume Shesagiri Rao reminds us that Gandhi was vitally interested in *practical* ecumenism. Rev. King, in his journey into Hindu belief, discovered not only Gandhi's practical principle of non-violent action but a side of the Christian tradition that had remained dormant and undeveloped. The principle of active non-violence unites the Christian virtues of love and justice. Too often and too long had the Christian notion of *charity* relegated the world's dispossesed to the position of passive acceptance of largesse from those more wealthy and more powerful. A charity that is just, King argued, allows for those formerly held down to stand up and act on their own behalf. In a special sense, Rev. King became a person of two faiths. Yet in no sense would we be permitted to say that he lost or even diminished his natal Christian faith. Rather, the elements of

Christian faith were reintegrated and transformed into a powerful religious commitment after Rev. King's encounter with Gandhi. In passing over to the otherness of Gandhi's reformed Hinduism, Rev. King arrived at a crossroad in Christian self-recognition and self-understanding.

Every achievement of self-identity, it seems, requires an exodus out of self-centeredness. We are asked to pass over into something different, unfamiliar and strange. In this volume, the Shinto and Sikh ways of faith presented to us by Yoshimine Komari and Avtar Singh certainly are not religious awarenesses into which Jews, Christians or Muslims can immerse themselves with ease and nonchalance. When we encounter them in sincere dialogue, however, we are asked to lose ourselves, at least a little bit, in order to search out the otherness in our neighbor and find the hidden otherness within ourselves. It is our hunch that this search lies behind the Buddha's teaching and practice of no-self and Jesus's preaching about a seed losing itself in the soil.

One of the emerging implications of the second axial turn in ecumenical relations is that the religions of the world, both great and small, are only now on the verge of attaining a rich self-recognition. This assertion may startle some. Yet the contributions in this volume, from established and non-established religions, from those well known and those little known, make clear that we are just now emerging into the clearing called dialogue with the other as other. No doubt devoted members of longstanding religious traditions are going to protest: "We have always known who we are? We are not searching for our identity." Will not the Christian claim that Jesus was once-for-all the final and all-sufficient revelation of God to humanity? Will not the devout Muslim assert that Muhammed was the final Prophet, exclusive and incomparable? There is little doubt that the historic religions of revelation—Judaism, Christianity and Islam—have all tended to be exclusive in their claims to self-identity. Thubten Losel has pungent things to say about this problem, while Pieter de Jong informs us that there may be widely differing responses toward other religions from within a classic religion of revelation. But, by and large, Judaism, Christianity and Islam have claimed to possess the one, true Law, the one, true Redeemer, or the one, true Prophet. These claims have bolstered the belief in a sole jealous God whose worship demands virulent missionizing and the undermining of belief in any other deities. It also smothers any motives for dialogue and, until late in this century, has suppressed the advancement of scriptural bases legitimating dialogue. In this regard, Badru

Kateregga's marshalling of the *Qur'anic* texts in favor of dialogue represents a significant breakthrough, as Islam has been perhaps the most exclusive of the religions of revelation in modern times.

In contrast with the exclusive religions of revelation originating west of the Indus, the religions of illumination in the East have tended to be inclusive in character and code. There is a common Far Eastern expression that a person tends to be a Confucianist in dealing with family and society, a Buddhist when philosophizing, and a Doaist (or shamanist) when in trouble! To the devout Hindu, Moses and Jesus can be true avatars of the Godhead, while such a formulation would be blasphemy to the strict Christian or orthodox Jew. What is interesting is that this kind of religious pluralism exists not simply between one group and another but even within one and the same person. In the West identity seems to come by excluding difference, whereas in the East it seems to come by including it.

These two tendencies are not absolute. The West often first persecutes religious innovations coming from the East, and then includes them into the kaleidoscope of its experience. Conversely, the East's inclusiveness can be peculiarly monistic, absorbing moral and religious trends from the West and effectively smothering them. On the horizon, but coming into focus, is a new kind of awareness, too easily described with the pejorative term "syncretistic" but more accurately portrayed as a blended consciousness arising from the encounter with otherness. In this volume I am struck by the contributions of Djohan Effendi, Ignatius Hirudayam and Swami Devananda. The first relates Islam to the unavoidable puralistic religious context of Southeast Asia and argues in favor of religious harmony. The second two discuss Christianity as a minority religion in Asia— a status inevitably requiring awareness of religious otherness and theological humility.

At this juncture, the essays in this volume invite us to ask the important question: Where are we ecumenically speaking? One of the remarkable features of this volume is that many religious voices from around the world are here speaking both with their strengths and their weaknesses. Almost all have crossed the threshold of authentic dialogue with those that are other. All speak with respect and some acceptance of living in a world of differences. But what does the approach of the third millennium have to say to us? Millennial thinking is not as peculiar to the West as some say to us. Millennial thinking is not as peculiar to the West as some believe. Many Hindus believe that we are nearing the end of the *kali yuga* or age of destruction in preparation for a cosmic regeneration. Many Far Eastern Buddhists look to the age of the Maitreya Buddha who will usher in a time of bliss. Maybe the important point of millennial hope is not that things will get perfect but that things can get better. From the Western perspective, however, certain features can be discerned.

Two credos have guided the western world in the second millennium. These two credos are the heartbeats of two major revolutions.[1] The first credo summed up the first millennium and served as the starter molecule for the second. It is embodied in St. Anselm of Canterbury's famous dictum: "I believe in order that I may understand." This credo established the dialogue between God and humanity. While this first credo raised aloft the effulgent spires of the medieval cathedral, it also eventually descended into that dungeon of torture wracks known as the Inquisition. The Inquisition paved the road toward faith colonialism, which reduced its subjects to objects capable of only machine belief. The essay by Wande Abimbola demonstrates that we are not wholly recovered from the distortions of this first credo.

The second credo arose out of the ashes of blinded faith. It is enshrined in the famous dictum of Rene Descartes: "I think, therefore I am." This creed defines our relation to the natural world. Although it anchored the modern sciences and gave humans autonomy over their environment, the second creed too had a fatal flaw. Where the first degenerated into violent religious persecution and intolerance, the second has propelled civilization into the armaments factory. In the degeneration of both the first and second creeds, what happened was that one of the terms of the dialogue—God, nature—was suppressed. The hope of the third millennium is to reopen the dialogue by appealing to the third term—society itself.

It is becoming clearer that the opening question for the third millennium will have to do with human society itself and that the reopening of the dialogue will depend upon our response to our fellow human beings. Rosenstock-Huessy suggests that the opening credo for the turn of the millennium be: "I will respond even though I will be changed." First, we are being called to respond to those who are other and different than we are. Second, our response means that we are going to be changed and altered. The witnesses in this volume are living examples of the new creed working the changes necessary for the third millennium to emerge.

Our response will need to be a response from the depth. When we encounter others who are not simply nationally and culturally different from ourselves but religiously other in their relation to the ultimate meaning of life, we encounter the farthest side of otherness. A heartfelt response to religious otherness challenges us at our very roots. The seriousness of this challenge explains one aspect of a response that can lead to religious intolerance and persecution. In the past many felt that the only responses possible were either victory over or capitulation to the other. The creed for the third millennium, however, challenges us not to give up our faith, nor to suppress the faith of our neighbor, but to be willing to have our faith transformed from within. The dialogue between faith and faith, as Pascaline Coff shows us, elicits and sharpens the dialogue between a faith and its innermost depths.

We are now getting glimmerings of where we are ecumenically speaking. The primary relation is no longer between subject and object, ego and it, but—in the words of Martin Buber, as Rabbi Rami Shapiro reminds us—between I and Thou. The emerging self is no longer an atom defending its space in a universe of whirling aliens, nor an Archimedean lever struggling to heave the world aloft by its own imagining, but a self whose identity emerges precisely and primarily by being in a give-and-take relationship with others above and beyond oppression and domination. In sum, the self of the third millennium is dialogue in its most fundamental sense. Paul Mojzes' essay opens avenues into the nature of dialogue. Dialogue has become important in the latter half of the the twentieth century because it is a key to identity today—an identity arising from teaching and learning, and listening and speaking to our fellow human beings. The universal dialogue with all types of humans who display all types of faith promises to be the archrelation for our relation to the ultimate and to nature.

The contributors to this volume represent as broad a spectrum of faiths as one can find between two covers. The writers also manifest various aspects of faith, including faith undergoing change. Recently there has been a lot of discussion about the stages of faith people pass through in the course of a life time. A change in faith in this sense is vertical. But this is not the only way faith is changed. In interfaith dialogue faith becomes enriched horizontally. In a certain sense, a person of faith in authentic dialogue becomes a person of two faiths. This does not mean that the person believes *what* the dialogue partner believes but *as* that partner believes. Furthermore, in having our faith expanded through dialogue we encounter the other side of our own faith acts. Thus, too, communities of believers in the coming millennium will attain full faith identity only by discovering the other side of their own faith acts through dialogue with others.

If the presentations in this volume say one thing, they say that we live in the Age of Dialogue. In this age a single faith understood as against the faith of others no longer suffices in the discovery of a full humanity. Colonialism in matters of faith, as in politics, is over with. Each of us is invited to encounter at least one believer of a different faith in tolerance and humility. In so doing, we will not lose any faith at all but find a re-enriched faith within ourselves and within others. We will find full human identity and dignity through dialogue.

At the beginning of the twentieth century Josiah Royce detected that in the West high social cultivation was the breeding ground for the spiritual emnity expressed in self-centered individualism.[2] On the other hand, the individual self is not a datum of individual perception or conception. Rather the self is an interpretation that emerges in the dialogue between past and future. The dialogue takes place within a *community* of memory and of hope.[3] The religious self, too, does not emerge in isolation but unfolds in the give-and-take of dialogue given in faith. The voices in this volume are responses to the coming millennium, voices—whether faint or resonant—beckoning all across the desert of wars and contentions to the universal and beloved community of dialogue.

Notes

1. For more on these credos, I refer the reader to Eugen Rosenstock-Huessy, *Out of Revolution* (Norwich, Vt.: Argo, 1969), 740-53.
2. Josiah Royce, *The Problem of Christianity* (Chicago: Univ. of Chicago Press, 1968), 113. Orig. published in 1918.
3. Ibid., 244-249.

Contributors

Wande Abimbola is Professor and Vice-Chancellor of Obafemi Awolowo University, Ile-Ife, Nigeria.

Odette Baumer-Despeigne is a Lecturer on East-West Dialogue, Abhishiktananda Society, Frauenfeld, Switzerland.

Pascaline Coff is Founder and Director of the Monastic Ashram Osage+Monastery Forest of Peace, Sand Springs, Oklahoma.

W. Owen Cole is a freelance lecturer and writer, lecturing at the West Sussex Institute of Higher Education, United Kingdom.

Ewert H. Cousins is Professor of Religious Studies at Fordham University, Bronx, New York.

Pieter De Jong is John Fletcher Hurst Professor of Theology, Rtd., Drew University, Madison, New Jersey.

Swami Devananda is a monk at the Osage+Monastery Forest of Peace, Sand Springs, Oklahoma.

Tsering Dhondup is Chairman of the Tibetan Young Buddhist Association, Dharamsala, India.

Djohan Effendi is a Lecturer on Islamology at Trisakti University, Jakarta, Indonesia, and Lecturer on Philosophy at Syafiiyah Islamic University, Jakarta, Indonesia.

A. Durwood Foster is Professor of Christian Theology at the Pacific School of Religion, Berkeley, California.

Ignatius Hirudayam is Director of the Interfaith Research Dialogue Center, Madras, India.

Gokul Chandra Jain is Head of the Department of Prakrit and Jaina Studies, Sanskrit Univeristy, Varanasi, India.

Badru Dungu Kateregga is H.E. the Ambassador of Uganda to Saudi Arabia.

Thomas Keating is a monk at St. Benedicts Monastery, Snowmass, Colorado.

T. James Kodera is Professor of Religion and Chairman of the Department of Religion at Wellesley College, Wellesley, Massachusetts.

Yoshimine Komori is Professor of Religion at Kokushikan University in Tokyo, Japan.

Thubten Losel is a monk at Sera Je Monastic University, Bylakuppe, India.

Paul Mojzes is Professor of Religious Studies, Rosemont College, Rosemont, Pennsylvania, and Co-Editor of the *Journal of Ecumenical Studies*.

Albert Nambiaparambil is Secretary of the World Fellowship of Inter-Religious Councils, New Delhi, India; and Secretary of the Catholic Bishops' Conference of India, New Delhi, India.

Anantanand Rambachan is Assistant Professor of Religion at St. Olaf College, Northfield, Minnesota.

K.L. Seshagiri Rao is Professor of Religious Studies at the University of Virginia, Charlottesville, Virginia.

Ki-Young Rhi is Director of the Korean Institute for Buddhist Studies, Seoul, Korea.

Rami Mark Shapiro is Rabbi of Temple Beth Or in Miami, Florida.

Avtar Singh is Dean of the Faculty of Humanities and Religious Studies, Punjabi University, Patiala, India.

Index